Motherhood confined

Manchester University Press

SOCIAL HISTORIES OF MEDICINE

Series editors: David Cantor, Anne Hanley and Elaine Leong

Social Histories of Medicine is concerned with all aspects of health, illness and medicine, from prehistory to the present, in every part of the world. The series covers the circumstances that promote health or illness, the ways in which people experience and explain such conditions, and what, practically, they do about them. Practitioners of all approaches to health and healing come within its scope, as do their ideas, beliefs, and practices, and the social, economic and cultural contexts in which they operate. Methodologically, the series welcomes relevant studies in social, economic, cultural, and intellectual history, as well as approaches derived from other disciplines in the arts, sciences, social sciences and humanities. The series is a collaboration between Manchester University Press and the Society for the Social History of Medicine.

To buy or to find out more about the books currently available in this series, please go to: https://manchesteruniversitypress.co.uk/series/social-histories-of-medicine/

Motherhood confined

Maternal health in English prisons, 1853–1955

Rachel E. Bennett

MANCHESTER UNIVERSITY PRESS

Copyright © Rachel E. Bennett 2024

The right of Rachel E. Bennett to be identified as the author of this work has been asserted in accordance with the Copyright, Designs and Patents Act 1988.

An electronic version is also available under a Creative Commons (CC BY-NC) licence, thanks to the support of Wellcome Trust, which permits non-commercial use, distribution and reproduction provided the author(s) and Manchester University Press are fully cited. Details of the licence can be viewed at https://creativecommons.org/licenses/by-nc/4.0/

Published by Manchester University Press
Oxford Road, Manchester M13 9PL

www.manchesteruniversitypress.co.uk

British Library Cataloguing-in-Publication Data
A catalogue record for this book is available from the British Library

ISBN   978 1 5261 6679 1   hardback

First published 2024

The publisher has no responsibility for the persistence or accuracy of URLs for any external or third-party internet websites referred to in this book, and does not guarantee that any content on such websites is, or will remain, accurate or appropriate.

Typeset
by New Best-set Typesetters Ltd

*Dedicated to the memory of
Frances Bennett
(1944–2019)*

Contents

List of figures	page viii
Preface	ix
Acknowledgements	xi
List of abbreviations	xiii
Introduction	1
1 Contesting women's health in the prison system	34
2 Maternity care in prison	72
3 Mothering in a carceral space	102
4 Born in prison: a heritage of woe?	137
Conclusion	174
Bibliography	184
Index	200

Figures

1.1 Mothers with their children exercising at Tothill Fields Prison, c. 1860s. John Johnson Collection of Printed Ephemera, Bodleian Libraries, University of Oxford, Wikimedia Commons *page* 43
2.1 The nursery, Holloway Prison, c. early twentieth century. Reproduced with kind permission of the Howard League for Penal Reform archives, Modern Records Centre, University of Warwick 79
3.1 Women in a mothercraft class at Exeter Prison, c. 1960s. Photograph reproduced with kind permission of the National Justice Museum 120

Preface

Britain has a long and storied history of crime and punishment, several chapters of which are dedicated to the experiences of those imprisoned for their crimes. Historically, prisons have been sites of intrigue and disdain and places of and for punishment. The conditions within have been staunchly defended, and rigorously criticised. The people occupying their cells have been variously viewed with curiosity, disdain, fear and pity. Women in prison, although consistently lower in number than men, have captured popular imagination and evoked medical, political and ideological debate. Cautionary tales of fallen women, and inspirational anecdotes of wayward women and rebels challenging the constraints placed upon them by society, have a long history. It is a history which has adapted in terms of context and language with the changing times, but one where the tropes of the mad, bad or sad female criminal have undoubtedly endured.

The modern prison system was created in the mid-nineteenth century. When we imagine life behind the high walls of the fortress-like prisons that were built or modified during that time, we conjure up scenes where strict regulation prevailed to control people in both body and mind, of locking and unlocking, of structures severe in both appearance and practice. An image that poses something of an antithesis, and one that can be difficult to reconcile with more popular imaginings of life in these carceral spaces, is that of mothers and their babies. Should pregnant women and mothers with babies be in prison? Are prisons appropriate places for their containment and care? Can they ever be? These are questions that continue to evoke debate today but have rarely been considered in a historical context.

This book is the first extensive historical examination of motherhood in prison. It has been written to offer a look behind the high walls of England's prisons and explore how mothers and their children posed distinct challenges to carceral spaces and penal regimes not designed with their containment in mind. It reveals the historic and enduring exigencies of confining motherhood, which even today have some resonance with current challenges facing the criminal justice system.

Rachel E. Bennett

Acknowledgements

Writing this book has been challenging but fascinating, intriguing but, at times, frustrating and difficult. Gathering the research materials and reading widely into Britain's history of crime and punishment has taken me down several different paths of enquiry. During the research and writing process I had valuable opportunities to share ideas with many people in different settings, which helped me to shape these ideas, find ways to articulate them and piece this study together.

I would like to acknowledge the generous support of the Wellcome Trust in funding the Investigator Award, 'Prisoners, Medical Care and Entitlement to Health in English and Irish Prisons, 1840–2000' (1003341/Z/13/Z), which provided the support for the research that underpins this book. Special thanks to the Principal Investigators Professor Hilary Marland at the University of Warwick and Associate Professor Catherine Cox at University College Dublin for their generosity with their advice, time and feedback while I navigated my research into health and medicine in women's prisons, and for enabling me to be a part of an exceptional team. Thank you to Margaret Charleroy, Nicholas Duvall, Flo Swann, Max Hodgson and Becky Crites at the University of Warwick, Fiachra Byrne, Holly Dunbar, Sinead McCann and Oisín Wall at University College Dublin, William Murphy at Dublin City University, and Virginia Berridge and Janet Weston at the London School of Hygiene and Tropical Medicine. Collaborating with this team and sharing ideas was a pleasure and a privilege that played a significant part in shaping the research underpinning this book. Thanks also to colleagues in Warwick's Centre for the History of Medicine for providing me with a strong and supportive community during my time as a Research Fellow, where I gained valued friends.

In addition to carrying out the research for this book, working as part of this project provided the team with invaluable opportunities to create a range of public engagement projects. These activities gave us the chance to collaborate with outstanding organisations and individuals, including those working in the arts and theatre, in prisons and in charities and organisations who work to reform conditions in prisons. These projects led to the production of theatre shows, exhibitions and policy events, among many other things. Having the chance to explore innovative and creative ways to illuminate the historical voices, themes and events we uncovered and to share them with a wide audience has been a real privilege. I would like to thank the project team and all of the people we collaborated with for these experiences, as they undoubtedly enriched this research as it took shape over the past few years.

Thanks also to the archivists and librarians in the various archives, libraries and museums I visited when gathering the materials for this book: Library of Birmingham, Hull History Centre, Liverpool Record Office, London Metropolitan Archives, the Modern Records Centre at the University of Warwick, the National Justice Museum in Nottingham, The National Archives in Kew and the Wellcome Library. They play a vital role in preserving invaluable historical records and allowing us to uncover the stories of the people and places we write about.

The greatest thank you goes to my family and friends for their unwavering and unconditional love and support, especially my parents, Ronnie and Alison, and Laura, Anthony and Sarah. I am extremely fortunate to have all of you in my life and you each share in the achievement of completing this book. Finally, I would like to thank my Nana Fay for all of the memories she gave me. She was a woman who was strong in will but always kind in spirit. The completion of this book is dedicated to her memory.

Abbreviations

BMJ	*British Medical Journal*
GP	General Practitioner
HDPAS	Holloway Discharged Prisoners' Aid Society
HHC	Hull History Centre
HO	Home Office
LB	Library of Birmingham
LMA	London Metropolitan Archives
LRO	Liverpool Record Office
Minute Book	Minute Book of the Visiting Justices for the House of Correction, Westminster
MRC	Modern Records Centre, University of Warwick
NSPCC	National Society for the Prevention of Cruelty to Children
Quarterly returns	Quarterly returns of prisoners in hulks and convict prisons
TNA	The National Archives, Kew
WL	Wellcome Library
WSPU	Women's Social and Political Union
WVS	Women's Voluntary Services

Introduction

Serving a sentence of fifteen years in prison in the late nineteenth century, Florence Maybrick lamented that to be sick in prison was a terrible experience. She recalled the desolation and indifference in treatment and vividly described 'lying in silence without the touch of a friendly hand, the sound of a friendly voice or a single expression of sympathy or interest'.[1] Between the mid-nineteenth and the mid-twentieth century many women fell ill in prison, their incarceration often causing or exacerbating their sickness. Meanwhile, hundreds of women entered prisons pregnant, and many of them gave birth to their babies behind bars. Countless others left children on the outside. Some of these women had been in prison several times and were perceived to be hardened to its toils, while others were stepping through the prison gates for the first time. Susan Willis Fletcher, reflecting upon the commencement of her year in Westminster Prison in the late nineteenth century, spoke of something that united them all. When the key turned in their cell door, women said a silent 'farewell to everybody and everything' they knew.[2]

The aim of imposing uniformity underpinned the creation of the modern prison system and shaped its administration thereafter. Despite this, carrying out research into the history of prisons and the experiences of the women who lived and worked within them reveals a skein of diverse narratives. There were those who completed their sentence without incident and others who constantly broke the prison rules and populated the tables of punishment, women who served only one sentence and others who entered into a cycle of recidivism. Some women bore the discipline of the prison with little evidence of it impacting on their health, while others were permanently damaged in body or mind by their time behind bars.

Many of the women who walked through the prison gates between the mid-nineteenth and the mid-twentieth century were mothers. It is their experiences that are explored in this book.

In 1919 an enquiry was carried out into medical provisions in Holloway Prison, England's largest women's prison at the time. Its report, which is addressed in greater depth in a later chapter, made a statement worthy of note here, speaking as it does to a question that permeates this study. When illuminating what they believed to be 'serious defects in the prison's administration' in terms of the availability of nursing staff and the conditions in which pregnant women were incarcerated, the enquiry committee explicitly expressed their belief that mothers, 'whatever their delinquencies', and their babies, who were innocent in the eyes of the law, were entitled to proper care while in the charge of the state.[3] However, the boundaries dictating this 'proper care' were subject to repeated drawing and redrawing by prison administrators, staff and reformers alike throughout this period.

Mary Size, reflecting upon her four decades serving as a prison officer, schoolmistress and deputy governor in the women's prison estate in the first half of the twentieth century, described each woman as 'a problem carrying a badge of shame, heartbreak, unhappiness and frustration'.[4] Female prisons confined women from all walks of life, both the 'pampered ladies and the verminous old drunks'.[5] However, incarcerating the first-time offender with the recidivist, the healthy prisoner alongside the sick, the refractory women with the mentally ill, created perennial difficulties for the prison system. Joanna Kelley, Governor of Holloway Prison between 1959 and 1966, elaborated on a specific issue facing female prisons when she stated, 'our problems were quite often different: problems of mothers and babies, problems of family visits impinged more on us, and we didn't have the problems of escapes and very violent prisoners'.[6] Since the inception of the modern prison system, pregnant women and mothers with babies have posed specific questions that it continues to grapple with. Is prison an appropriate place for their confinement? And how do we ensure their safe custody?

This book provides the first extensive historical examination of the incarceration of mothers in England. It begins in 1853, with the opening of England's first female-only establishment in Brixton, and explores the period up to the late 1950s, when prison policy changed to remove women to hospitals outside the prison estate to give birth. Each chapter takes the reader behind the prison walls to examine how motherhood, including pregnancy and childbirth, was managed in physical spaces and as part of penal regimes that were designed and administered without proper consideration of the specific health needs of mothers. Drawing on this evidence, it addresses and refines scholarship in the medical humanities and prison history that explores the inherent challenges and contradictions of providing for prisoners' health while also enforcing discipline.[7] The book tracks the oscillating debates about the purpose and role of prisons and explores the blurring of the line between the punitive, reformatory and medical treatment of their female inmates, shaped by regimes determined to exercise uniformity and deterrence but also mindful of the fact that prisoners' health was meant to be maintained and anxious to avoid public accusations of injuring prisoners in body and mind.

Tracing official debates and shifts in penal policy, the book examines what we can glean about the aims of those conceiving and designing prisons and their regimes, while also providing a fresh insight into how they worked in practice. By uncovering the previously neglected voices of those who lived and worked in prisons, the chapters explore how obdurate prison regimes were negotiated in practice by prison staff and the women themselves. Advancing our understanding of prisons as medical as well as disciplinary institutions allows the book's scope to transcend the confines of penal history. By exploring the intersecting debates about criminality, motherhood and institutional health, it offers new ways of understanding ideas, beliefs and practices surrounding maternity care, motherhood and femininity in the modern period.

History, health and medical provision in English prisons

Prior to the late eighteenth century, people were largely incarcerated for short periods of time if they were debtors or while they either awaited their trial or the imposition of another punishment, including the death penalty or transportation overseas. They would be held in bridewells, lock-up houses and gaols that were run by gaolers, and conditions were often squalid, unsanitary and disordered. A variety of criticisms were levelled at these places of confinement. It was lamented that drinking, gambling, vice and corruption were rife and there were no reformatory ambitions underpinning the imprisonment of Britain's criminals. Provisions for health and sanitation were almost non-existent. In the late eighteenth century criticisms of this disorganised system became louder.

John Howard is one of the main figures associated with prison reform and an early protagonist in the story of prison health. Howard was appointed as the Sheriff of Bedfordshire in 1773 and part of his role in office was to inspect the county gaol. He did so in 1773 and 1774 and was shocked and appalled by what he found. He later wrote what became a well-known indictment of these institutions, *The State of the Prisons in England and Wales* (1777), which lamented the health ramifications of poor prison conditions and the moral dangers resulting from of all classes of prisoners being confined together: men and women, debtors and felons, and habitual criminals with young offenders. He encapsulated an issue that would rage on throughout the nineteenth and twentieth centuries when he stated that 'a gaol is not designed for the final punishment [death] ... but for the safe custody of the accused to the time of trial; and of convicts till a legal sentence be executed upon them'.[8]

In response to the growing criticisms levelled at prison conditions, the Health of Prisoners Act was passed in 1774. It empowered the Justices of the Peace in a given area to intervene in prison administration to ensure the maintenance of health standards. For example, they could order the white-washing of walls, make provision for sick-rooms, regular washing and cleaning facilities, and appoint a surgeon to report back to them on prisoner health. Higgins' study of health care in prisons commences with John Howard and the debates about prison reform in the late eighteenth century, before charting the growing calls for the more systematic provision of prison doctors by the magistrates and officials administering England's places of confinement in the decades that followed. He examined the role of the prison doctor in attempting to combat and treat specific diseases, including periodic outbreaks of typhus and cholera in several prisons in the early nineteenth century.[9] The Act of 1774 and subsequent efforts to improve health and sanitation were important in that they made the health of prisoners a more publicly visible issue and made the institutions themselves responsible for it on a very basic level. However, many of the recommendations made by Howard and other early penal reformers were not adequately addressed and thus they are perhaps best viewed as an early chapter in a much longer story of deciding upon a prisoner's entitlement to health. With its focus upon mothers and their children, this book provides a previously underexplored chapter in this long and complex story. Demonstrating that, while prison health has not featured as a major area of study within medical humanities until recently, and women's health remains a notable chasm, the experiences of mothers challenged how prisons reconciled their roles of containment and medical care.[10]

Jeremy Bentham's Panopticon prison design of the late eighteenth century was based upon the principle that the structure itself would allow inmates to be subject to close surveillance at all times from the prison's central point, thus facilitating a system of control reinforced by the fact that inmates never knew when they were being watched. British prisons were never fully Benthamite in their construction or administration. Yet the health experiences of those incarcerated were shaped by key principles espoused by Bentham, including severity, strict management and economy, which placed responsibility on the state to preserve prisoners' health while emphasising the need to make prison conditions of a standard lower than those facing its poorest free citizens. Within his research into the history of health in prisons, Wiener placed the prison medical officer at the centre of this conundrum as they had 'an essentially Benthamite task' of balancing these aims that were 'neither completely separable nor reconcilable'. This dilemma meant that a 'permanent process of struggle and negotiation ensued'.[11]

By virtue of their office, prison medical officers were constables as well as doctors. They determined a prisoner's fitness for work and subjugation to the prison regime, including certifying them as fit or unfit for labour, dietary punishment and restraint. Wiener labelled this decision-making process as a form of moral categorisation that involved the interpretation of behaviour as well as the identification of ill health.[12] In their respective significant studies of the Victorian prison system, Sim and Priestley critiqued what they concluded was the prison doctor's fundamentally disciplinary task, which placed them more on the side of the state than of the sick.[13] Broader prison policy played a part in dictating not only attitudes among prison doctors but also the rules, resources and context in which they had to identify and treat ill health in prison. For example, the 1860s and 1870s witnessed a commitment to a more penal approach on the part of the Prison Directorate, in response to intensified debates about recidivism, to ensure that prisons were characterised by deterrence and economy. However, the 1890s post-Gladstone era witnessed a recommitment to the reformist aims of the modern prison system when it was first established in the 1840s and 1850s. This was driven by evidence gathered during enquiries into the administration of the prison system, which were more concerned with the potential causes of crime, the circumstances from which criminals had come and potential methods of reform.

The treatment of mental ill health has been richly explored to illuminate the complexity of the disciplinary task of the prison medical officer. As part of his study of the history of identifying and treating mental illness following the inception of the modern prison system, Watson argued that negotiating their statutory duty meant prison doctors produced knowledge and debates about categories of mental behaviour that were unique to the prison setting.[14] Davie's research added that it was both practical and crucial for prison doctors to establish objective criteria to reflect upon the distinct nature and extent of physical and mental disabilities among prison inmates so as to not only decide upon their fitness to undergo the full rigours of the regime but also pre-empt any challenges to their diagnoses from other quarters of the prison hierarchy.[15] One aspect of prison history that has been the subject of extensive research is the system of separate confinement. Based on the model set out in Philadelphia's Eastern State Penitentiary, this was first introduced to Britain in Pentonville Prison, for male convicts, in 1842. Although the system had notable detractors from the outset, it was implemented, though often in a modified form, in the majority of prisons in the mid-nineteenth century and retained until the early twentieth century.

As part of a significant portfolio of recent historical research into the identification and treatment of mental ill health in English and Irish prisons, Cox and Marland explored the links drawn by prison officials, external reformers and prisoners themselves between the rigours of the separate system and cases of mental breakdown. They demonstrated how the identification of mental ill health in prison was subject to intense scrutiny to refute these criticisms and, crucially, to detect efforts on the part of prisoners to receive some relaxation of the prison regime.¹⁶ This was a particular issue in the 1860s and 1870s with the pursuit of greater uniformity, severity and economy. In addition, Shepherd's study argued that feigning insanity was used by prisoners when other attempts at resisting the system failed.¹⁷ Elsewhere, my work has identified how notable ameliorations were made to the system, prompted by concerns that female prisoners could not safely withstand its full rigours.¹⁸ The first two chapters of the book deepen this scholarship by demonstrating the impact of separation and isolation upon the health of pregnant women and new mothers and illuminating the particular criticisms levelled at its use for these women by prisoners, staff and prison reformers.

Exploring women's health and maternity care in English prisons

The central theme explored throughout the book is that containing and caring for mothers posed distinct, but underexplored, challenges for prison doctors and staff. The prison system and policy makers did not provide consistent criteria to govern their treatment. Instead, the care of mothers was dependent upon a range of factors including the circumstances within individual prisons, the ability and inclinations of prison staff to provide adequate care and, in some cases, the women themselves.

Oakley's pioneering sociological study of medical care during childbirth in the late twentieth century argued that mothers were not only treated as 'passive patients' but also as being 'manipulable'.¹⁹ Cahill's historical examination of the long-term medicalisation of childbirth subsequently provided a deeper exploration of the consequences of this assumed female inferiority, concluding that maternity care is an area in which the ability of women to exercise real choice and make informed decisions about the conditions of their care is limited.²⁰ While it is vital to acknowledge that concepts such as choice and informed decision making in maternity care are constructs of the later twentieth century and cannot be directly applied to nineteenth-century experiences, this book argues that the longer historical narrative of the prison setting adds a unique dimension to this question of the agency of mothers in prison. When exploring the question of separation from family for women in prisons, Baunach argued that incarceration has historically been regarded as a manifestation of mothers' abandonment of their responsibilities.[21] This study delves further to argue that physical carceral spaces and the regimented regimes within them impacted on how women cared for their children. In addition, perceptions of the maternal failings of female prisoners were held up as indicators of the need for the prison regime to intervene to address loss of femininity, and shaped debates about whether mothers in prison should retain or relinquish their ability to make choices in the care of their children.

In his 1907 work *The Female Prisoner*, Captain Vernon Harris, an inspector of prisons, voiced a long and widely held belief that 'a bad woman is the worst of all creations'.[22] Women have historically accounted for a much smaller proportion of the people arrested, convicted and punished by the criminal justice system than men. However, 'in them one sees the most hideous picture of all human weakness and depravity', a picture of the 'coarsest and rudest moral features' made more striking because it has occurred among those supposed to be the gentle sex.[23] Illuminative of fears about the dangers of female criminality, these nineteenth- and early twentieth-century views also play a part in shaping how the story of the women who populated England's prisons has been told since. Tales of 'bad girls' and 'wayward women' have long captured the public's interest and continue to interest scholars and writers.[24]

Bosworth's criminological research into female imprisonment reveals the importance of unacknowledged gender bias within accounts of the development of the prison system throughout the twentieth century. She argues that this is because exploring the system's development as a transformation in ideologies about the purpose of punishment is more applicable for male prisoners. By contrast, Bosworth notes key continuities in attitudes towards women who commit crime, notably the questions of morality and the offending of certain gender norms and how these things are used to legitimise the imprisonment of women, including mothers.[25] While Bosworth's argument was mainly concerned with the field of criminology, it is also applicable to historical accounts of prisons. Within the history of crime and punishment, prison history is a sub-genre, with seminal works dedicated to examining the development and administration of the prison system since the mid-nineteenth century.[26] However, within these larger works, the provisions for and experiences of women are primarily confined to a single, stand-alone chapter or ignored entirely. Despite their absence or limited place in broader studies of prison history, women have been the subject of more specific research by historians of crime whose work explores how responses to female criminals intersected with, and were shaped by, questions of gender and femininity, including Zedner, Dobash, Dobash and Gutteridge, Forsythe and Davie. They have provided detailed discussions of beliefs and fears surrounding female criminality and their impact on the running of women's prisons in nineteenth-century England.[27] These studies offer in-depth considerations of the supervision of behaviour and provide valuable insight into daily prison life, but they say relatively little about the management of health, including that of the hundreds of women who entered prisons pregnant and gave birth behind bars. Within scholarship dedicated to the organisation of the prison system in the late twentieth and early twenty-first century, gender has increasingly become a central tenet of understanding the conditions of imprisonment in Britain.[28] Research on the impact of imprisonment upon mothers, and the health-care provisions in place within the women's prison estate, has become increasingly rich in the twenty-first century.[29] The recent and ongoing research of Lucy Baldwin, among others, delves deeply into the encounters of mothers with the criminal justice system, including the courts and the prison estate, and weaves together the first-hand accounts of mothers and of practitioners who have cared for and worked with them to provide a series of reflections and recommendations.[30] However, when reading these works, it becomes clear that the questions raised, the contentions between containment and care, and the experiences of the mothers behind the cell doors have a much longer history.

Zedner's work explores nineteenth-century views about mothers who committed crime, and debates within legal and social commentaries about the effects of female criminality and maternal alcoholism upon the home and upon children.[31] However, it provides only a limited discussion of how these debates impacted upon provisions for the containment of mothers and their babies. More recent research has begun to illuminate the experiences of mothers in prison. Johnston drew upon several case studies to explore how women used their limited agency in prison to reassert their identities as mothers and how they attempted to maintain contact with, and control the fate of, their children on the outside.[32] Farrell's study of Irish convict prisons between 1853 and 1900 argued that the reception of infants into prisons with their mothers and the care of those born to women in prisons became increasingly regulated in the second half of the nineteenth century, due to debates about the effect of their presence upon the prison regime.[33]

The current study is primarily focused upon England and draws largely upon material and scholarship focused on the country's penal history. Although limited, there are brief discussions of the experiences of mothers that can be used to offer parallels with other countries. For example, Wingfield and Bucur briefly used the example of women and children imprisoned in Eastern Europe during wartime in the twentieth century to further demonstrate how the lack of provision for them, including in some prisons the lack of separation from male prisoners and being under the sole custody of male officers, resulted in the exacerbation of women's feelings of shame and humiliation.[34] Tucker's study of women in Egyptian prisons in the nineteenth century explored how some reforms were introduced by the colonial government to reflect changes in Britain. However, Tucker demonstrates how several of the inadequacies in Britain, including the lack of proper consideration of women who brought children into prison with them, were also transferred and meant that their incarceration placed greater pressure on an already insufficient system. Tucker does briefly suggest that women in the ninth month of pregnancy and those very recently delivered were not sent to prison in Egypt.[35] However, this marks a notable difference from practices in Britain, as the current study has uncovered cases of women giving birth within days of their committal. Farrell's work on Ireland and O'Brien's study of France both explored how women were more likely than their male counterparts to be forced to leave behind children when they went to prison and how ruminations over female criminality and its impact upon families, including that of unwed mothers, shaped discussions about the appropriate treatment of women in convict prisons in the nineteenth century.[36]

Similar to eighteenth- and nineteenth-century British history, the development of American prisons in this period has also been the subject of significant study. Studies have demonstrated that, similar to Britain, consideration of the distinct needs of women and children did not feature heavily within official policy shaping the prison system. However, the importance of place and environment was more greatly identifiable in shaping the experiences of American women in prison, including mothers and their children. The works of Derbes and Coulson both explore the distinct experiences of women based on race and gender prior to the Civil War and in the Reconstruction era in the South, which was more committed to punitive restitution compared to the notion in the North that prison labour should be reformative.[37] This led to poor health outcomes for pregnant women and their infants who, like in Britain, were born and remained with their mothers in prison. Coulson highlighted a high death rate among babies born in Virginia Penitentiary, due to the poor conditions and lack of care.[38] With a focus on the American West after the 1860s, Butler explored the mirroring of the development of the penitentiary with the social, economic and political struggles that accompanied western change. Butler made clear that while male convicts certainly did not escape the harsh reality of penitentiary life, for women prisoners incarcerated in male institutions, their womanhood exposed them to an additional 'penal burden' that encompassed both physical and mental violence.[39] As in Britain, these studies show how it was not just the physical structure of the prison that impacted upon the health experiences of women, but also the people who were placed in charge of their custody.

Until the mid-twentieth century, the positions of governor and medical officer were mainly occupied by men across the prison estate. However, the daily running of female prisons and female wings was placed in the hands of lady superintendents, matrons and female prison officers throughout the nineteenth and twentieth centuries. Elizabeth Fry, now regarded as one of Britain's most eminent penal reformers, provided the first major recommendations on the governance of female offenders. She argued that not only would the superintendence of women over female inmates be a check on the abuses she highlighted, including overcrowding, women and children being kept in squalid sanitary conditions and being at the mercy of male gaolers, but they would also exert a moral influence over their fallen sisters.[40] Chapter 1 will extend the analysis of the appointment, position and gendered role of female prison officials initiated by Forsythe and Johnston.[41] It will introduce the reader to

Fry's less familiar successors who continued to advocate for one of the core principles at the heart of her early reformatory efforts, namely that female offenders required the more personalised attentions, including the moral, educational and, eventually, medical guidance, of members of their own sex. Emma Martin, the Lady Superintendent of Brixton, England's first female convict prison, lived in the prison with her children in the 1850s and 1860s. She continually petitioned the Prison Directorate regarding the specific health and disciplinary needs of the women in her charge. Cicely McCall, a psychiatric social worker who served as a prison officer in Holloway and Aylesbury in the 1930s, Mary Size, who instituted important reforms during almost five decades in the prison service between 1906 and 1952, and Dr Mary Gordon, appointed the first female Inspector of Prisons and Inebriate Reformatories in 1908, offer some examples included in this study of female officials who advocated for women's prisons to be sites of reform and health intervention instead of purely penal institutions in the early twentieth century. Mothers, including those who gave birth in prison, brought their babies in with them, and those who left behind children on the outside were at the forefront of these efforts.

The overwhelming majority of people who populated penal institutions came from the most impoverished sections of society, with male and female prisons being confronted with inmates who were in poor physical and mental health when they entered the system. They were variously described as aged, debilitated, alcoholics or weak minded and in need of immediate medical treatment. Medical officers treated cases of ulcers, abscesses, diseases of the joints and bones, digestive complaints, kidney, lung, heart and brain disease, epilepsy and respiratory issues as well as venereal disease, menorrhagia (abnormally heavy menstrual bleeding), prolapses uteri and pregnancy. Many of these ailments were treated in a prisoner's cell. However, in some cases they required admission into the prison hospital and some amelioration of the strict penal regime, whether this was an improvement in diet, the relaxation of labour requirements or being placed in greater association. However, a group of prisoners who posed distinct challenges to the prison authorities in terms of their containment and, crucially, their care were mothers.

Before delving into how each of the book's chapters explore different facets of motherhood in prison, it is beneficial to first provide a brief discussion of how the book uses terms such as pregnancy, childbirth and motherhood. Pregnancy and childbirth are generally accepted to describe biological states or entities, namely the period in which a foetus develops in the womb following conception, for around forty weeks or nine months, and the process of giving birth at the end of this period. However, the term motherhood needs to be further deconstructed. Historically, the chain of events from sexual intercourse to pregnancy to motherhood has largely been considered to be so natural that they are inevitable and unquestionable. However, in her sociological study of White, British motherhood in the second half of the twentieth century, Smart argues that, rather than simply being an unfolding of nature, there are a range of more complex channels, choices and events taking place that have historically and culturally impacted on this journey to motherhood, especially expectations of 'proper' motherhood.[42] Similarly, work which frames motherhood as a social construct challenges the assumption that the traits and practices of mothers are inevitable, and instead makes visible the means by which dominant meanings of motherhood have emerged, changed and been socially reproduced over time.[43] Within this, the virtues presupposed to be provided by motherhood and the appropriate cultural conditioning of mothers are not universally agreed, no more today than in the past.[44] Motherhood has a long history of being labelled, sometimes simultaneously, as 'a handicap but also a strength; a trial and an error; an achievement and a prize'.[45] The prison setting offers a unique microcosm to explore the marking out and patrolling of the boundaries of 'proper' or 'good' motherhood and the impact of its physical spaces and regimes upon the management and experience of pregnancy, childbirth and mothering.

The period between the mid-nineteenth and mid-twentieth century not only witnessed profound changes in England's penal system, but was also a time of seminal development in maternity care. The chapters of this book seek to situate debates and shifting practices in prison births and the care of mothers within this wider narrative. Towler and Bramall's work provides an examination of the evolution of midwifery in particular over the four centuries leading to the nineteenth century to illuminate the profound institutional, legislative and social shifts in the role of the midwife which continued into the twentieth century.[46] The Midwives Act 1902 meant that midwifery became legally recognised and led to the creation of the Central Midwives Board and the formalising of the registration and education of midwives in England. This regulation occurred against a backdrop of concerns about the health of the nation more broadly, and in its wake increased debate about its links with maternal mortality, the place of birth and the care and education of mothers.[47]

Most women in the early twentieth century were unlikely to receive antenatal care until their delivery, when a midwife would be called for, and the safest place to give birth was at home, due to the dangers of infection and fever posed by lying-in hospitals.[48] Loudon identifies the period between the mid-nineteenth century and the mid-1930s as one of high maternal mortality and argues that the main determinant of this was the overall standard of care provided by birth attendants, with poverty and associated malnutrition playing a key role.[49] The health of women when they entered prison, including those who entered pregnant, was repeatedly ruminated on by prison doctors and played a part in debates about the role of the prison in providing care for these women. Interviews carried out with a sample of women who gave birth between the 1940s and 1990s as part of an oral history study by Davis revealed that for most women the quality of their relationship with medical professionals was what they recalled to be the most important aspect of their care.[50] Within the prison environment, it was often the case that the prison staff, as well as the physical environment itself, could be pivotal in shaping women's experiences of birth in prison.

After the mid-1930s there was a sharp reduction in maternal mortality rates, with reasons including the development of sulphonamides, the use of blood transfusions and an accompanying improvement in the use of anaesthesia, the latter also being linked to the increased expectations placed upon medical intervention during delivery on the part of both birth attendants and women themselves.[51] Before the Second World War, the majority of births occurred at home. However, the mid-twentieth century witnessed a major increase in hospital births, rising from around two-thirds between the late 1940s and mid-1960s to around 95 per cent by 1975.[52] At the same time as this post-war uptick in hospital births, debates about whether babies should be born within the confines of a prison intensified, encompassing debates about not only the standard of care but also the social ramifications of the place of birth. They led to the reduction of prison births and the establishment of the practice of sending women to outside hospitals for their delivery. It is worth noting that it remains the case today that women should be sent to outside hospitals to have their babies, but continue to give birth in prison if they are not transferred to hospital in time, due to the onset of premature labour and complications with their care posed by medical and institutional complexities and inconsistencies.

Researching experiences 'on the inside'

There is no one set of comprehensive records that can fully illuminate the complex past of the establishment, administration and the experiences of the people confined in England's prison system. Therefore, the book adopts a broad chronological and thematic approach to exploring the many ways mothers experienced the criminal justice system. Using records relating to convict prisons, intended to contain women sentenced to longer terms of penal servitude, and local prisons, for those serving shorter sentences, it pieces together a wide composite of archival material, personal testimonies and publications to breach the often-impenetrable prison walls. Piecing together these records allows the study to open up the regimes within to examination, to track how penal policy was translated into everyday practice and to identify shifts and continuities in the punitive, reformatory and medical treatment of women, especially mothers, between the mid-nineteenth and the mid-twentieth century.

The Directorate of Convict Prisons was established in 1850 under the chairmanship of Sir Joshua Jebb. Its annual reports collated information received from each convict prison, including reports delivered by governors, chaplains and doctors. Following the Prison Act 1877 and the creation of the Board of Prison Commissioners, annual reports summed up the operation of local prisons. In the late 1890s the Prison Commission decided to issue one annual report dealing with all prisons. These records offer voluminous information on the organisation of prisons and their regimes and the viewpoints of those administering them on a daily basis. They provide valuable information on the numbers of prisoners committed and released each year, details of medical provisions and records related to subjects including discipline, punishments, diet and accommodation.[53] Home Office records housed in The National Archives offer an additional extensive collection of records relating to individual prisons and prisoners.[54] In addition, this book is able to illuminate key debates in penal policy through a close analysis of parliamentary select committees, Royal Commissions and enquiries into the operation of the prison system that were carried out throughout this period and that included evidence from prison staff, senior members of the prison hierarchy and, in some cases, ex-prisoners. It is important to acknowledge that, within these official records and parliamentary documents, the prisoner's voice was often either absent or mediated by those recording the information. Furthermore, it was very often not the aim of such records to illuminate the viewpoint of prisoners or to offer a means for them to share their experiences of, or indeed their opinions about, their imprisonment. However, a reading of the content of reports and records compiled within individual prisons enables an assessment of the ways in which prison officials identified, categorised and rationalised health and disciplinary needs and, crucially, how these assessments impacted upon the punitive and medical treatment of mothers in prison.

Previously underexplored records related to several prisons across England, held in local archives and libraries, offer further valuable insights into the operation of women's prisons.[55] These records reveal debates between the prison staff, including the doctor, about containing women, and information on medical and sanitary provisions, and describe the spaces and regimes in which pregnant women were imprisoned and gave birth. They are of great value in exploring variations in provision and practices of maternity care in convict prisons including Brixton, Millbank, Parkhurst, Woking and Aylesbury, and in some of England's largest local prisons, including Liverpool, Westminster, Birmingham, Manchester and Holloway, England's only local prison designated exclusively for women. To provide the fullest possible picture of prisons across England, the comparatively limited, but nonetheless valuable, material related to the smaller female populations in prisons such as Hull, Durham and Exeter has also been drawn upon.

Prisons and prisoners were the subject of extensive legal, social and medical commentary, with the causes of crime and their remedy at the centre of debates. The book draws upon this extensive discourse to illuminate pervasive themes discussed in relation to female criminality. These included the difficulties women faced reclaiming respectability once tainted by incarceration, the problem of recidivism and, crucially, the moral and social effect of maternal imprisonment. In addition, the book incorporates the work of journalists and social reformers who described their visits into prisons, and newspaper articles reporting upon prison conditions, as they yield valuable insight into how the outside looked in. They reveal shifting public perceptions about prisons and those who populated them and can be used to uncover contemporary criticisms of the prison system, including provisions for health care and sanitation. These were also subjects regularly written about in the medical press, with doctors working inside and outside of the prison estate contributing articles to the *Lancet* and the *British Medical Journal* on subjects ranging from the treatment of mental disorders, prison diet and labour to provisions for childbirth and the physical state of women who entered the prison system pregnant.

Since the inception of the modern prison system in the mid-nineteenth century there have been calls for its reformation and for greater provisions to support prisoners during and after their sentence. To explore these themes further in relation to mothers in particular, the book delves into rich material held at the Modern Records Centre at Warwick University. This includes the records of the Howard League for Penal Reform, an organisation which has campaigned widely and vigorously for reform on issues including education, work and health for over 150 years.[56] The Holloway Discharged Prisoners' Aid Society (HDPAS) was established in March 1904 and was the only branch of the organisation to focus exclusively upon women. Certified by the Prison Commission and subsidised by the Treasury along with charitable donations, agents from the Society visited women in Holloway to help make arrangements to aid them on release. When women walked back through the prison gates into society they often faced it penniless, friendless and without character. A detailed reading of the Society's annual reports reveals that they offered women vital support to find employment, to improve their home conditions, to care for their children and to manage debts. They also provided material support in the form of cash grants, clothes, food and furniture. The reports documented the 'typical cases' the Society encountered time and again, of women entering prison due to poverty and poor home conditions, to reinforce their calls for women, especially mothers, to receive greater education and support during their imprisonment to better prepare them for release.[57]

Prison reports and parliamentary committees enable interrogation of the conception and intentions behind the imposition of penal power and how this impacted on the daily running of prisons. A reading of the recollections of their time in prison written by ex-prisoners and staff offers a contrasting and valuable insight into the lived experience of these institutions. Between the late nineteenth and mid-twentieth century, women chronicled their feelings of isolation, sensory deprivation, despair and anger. They wrote about the realities of prison life and their interactions with the other prisoners and staff around them and described their experiences of seeking and receiving medical treatment. They spoke about the deleterious effects of prison regimes to contest their legitimacy and to highlight their potential to harm prisoners in body and in mind. In the late nineteenth century, ex-prisoners such as Florence Maybrick, who served fifteen years in prison for the alleged murder of her husband, and Susan Willis Fletcher, who served twelve months in prison for fraud, provided detailed observations of the effects of rigorous prison regimes upon themselves and other prisoners.[58] Similarly, Joan Henry, imprisoned in Holloway and Askham Grange prisons in the mid-twentieth century, spoke about the impressions she had formed of the women around her.[59] Political prisoners in the first half of the twentieth century, notably suffragettes and conscientious objectors, employed their prison accounts to promote their respective causes, but also to highlight the plight of the ordinary female prisoners they encountered behind bars.[60]

There are some caveats we must acknowledge when using prisoner memoirs. They tended to be written by literate, middle- or upper-class inmates, particularly in the case of women, and there was the potential for publishers to push these authors to emphasise certain themes, such as immorality and 'fallen women', for commercial purposes.[61] However, Anderson and Pratt and, more recently, Marland argue that what lends these accounts authenticity is the recurrence of themes and descriptions such as the horror of the separate cell or the monotony of prison life. In addition, they demonstrate that, in advocating for reform, these accounts offer a look behind the often impenetrable prison gates and expose the regimes within to outside scrutiny.⁶² They are drawn on to gain insight into how regimes, intended to be strict and unwavering in principle, were adapted and negotiated in practice in response to the distinct health needs of mothers and their children.

Published accounts written by prison officers, governors and doctors provide a vital means of understanding the role of prison staff in shaping the experiences of women and children in prison. They include detailed observations, defences and criticisms of the institutions and regimes their writers worked within. In addition, the authors provide vivid descriptions of the women under their charge and talk not only about their behaviour, demeanour and responses to incarceration but also about the circumstances that had led them to the prison gates and their lives outside prison. These accounts enable an exploration of the importance of the gender and class of the observers who wrote them and how this shaped their recollections and opinions of those they observed. Some, such as George Laval Chesterton, Governor of Coldbath Fields in the midnineteenth century, Mary Carpenter, a penal and educational reformer, and Arthur Griffiths, Deputy Governor of Millbank and later a prison administrator, spoke about the women they encountered in the harshest of terms and roundly condemned their lack of femininity.⁶³ However, by the 1920s and 1930s those working in the female estate, including Dr Mary Gordon, Cicely McCall and Mary Size, talked more about the social and environmental causes of female criminality, such as poverty and the negative influence of husbands, and placed greater emphasis upon the reformative and remedial role of the prison.⁶⁴ When exploring the significance of the accounts left by prisoners for our understanding of life behind bars, Brown and Clare found that, in contrast to official discourse, prisoner accounts capture the manner in which prison regimes imprisoned staff as well as inmates.⁶⁵ This is a paradox further explored here using the accounts of those who worked in prisons to illuminate how people in positions of power and on the front line in enacting penal policy felt bound by it but also sought to negotiate and reform often obdurate regimes from within. In some cases this was believed to be a necessity to preserve the health of prisoners, and their children, due to the immediate circumstances. Yet, in others, criticisms of the prison system itself can be clearly gleaned.

The book is thematically organised to first examine the physical spaces and regimes in which mothers and babies were confined before exploring shifting provisions for their education and training in mothercraft while in prison and debates about the practice of having babies within the prison environment at all. The disciplinary regimes established with the inception of the new prison system in the mid-nineteenth century were designed by male authorities, with the containment of male prisoners in mind with little consideration at policy level of the specific requirements of containing women. Chapter 1 reveals that female prisoners' access to care in practice was subject to a chain of decision-making processes, including prisoners themselves, governors, officers and doctors as well as officials beyond the gates. These decisions could and did have life-threatening ramifications for mothers and their babies. A question that endured was whether prisoners, regardless of their crimes, were entitled to a certain standard of medical care and to an assurance that their health would not be injured by the prison regime.

Throughout this period, births were regular events in women's prisons, sometimes numbering between twenty and thirty deliveries a year in one institution alone. When they walked through the prison gates, hundreds of women knew they would give birth behind bars, but their experiences have remained largely absent from studies of the history of female prisons and do not feature in the expansive scholarship exploring the developments in maternity care in nineteenth- and twentieth-century England. Chapter 2 reveals the conditions in which pregnant women and mothers with children were imprisoned, including the impact of separation and prolonged cellular confinement on their health. It demonstrates how the often perfunctory nature of medical examinations upon entry into prison, combined with the difficulties of identifying pregnancy due to poor nutrition and irregular menstruation, meant that some pregnancies went undetected for months. Others were deliberately concealed by the women and became known only when they gave birth in their cells. Pregnant women were placed in separate confinement, due to the pervasive principle of limiting and closely regulating association and communication between prisoners. In cases of emergency, including when women went into labour, calls for help were not always answered in time and women gave birth alone within the confines of their cells. The isolation and feeling of helplessness prompted mental distress and anxiety, especially as women approached the time of birth. The trauma caused to pregnant women and those in the cells around them who heard their cries pierce the silence but were unable to help was frequently commented upon in the memoirs of ex-prisoners.

A close reading of individual prison records and the accounts of ex-prisoners and staff enables the chapter to uncover adaptations to the regime by the doctor and female prison officers if the health of mothers or their babies was in danger. These adaptations included designating specific observation cells for women at an advanced stage of pregnancy and accommodating them two or three to a cell so they could alert the officer on duty in case of an emergency. In addition to the day-to-day efforts of small numbers of prison staff to adapt the regime, efforts were also driven by reformers outside. In the early twentieth century, cases of women suffering miscarriages and giving birth in their cells were increasingly held up as indictments of the inadequacies of medical provision in prisons, in petitions sent to the Home Office and in newspaper reports. They were reported at a time of intense debate about the physical and mental condition of the population more broadly, especially mothers and children, and when motherhood was held up as a national as well as a moral duty, one that required greater education and regulation.

These debates have been the subject of detailed examination by historians of maternity and motherhood, with the respective studies of Lewis, Davin and McIntosh in particular illuminating the impact of these debates and the policies implemented thereafter upon mothers.[66] However, their resonance within the prison system is one that has been largely ignored within medical humanities and the social history of motherhood. This study demonstrates that prisons were increasingly viewed as potential sites for the reconstruction of respectable motherhood by reformers and some of those working within the system. In turn, the historical works of Marks and Bryder explore how circumstances or opportunities for public debate at a given time, including wartime, or in response to specific circumstances, including shifting attitudes towards the administration of the Poor Law, had the potential to drive changes in policy towards mothers and children. However, these studies do not extend to exploring the impact on provisions for, and rules dictating, the care of mothers and children in prisons at these key moments.[67]

One such event that has been widely regarded as a significant prompt for an intensification of debates about motherhood was the outbreak of the First World War in 1914 and its far-reaching consequences. Dwork's study illuminated how the wartime circumstances provoked concern about physical degeneracy and provided an impetus to improve the health of children through closer scrutiny of their mothers.[68] However, this study reveals that calls to address the health of the nation more broadly penetrated the prison walls and prompted shifts in attempts to educate women in mothercraft. While mothers in prison are largely absent within the rich historical field dedicated to motherhood, especially in the first half of the twentieth century, reading widely in this field makes clear how the prison environment offers a unique site, and notable chasm, to explore how these broader social, class and political debates, which have been the subject of in-depth examination for mothers outside of the prison gates, impacted on the direction of penal policy towards maternity care in prisons. This includes developments in the staffing of prisons.

Midwifery in women's prisons has not featured within broader scholarship charting the history of the profession, its legal regulation and the quality of care offered by midwives in the early twentieth century.[69] In some of the larger prisons in the early twentieth century there was a trained midwife on the staff, although she would not always be on call. In other prisons, arrangements were made to call in a midwife when a prisoner went into labour. This practice varied considerably from case to case and across different prisons. More consistent access to midwives was an intensely debated issue in women's prisons, as it was outside of them, particularly following the end of the First World War. Debates were nuanced and practices were shaped by the distinct context and disciplinary requirements of the prison setting, but were informed by broader efforts to tackle infant welfare, to reduce maternal mortality and to regulate maternity care in Britain. A significant section of Chapter 2 will explore the outcomes of a landmark enquiry into health and maternity care provisions in Holloway Prison in 1919, chaired by notable penal reformer Adeline Marie Russell, Duchess of Bedford. The committee's recommendations included improving the conditions in which mothers and babies were accommodated and the gradual appointment of full-time midwives in all women's prisons and the introduction of financial incentives to encourage other female members of staff to undergo the necessary training to acquire the Certificate of the Board of Midwives. By the mid-twentieth century, prison authorities argued that accessibility to maternity care was equal to, if not better than, that available to women in their communities, especially those from the poorest social backgrounds, prior to the establishment of the National Health Service in 1948.

While the first half of the book explores how pregnancy and childbirth were incorporated and managed in prison, Chapter 3 examines the opportunities women had to be mothers during their sentence. This includes attempts made to mould them into what would be deemed a 'good' mother. To do this we must first return to the question of how we define motherhood and the extent to which women could be mothers in prison. One of the most significant questions explored by Baunach in her study of mothers in prison in the late twentieth century is that of loss. Whether their relationship with their children was considered to be positive and caring or strained and unhealthy, the imprisonment of mothers has long engendered feelings of loss and failure. This loss and the resulting separation from their children was and is unique for women in prison, and made potentially more traumatic as it was perceived to be a consequence of their own behaviour and a manifestation of their inability to be, or abandonment of their role as, mothers.[70] The chapter assesses the role of the prison regime itself in addressing the behaviour and characteristics of the 'bad' mothers who entered the prison and the attempts made to mould these women into 'good' ones before they walked back out.

Rich scholarship in gender history has identified the Victorian period as one in which motherhood emerged as a dominant social construct and concern. It has demonstrated how institutions, from the church to the government, used the family as a metaphor and a justification for the imposition of their authority,[71] or, indeed, the role of motherhood as a 'moral force'.[72] When examining the difficulties of reconciling women's identity as mothers and their status as prisoners, the chapter uncovers the efforts made to educate mothers in prison in domesticity and mothercraft. It charts how this education developed between the 1850s and 1950s and argues that, alongside the long-standing issue of the moral instruction of mothers, the potential to use prison sentences to achieve more medically focused intervention and practical advice to help with the implementing of this education in the home was slowly acknowledged.

Bad mothers were held up as an indictment on the nation in the early twentieth century which required redress. Although overtly eugenic or social Darwinist ideals were not fully translated into policy, the interaction between these and questions of public health has been examined in relation to attempts to develop state control over motherhood.[73] The 1904 *Report of the Inter-Departmental Committee on Physical Deterioration* accused mothers of having no knowledge of treating their children's ailments and of lacking the skills to provide a healthy home environment for their families.[74] Chapter 3 demonstrates that around the time of the report's publication there were already calls from within and outside the prison system to offer greater provision for the education of female inmates in domesticity and mothercraft, and which continued in the interwar period and became more pronounced in the decade following the end of the Second World War.

The post-1945 period was an age in which motherhood was idealised in order to lure women back from the workplace to the home, but it was also a time of intense scrutiny of mothers.[75] They were believed to be culpable in creating the social evil that was the 'problem family', which lived in cramped and unsanitary conditions and produced unhealthy and poorly educated children, and to be in need of education to combat these issues.[76] Chapter 3 demonstrates how women's prisons present key, but previously underexplored, spaces in which these efforts were concentrated. Courses in mothercraft were established in each prison holding women in the early 1950s and were delivered on a more consistent basis than ever before. Although they differed slightly in each prison, their composition and teaching was the result of a sharing of ideas, experiences and best practice between prison officials, charities and organisations such as the National Society for the Prevention of Cruelty to Children and the Women's Voluntary Services and, crucially, with the Ministry of Health and local health authorities, including health visitors and the newly expanded maternity and child welfare services. Analysing the content of courses enables the chapter to demonstrate how policy makers and medical practitioners attempted to abstract the problem of maternal ignorance from issues of poverty and environmental circumstances when attempting to educate women to be 'good' mothers and to demonstrate how this marked a change from previous prison policy.

A key theme running throughout the book and a quandary that perennially troubled prison authorities and reformers alike was the question of whether prison was, or indeed could ever be, a suitable environment for mothers and babies. To address the complexity of this question, Chapter 4 delves into the shifting medical, social and legal debates about whether babies should be born in prison and the impact of their presence upon their mothers, the other women around them and the institution itself. In 1903 Arthur Griffiths, who had worked in several prisons in the late nineteenth century and became Inspector of Prisons in 1878, lamented that to be born in prison was an 'inalienable heritage of woe'. However, he captured the long-standing inconsistency surrounding views about the presence of children in prison when he added that, despite the stigma, in many cases 'the prison born are better off than the free born – more cared for, more delicately nurtured' than those dragged up in the 'dark dens of the town'.[77] The chapter provides a reading of debates which acknowledged that for some women prisons were places of refuge from the harsher conditions they faced outside, but persistently warned of the danger of moral contagion for children born in prison.

Prisoners, their families and reform organisations petitioned the government to prevent the social stigma of a prison birth. A reading of these petitions allows the chapter to expose the legal, social and medical arguments that were levied to support them, as well as to identify the increasing emphasis that was placed upon the rights and needs of the unborn babies of women in prison. In doing so it adds a new voice to the historical field that has identified the twentieth century as one in which the rights of children and their specific health needs were more carefully defined and provided for and more rigorously protected.[78] Section 60 of the 1948 Criminal Justice Act empowered the Secretary of State to authorise the temporary release, to a hospital outside the prison estate or a maternity home, of any pregnant women who wished for their confinement to take place outside the prison. While the legislation led to a notable decline in the number of babies born in prison, it did not initially end the practice completely, as some women stated their preference to remain in the prison hospital due to a familiarity with the surroundings and the staff. This raised complex questions about the mother's right to choose the circumstances in which she gave birth and led to calls for this choice to be removed for the good of the child. However, it would be another decade before the official sanctioning of prison births ended.

Before delving into the chapters that follow, it is important to note that this book uncovers the personal experiences of some of the mothers who walked through the prison gates during this period, including those who were pregnant, gave birth and attempted to be mothers in prison. However, it cannot tell every mother's story. The experiences of many women remain hidden, or they form part of the broader discussions in each chapter. In addition, the nature of the subject area of mothers and babies in prison has historically been a complex and emotive one which has evoked medical, legal, social and ideological debates that in many ways rage on in our criminal justice system today. Although the book provides the first extensive history of these debates, it seeks neither to be an indictment nor a defence of women's prisons or those who worked or were confined within them between the mid-nineteenth and the mid-twentieth century. Instead, each chapter aims to disentangle the exigencies of providing for the health of mothers in prison due both to the constraints of the environment itself and also to the difficulties of caring for this group of prisoners who, like many of the other women around them, were in poor physical or mental health when they entered the prison system and faced financial difficulties and poor home conditions when they left it.

Notes

1 Florence Elizabeth Chandler Maybrick, *Mrs Maybrick's own story: My fifteen lost years* (London: Funk & Wagnalls Company, 1905), p. 126.
2 Susan Willis Fletcher, *Twelve months in an English prison* (New York: Charles T. Dillingham, 1884), p. 343.
3 The National Archives, Kew (hereafter TNA) PCOM 7/40, Report of committee presided over by Adeline, Duchess of Bedford to inquire into various matters concerning Holloway Prison, May 1919, p. 44.
4 Mary Size, *Prisons I have known* (London: George Allen and Unwin, 1957), p. 95.
5 Cicely McCall, *They always come back* (London: Methuen & Co., 1938), p. 35.

6 Quoted in Paul Rock, *Reconstructing a women's prison: The Holloway Redevelopment Project, 1968–88* (Oxford: Oxford University Press, 1996), p. 87.
7 For select key works see Joe Sim, *Medical power in prisons: The Prison Medical Service in England 1774–1989* (Milton Keynes: Open University Press, 1990); Michael Clark and Catherine Crawford (eds), *Legal medicine in history* (Cambridge: Cambridge University Press, 1994). For more recent scholarship see Catherine Cox and Hilary Marland, '"He must die or go mad in this place": Prisoners, insanity, and the Pentonville Model Prison experiment, 1842–1852', *Bulletin of the History of Medicine*, 92:1 (2018), 78–109, https://doi.org/10.1353/bhm.2018.0004; Catherine Cox and Hilary Marland, 'Broken minds and beaten bodies: Cultures of harm and the management of mental illness in mid- to late nineteenth-century English and Irish prisons', *Social History of Medicine*, 31:4 (2018), 688–710, https://doi.org/10.1093/shmhky038.
8 John Howard, *The state of the prisons in England and Wales* (Warrington: William Eyres, 1777), p. 38.
9 Peter McRorie Higgins, *Punish or treat? Medical care in English prisons 1770–1850* (Victoria: Trafford Publishing, 2007).
10 For a recent study of health in prisons see Catherine Cox and Hilary Marland, *Disorder contained: Mental breakdown and the modern prison in England and Ireland, 1840–1900* (Cambridge: Cambridge University Press, 2022).
11 Martin J. Wiener, 'The health of prisoners and the two faces of Benthamism', in Richard Creese, W.F. Bynum and J. Bearn (eds.), *The health of prisoners* (Amsterdam: Rodopi, 1995), pp. 44–58, pp. 47–49.
12 Martin J. Wiener, *Reconstructing the criminal: Culture, law, and policy in England, 1830–1914* (Cambridge: Cambridge University Press, 1990), pp. 122, 126.
13 Sim, *Medical power in prisons*; Philip Priestley, *Victorian prison lives: English prison biography, 1830–1914* (London: Pimlico, 1985), p. 190.
14 Stephen Watson, 'Malingerers, the "weak-minded" criminal and the "moral imbecile": How the English prison medical officer became an expert in mental deficiency, 1880–1930', in Michael Clark and Catherine Crawford (eds), *Legal medicine in History* (Cambridge: Cambridge University Press, 1994), pp. 223–241, p. 224.
15 Neil Davie, *Tracing the criminal: The rise of scientific criminology in Britain, 1860–1918* (Oxford: The Bardwell Press, 2005), p. 71.
16 Cox and Marland, '"He must die or go mad in this place"', p. 81; Cox and Marland, 'Broken minds and beaten bodies'.

17 Jade Shepherd, 'Feigning insanity in late-Victorian Britain', *Prison Service Journal*, 232 (2017), pp. 17–23, p. 19.
18 Rachel Bennett, 'Bad for the health of the body, worse for the health of the mind: Female responses to imprisonment in England, 1853–1869', *Social History of Medicine*, 34:2 (2021), 532–552, https://doi.org/10.1093/shm/hkz066.
19 Ann Oakley, *Women confined: Towards a sociology of childbirth* (New York: Schocken Books, 1980), p. 34.
20 Heather A. Cahill, 'Male appropriation and medicalisation of childbirth: An historical analysis', *Journal of Advanced Nursing*, 33:3 (2001), 334–342, https://doi.org/10.1046/j.1365-2648.2001.01669.x.
21 Phyllis Jo Baunach, *Mothers in prison* (New York: Transaction Publishers, first edition 1983, this edition 2020), p. 2.
22 Vernon Harris, 'The female prisoner', *The Nineteenth Century and After*, 363 (1907), p. 783.
23 Henry Mayhew and John Binny, *The criminal prisons of London and scenes of prison life* (London: Griffin, Bohn and Company, 1862), p. 464.
24 For a recent history of Holloway Prison see Caitlin Davies, *Bad girls: A history of rebels and renegades* (London: John Murray, 2018). For a recent collection of life histories of select women who experienced the prison system between the mid-nineteenth and the early twentieth century see Lucy Williams and Barry Godfrey, *Criminal women 1850–1920: Researching the lives of Britain's female offenders* (Barnsley: Pen & Sword, 2018); Lucy Williams, *Wayward women: Female offending in Victorian England* (Barnsley: Pen & Sword, 2016).
25 Mary Bosworth, 'Confining femininity: A history of gender, power and imprisonment', *Theoretical Criminology*, 4:3 (2000), 265–284, 265–267, https://doi.org/10.1177/1362480600004003002.
26 For select and widely cited key studies dedicated to the rationale underpinning the design of the modern prison system and its administration see Seán McConville, *A history of English prison administration, Vol. I 1750–1877* (London: Routledge & Kegan Paul, 1981); Norval Morris and David J. Rothman (eds), *The Oxford history of the prison: The practice of punishment in Western society* (Oxford: Oxford University Press, 1995); Priestley, *Victorian Prison Lives*.
27 Lucia Zedner, *Women, crime and custody in Victorian England* (Oxford: Oxford University Press, 1991); Russell P. Dobash, R. Emerson Dobash and Sue Gutteridge, *The imprisonment of women* (Oxford: Basil Blackwell, 1986); Bill Forsythe, 'Women prisoners and women's penal officials 1840–1921', *British Journal of Criminology*, 33:4 (1993), 525–540, https://doi.org/10.1093/oxfordjournals.bjc.a048357; Neil Davie, 'Business

as usual? Britain's first women's prison, Brixton 1853–1869', *Crimes and Misdemeanours*, 4:1 (2010), 37–52.

28 For select works see Bosworth, 'Confining Femininity'; Pat Carlen, *Sledgehammer: Women's imprisonment at the millennium* (Basingstoke: Palgrave Macmillan, 1998), in particular pp. 46–99. For a study of the interaction between beliefs about masculinity and prison management see Eamonn Carrabine and Brian Longhurst, 'Gender and prison organisation: Some comments on masculinities and prison management', *The Howard Journal of Criminal Justice*, 37:2 (1998), 161–176, https://doi.org/10.1111/1468-2311.00088.

29 Baunach, *Mothers in prison*; Laura Abbott and Kelly Lockwood, 'Negotiating pregnancy, new motherhood and imprisonment', in Kelly Lockwood (ed.), *Mothering from the inside: Research on motherhood and imprisonment* (Bingley: Emerald Publishing, 2020), pp. 49–66.

30 Lucy Baldwin (ed.), *Mothering justice: Working with mothers in criminal and social justice settings* (Hampshire: Waterside Press, 2015).

31 Zedner, *Women, crime and custody*, pp. 13–14, 47–48, 222–226.

32 Helen Johnston, 'Imprisoned mothers in Victorian England, 1853–1900: Motherhood, identity and the convict prison', *Criminology & Criminal Justice*, 19:2 (2019), 215–231, https://doi.org/10.1177/1748895818757833.

33 Elaine Farrell, 'Poor prison flowers: Convict mothers and their children in Ireland, 1853–1900', *Social History*, 41:2 (2016), 171–191, https://doi.org/10.1080/03071022.2016.1144312.

34 Nancy M. Wingfield and Maria Bucur (eds), *Gender and war in twentieth-century Europe* (Bloomington: Indiana University Press, 2006).

35 Judith E. Tucker, *Women in nineteenth-century Egypt* (Cambridge: Cambridge University Press, 1985).

36 Elaine Farrell, *Women, crime and punishment in Ireland: Life in the nineteenth-century convict prison* (Cambridge: Cambridge University Press, 2020); Patricia O'Brien, *The promise of punishment: Prisons in nineteenth-century France* (Princeton: Princeton University Press, 1982).

37 Brett Josef Derbes, '"Secret horrors": Enslaved women and children in the Louisiana State Penitentiary, 1833–1862', in Erica Rhodes Hayden and Theresa R. Jach (eds), *Incarcerated women: A history of struggles, oppression, and resistance in American prisons* (London: Lexington Books, 2017), pp. 3–16; Hilary L. Coulson, '"In the care of the supposed powerful state": Women and children in the Virginia Penitentiary, 1800–1883', in Erica Rhodes Hayden and Theresa R. Jach (eds), *Incarcerated women: A history of struggles, oppression, and resistance in American prisons* (London: Lexington Books, 2017), pp. 17–36.

38 Coulson, '"In the care of the supposed powerful state"', p. 25.
39 Anne M. Butler, *Gendered justice in the American West: Women prisoners in men's penitentiaries* (Chicago: University of Illinois Press, 1997), quote taken from p. 6.
40 Elizabeth Fry, *Observations on the visiting, superintendence and government of female prisoners* (Norwich: S. Wilkin, 1827), p. 3.
41 Forsythe, 'Women prisoners and women's penal officials'; Helen Johnston, 'Gendered prison work: Female prison officers in the local prison system, 1877–1939', *Howard Journal of Criminal Justice*, 53:2 (2014), 193–212, https://doi.org/10.1111/hojo.12043.
42 Carol Smart, 'Deconstructing motherhood', in Elizabeth Bortolaia Silva (ed.), *Good enough mothering? Feminist perspectives on lone motherhood* (London: Routledge, 1996), pp. 37–57, p. 39.
43 Karin Sardadvar, 'Social construction of motherhood', in Andrea O'Reilly (ed.), *Encyclopaedia of motherhood* (London: SAGE, 2010), pp. 1134–1135.
44 Elisabeth Badinter, *The conflict: Woman and mother* (Melbourne: Text Publishing, 2010); Elisabeth Badinter, *Mother love: Myth and reality: Motherhood in modern History* (Basingstoke: Macmillan, 1981).
45 Ann Oakley, *Becoming a mother* (London: Penguin Books, 1979), p. 308.
46 Jean Towler and Joan Bramall, *Midwives in history and society* (London: Croom Helm, 1986).
47 For a detailed overview of this period see Tania McIntosh, *A social history of maternity and childbirth: Key themes in maternity care* (Abingdon: Routledge, 2012).
48 McIntosh, *A social history of maternity and childbirth*, p. 38.
49 Irvine Loudon, 'Maternal mortality in the past and its relevance to developing countries today', *The American Journal of Clinical Nutrition*, 72:1 (2000), 241S–246S.
50 Angela Davis, 'Choice, policy and practice in maternity care since 1948', *History & Policy* (May 2013).
51 Hilary Marland, 'Childbirth and maternity', in Roger Cooter and John Pickstone (eds), *Medicine in the twentieth century* (London: Routledge, 2000), pp. 559–574; Irvine Loudon, 'On maternal and infant mortality 1900–1960', *Social History of Medicine*, 4:1 (1991), 29–73; Irvine Loudon, *Death in childbirth: An international study of maternal care and maternal mortality 1800–1950* (Oxford: Oxford University Press, 1992).
52 Davis, 'Choice, policy and practice'.
53 The annual reports of the Directors of Convict Prisons, the annual Report of the Commissioners of Prisons and the combined annual

Report of the Commissioners of Prisons and the Directors of Convict Prisons can be found among the Parliamentary Papers collection.

54 For an extensive collection of Prison Commission records see TNA PCOM 2.
55 For a comprehensive digital guide to many of the other penal institutions operational in nineteenth-century England see prisonhistory.org.
56 The Howard League for Penal Reform is the oldest prison reform charity in Britain. Founded as the Howard Association in 1866, taking its name from influential late eighteenth-century penal reformer John Howard, it became the Howard League for Penal Reform in 1921 when it was merged with the Prison Reform League. The collection of Howard League records at the MRC includes annual reports, committee meeting minutes, specific subject files, research materials and photographs.
57 The HDPAS annual reports between 1918 and 1964 can be found among the National Association for the Care and Resettlement of Offenders (NACRO) records at the MRC, catalogue reference MSS.67/4/24.
58 Maybrick, *Mrs Maybrick's own story*; Fletcher, *Twelve months in an English prison*.
59 Joan Henry, *Women in prison* (London: White Lion Publishers, 1952).
60 Constance Lytton and Jane Warton, *Prisons and prisoners: Some personal experiences* (London: William Heinemann, 1914); Lonsdale et al., *Some account of life in Holloway Prison*.
61 Anne Schwan, *Convict voices: Women, class, and writing about prison in nineteenth-century England* (New Hampshire: University of New Hampshire Press, 2014), p. 94.
62 Sarah Anderson and John Pratt, 'Prisoner memoirs and their role in prison history', in Helen Johnston (ed.), *Punishment and control in historical perspective* (Houndmills: Palgrave Macmillan, 2008), pp. 179–198, pp. 179–181; Hilary Marland, '"Close confinement tells very much upon a man": Prison memoirs, insanity and the late nineteenth- and early twentieth-century prison', *Journal of the History of Medicine and Allied Sciences*, 74:3 (2019), 267–291, https://doi.org/10.1093/jhmas/jrz027, pp. 288–291.
63 George Laval Chesterton, *Revelations of prison life with an enquiry into prison discipline and secondary punishments* (London: Hurst and Blackett Publishers, 1856); Mary Carpenter, *Our convicts, Vol. II* (London: Longman, 1864); Arthur Griffiths, *Memorials of Millbank and chapters in prison history* (London: Chapman and Hall, 1884).
64 Mary Gordon, *Penal discipline* (New York: George Routledge & Sons, 1922); Size, *Prisons I have known*.
65 Alyson Brown and Emma Clare, 'A history of experience: Exploring prisoners' accounts of incarceration', in Clive Emsley (ed.), *The persistent*

prison: Problems, images and alternatives (London: Francis Boutle, 2005), pp. 49–73, p. 67.

66 For select key works see Jane Lewis, *The politics of motherhood: Child and maternal welfare in England, 1900–1939* (London: Croom Helm, 1980); Anna Davin, 'Imperialism and motherhood', *History Workshop*, 5:1 (1978), 9–65, https://doi.org/10.1093/hwj/5.1.9; Ellen Ross, *Love and toil: Motherhood in outcast London, 1870–1918* (Oxford: Oxford University Press, 1993); Tania McIntosh, *A social history of maternity and childbirth: Key themes in maternity care* (Abingdon: Routledge, 2012).

67 Lara Marks, 'Medical care for pauper mothers and their infants: Poor Law provision and local demand in East London. 1870–1929', *Economic History Review*, 46:3 (1993), 518–542, https://doi.org/10.1111/j.1468-0289.1993.tb01347.x; Linda Bryder, 'Mobilising mothers: The 1917 National Baby Week', *Medical History*, 63:1 (2019), 2–23, https://doi.org/10.1017/mdh.2018.60.

68 Deborah Dwork, *War is good for babies and other young children: A history of the infant and child welfare movement in England 1898–1918* (London: Tavistock Publications, 1987).

69 McIntosh, *A social history of maternity and childbirth*; Lucinda Beier, 'Expertise and control: Childbearing in three twentieth-century working-class Lancashire communities', *Bulletin of the History of Medicine*, 78:2 (2004), 379–409, https://doi.org/10.1353/bhm.2004.0056; Alice Reid, 'Birth attendants and midwifery practice in early twentieth-century Derbyshire', *Social History of Medicine*, 25:2 (2012), 380–399, https://doi.org/10.1093/shm/hkr138.

70 Baunach, *Mothers in prison*, pp. 1–2.

71 Claudia Nelson and Daniel Nelson, *Family ties in Victorian England* (Westport, CT: Praeger Publishers, 2007), p. 7.

72 Ann Sumner Holmes and Claudia Nelson, 'Introduction', in Claudia Nelson and Ann Sumner Holmes (eds), *Maternal instincts: Visions of motherhood and sexuality in Britain, 1875–1925* (Basingstoke: Macmillan, 2007), pp. 1–12, p. 1.

73 Carol Dyhouse, 'Good wives and little mothers: Social anxieties and the schoolgirl's curriculum, 1890–1920', *History and Education*, 3:1 (1977), 21–35, https://doi.org/10.1080/0305498770030102; Davin, 'Imperialism and motherhood'; McIntosh, *A social history of maternity and childbirth*, for a discussion of the Edwardian period see pp. 24–44.

74 Report of the Inter-Departmental Committee on Physical Deterioration (London: 1904).

75 Ann Dally, *Inventing motherhood: The consequences of an ideal* (London: Burnett Books, 1982); Angela Davis, *Modern motherhood: Women and*

family in England, c. 1945–2000 (Manchester: Manchester University Press, 2012).

76 Pat Starkey, 'The feckless mother: Women, poverty and social workers in wartime and post-war England', *Women's History Review*, 9:3 (2000), 539–557, https://doi.org/10.1080/09612020000200259; John Welshman, *Underclass: A history of the excluded 1880–2000* (London: Hambledon, 2006); Becky Taylor and Ben Rogaly, '"Mrs Fairly is a dirty, lazy type": Unsatisfactory households and the problem of problem families in Norwich 1942–1963', *Twentieth Century British History*, 18:4 (2007), 429–452, https://doi.org/10.1093/tcbh/hwm019.

77 Major Arthur Griffiths, 'In Wormwood Scrubs Prison', in George Sims (ed.), *Living London: Its work and its play, its humour and its pathos, its sights and its scenes*, Vol. III (London: Cassell, 1903), pp. 126–131, p. 127.

78 Roger Cooter, *In the name of the child: Health and welfare 1880–1940* (London: Routledge, 1992); Harry Hendrick, *Child welfare: England 1872–1989* (London: Routledge, 1994); Harry Hendrick, *Children, childhood and English society 1880–1990* (Cambridge: Cambridge University Press, 1997); Marijke Gijswijt-Hofstra and Hilary Marland (eds), *Cultures of child health in Britain and the Netherlands in the twentieth century* (Amsterdam: Rodopi, 2003).

1

Contesting women's health in the prison system

Prison reformer Mary Carpenter encapsulated a difficulty that has long faced the justice system when confining women, labelling it as 'a subject of great importance and of peculiar difficulty'.[1] When they walked through the prison gates women brought with them a skein of stories and experiences. Some entered prison to serve a sentence of a few days. Others faced several years behind bars. Prisons for women accommodated the young and the old; the healthy alongside the sick; the first-time offender entering prison with trepidation, along with the recidivist, perceived to be hardened to the toils of incarceration. Some women began and ended their prison sentences without family, friends or character. Some began their sentence pregnant, hundreds of others left children and lives on the outside. Historically, mothers in prison have been doubly ostracised by society for their criminal behaviour and for their seeming failure as mothers, exacerbating the impact of the separation from their children.[2] This chapter demonstrates that for each one of them, their experiences of health and discipline were heavily regulated – yet often contested – by those tasked with their custody and care.

Exploring the creation of female prisons and female-only sections in mixed prisons in the mid-nineteenth century, this chapter argues that the physical prison spaces and penal regimes established in these institutions were designed by male prison administrators with the containment of men in mind. It uncovers the ongoing tensions in the century that followed between policy and practice when women were subjected to these regimes, exploring the equally problematic, but underexplored, question of providing for women's health behind bars. The chapter identifies chains of formal and informal decision-making processes that sometimes conflicted with prison policy and regulations and could have a major impact upon prisoners' health. The people involved included the prisoners themselves, prison officers and medical officers as well as prison administrators. Health in prison was also shaped by discussions of the condition of the women who walked through the prison gates and ruminations about their appropriate treatment that were often steeped in gendered and class debates. Within a discussion of the importance of the staff who worked in women's prisons, the chapter introduces readers to the less familiar successors of eminent prison reformer Elizabeth Fry who continued to advocate for one of the core principles at the heart of her early reformatory efforts, namely that female offenders required the moral, educational and, eventually, medical guidance of members of their own sex.

A new departure? Establishing the female prison estate

Britain has a long and storied penal history in which the eighteenth and nineteenth centuries feature heavily, due to fundamental shifts in the infliction of punishment that occurred. Prior to their move behind the prison walls in 1868, those convicted of capital crimes could be publicly executed on one of the many scaffolds scattered across Britain. By the 1830s, the last punishment of the law was largely reserved for those convicted of murder. Thousands of others were transported to Australia, a penal option which had commenced with the sailing of the First Fleet in 1787. As discussed in the Introduction, old gaols and houses of correction were gradually replaced with prisons in the early nineteenth century as incarceration became a secondary penal option for serious offenders, alongside transportation, as well as a punishment for more petty offences.

The Gaol Act 1823 placed stricter restrictions upon local authorities regarding the administration of places of confinement. It directed that prisoners be divided by sex and required that every prison containing women should have a matron to maintain the female side of the prison. However, the mid-nineteenth century marked a seminal moment in Britain's penal narrative when transportation for women ceased to be an option in 1852 and the practice ended completely in 1868. The Penal Servitude Act 1853 replaced sentences of transportation with those of penal servitude. Initially, the minimum length of a sentence was four years, but, following the passing of the Penal Servitude Act 1857, sentences ranged between three years and life. They were served in a government-controlled convict prison.

The Surrey House of Correction was purchased and adapted by the government in 1852 to create Brixton, Britain's first female convict prison. Two wings were added to each end of the old crescent-shaped building along with a new chapel, laundry and accommodation for staff. Separate cells, punishment cells and association rooms were adapted within the buildings. It was designed by the Chairman of the Directors of Convict Prisons, Sir Joshua Jebb, who was often consulted by the Home Office in matters of prison construction in the mid-nineteenth century due to his prior positions in the Royal Engineers and as Inspector-General of Military Prisons. At the outset of this new penal regime in November 1853, 75 prisoners were transferred in from Millbank, and by June 1854 there were over 550 prisoners incarcerated in Brixton. However, overcrowding prompted the decision to reallocate one of Millbank's pentagons to women in February 1855.

In the initial decade following 1853, it was intended that women would undergo the probation stage of discipline and the third class in Millbank before progressing on to Brixton to complete the second- and first-class stages. The classes began with the probation stage, for prisoners beginning their sentence. As women progressed through the classes they would receive additional privileges such as an improved diet or more regular letters. Prisoners would be lectured on the nature of classification and the means of progression by showing industriousness and maintaining good behaviour. Fulham Refuge was opened in 1856 to receive those women who had shown impeccable behaviour and to provide them with industrial training in the final months of their sentence, with the aim of helping them to find respectable employment upon release, usually in domestic service. Additional refuges were opened as the nineteenth century progressed. However, my recent research elsewhere has shown that, while the early convict system for women did become a system wherein they were moved between prisons, it was not the efficient system initially envisaged by Jebb based solely upon progression as a result of compliance with the prison rules. Instead, the regime had to be negotiated and adapted by prison officials due to concerns about prisoners' health.[3] Some women were deemed unfit for the discipline in Millbank and removed to Brixton despite their conduct not warranting such progression. In contrast, women who had earned their progression to Fulham Refuge due to good behaviour were deemed unfit for a place there, often due to age or debility, and were thus detained in Brixton until the expiration of their sentence, to be cared for in the prison's infirmary.

In 1864, in response to the issues of overcrowding and the pressures placed upon prisons for women, the Directors of Convict Prisons acknowledged, 'it is scarcely possible to expect that the best results of prison discipline can have been as yet attained in prisons of a makeshift character'.[4] They were referring to the fact that prisons for women had not been specially constructed and were instead modifications of the arrangements in place for male convicts. Therefore, the Directors gained government approval to construct a new female convict prison at Woking. When reporting upon its progress in 1865, the Directors provided further justification for the closure of the other female convict establishments by stating that all due diligence had been exercised to ensure that the new prison addressed the 'many deficiencies' of the old system.[5] This included building an infirmary to cater for 'all that can be desired for the reception and treatment of the sick'.[6] In December 1869 Brixton closed as an establishment for women and reopened in February 1870 as a light labour prison for men. From April 1869 Parkhurst, which had accommodated women for only six years, became a male convict prison for invalids. The female inmates of these two prisons were transferred to Woking, which served as England's main female convict prison. Fulham was redesignated as a prison in 1869 instead of a refuge. However, Discharged Prisoners' Aid Societies continued to set up and manage refuges elsewhere.

Despite the convict prison estate often featuring at the centre of criminal debate in the mid-nineteenth century, the vast majority of prison sentences handed down to offenders were served in one of the country's local prisons. These sentences could be for a few days or for years. Zedner estimated that 98 per cent of prison sentences for women were served in a local prison in the second half of the nineteenth century.[7] In 1850 Westminster Prison, also known as Tothill Fields, was redesignated to confine women and juvenile boys (under the age of seventeen). After 1860 it was exclusively for women. Liverpool and Birmingham prisons also designated sizeable portions of their prison to women. Holloway Prison was opened in 1852 as a local prison for men and women. In 1902 it was decided that Holloway would become female-only to address the need for greater provision for female prisoners, which was partly exacerbated by the closure of Newgate Prison. Modelled on Warwick Castle, the prison gained the moniker of 'The Castle'; it was an imposing structure in London's landscape and became a central location in the history of female imprisonment in England until its closure in 2016.

Smaller local prisons were adapted to accommodate women but faced repeated difficulties in managing their incarceration, due to issues of space and provision. Some local prisons were so small that they may have only had a handful of women at any one time, meaning provision for them could be makeshift at best. Zedner argued that this could mean women suffered worse conditions than their male counterparts.[8] In Hull Gaol female prisoners were accommodated in a ward adjoining the debtors. Governor Neill remarked to the Gaol Committee in 1857 that this meant the noise in the yard and the daily visitors to the debtors' part of the prison disrupted the orderly management of the female prisoners. It was proposed to alter another part of the prison to remove the debtors and thus double the accommodation available for the female prisoners. It was suggested that a work room be added, along with additional cells for the more effective classification of different groups of prisoners.[9]

During the second half of the nineteenth century, women made up one fifth of those convicted of crime and accounted for approximately 17 per cent of the total prison population.[10] In 1870 they accounted for around 22 per cent of the population in local prisons. This fell to 16 per cent in 1895 and fell further still with the turn of the twentieth century. In convict prisons, women accounted for 14 per cent of inmates in 1878, dropping to an average of one in eight in the 1880s and just three per cent by 1912.[11] Around two-thirds of the women in Westminster Prison in the 1870s were committed for drunk and disorderly offences.[12] When the Prison Act was passed in 1877 to provide more central government control over local prisons, over half of the women entering Westminster were serving sentences of less than fourteen days. Only around one in ten had been sentenced to terms longer than six months.[13] By 1900, the average daily population in local prisons was 2,699 women, as compared to 11,795 men. In convict prisons the figures were 128 women, as compared to 2,588 men.[14] The daily average number of women prisoners in 1913–14 was 2,236 in local prisons and 95 in convict prisons. By 1920–21 the figure was 1,235, of whom 76 were in convict prisons.[15] In her work on the organisation of the prison estate, Johnston offers several reasons for the declining overall prison population in the first three decades of the twentieth century, notably a decline in recorded crime, a reduction in the minimum sentence lengths for penal servitude and an increase in non-custodial practices, including allowing longer for the payment of fines.[16]

By July 1868 the total number of prisons had decreased from 113 to 69, of which 62 held women, although the size of the female portion of the prison and the numbers incarcerated at any one time varied greatly. Following the centralisation of prisons by the Prison Act 1877, the total number of prisons was further reduced. By 1901 there were fifty-two local prisons that held women, with one convict prison for women at Aylesbury. In his historical examination of the shifting policies and debates about rebuilding the physical structure of Holloway Prison, Rock stated that among the criticisms of the prison system in the early twentieth century, the prison commissioners presiding over it were 'likened to slum landlords administering a dilapidated Victorian estate'.[17] Further closures and redesignations of prisons meant that by the 1920s there were only thirty local prisons accommodating women, along with the one convict establishment. The number was reduced further in the 1930s with the decline in the overall female prison population and only nine local prisons held women, along with convict prisons in Aylesbury and Liverpool.[18] Holloway remained the only local prison designated exclusively for women. Further closures of female wings in the second half of the twentieth century led to a broader geographical spread of prison provision for women across England.

Experience is wanting: women and the prison regime

The public nature of punishment had undergone significant changes between the eighteenth and early nineteenth century.[19] Foucault's opening chapter in his seminal study *Discipline and Punish* detailed the prolonged public execution by quartering of the would-be regicide

Robert Damiens in 1757, contrasting this very public punitive spectacle with the heavily regimented running of an institution for young prisoners in Paris in the early nineteenth century. This formed the foundation of Foucault's analysis of the long-term shift from the public punishment of the body to the more regimented attempts to reform criminal behaviour in the prison system.[20] A persistent element running through Victorian penal policy was the imperative to remove uncertainty and variability from punishment.[21] During early discussions about the establishment of the modern prison system in the 1840s and early 1850s, reform was positioned as the central aim around which to build the system. However, in the 1860s, pressures on the prison service and intense debate about recidivism meant that Edmund Du Cane's Directorate of Convict Prisons between 1869 and 1895 was characterised by 'an inflexible adoption of deterrence as the primary aim of punishment and a rigid adherence to its uniform enforcement'.[22]

When reflecting upon his early tenure as Brixton's Medical Officer in 1856, James Rendle remarked that 'the collecting of so large a number of female prisoners in a prison expressly prepared for women are circumstances altogether new in this country'. He continued, 'a system of management is unknown, and experience is wanting'.[23] Within this system of management a recurring question was that of health. John Lavies, Westminster's Medical Officer, remarked in 1863 that women were less robust than their male counterparts and 'are liable to many ailments peculiar to themselves'.[24] Despite acknowledgements that female prisoners posed specific questions within the higher echelons of the prison hierarchy, as well as within individual institutions, this chapter argues that there was limited impact upon actual policy. Forsythe labelled Brixton's regime as a '(mal)adaptation of prison regimes for men' that was informed by male beliefs about female respectability.[25] Recent research has demonstrated that, despite this, the regimes for women in the convict estate were adapted by those working within them and that the disciplinary system was impacted upon by questions of prisoner health. The lack of official policy directed exclusively at women was also an issue raised within debates about the closure of Brixton in 1869, but one that remained in many ways unanswered with the opening of Woking convict prison for women thereafter.[26]

An area of prison policy that attracted criticism and intense debate was the system of separate confinement. Reflecting upon his detention in Reading Gaol in the 1890s, Oscar Wilde wrote of the separate system, 'the production of insanity is, if not its object, certainly its result'.[27] Sentences of penal servitude were for a minimum of three years and were intended to reform convicts before their release back into society. This process of reformation began with prisoners being placed in separate confinement. The separate system was based on the principle that inmates would spend a large proportion of their day alone in their cells and would have time for individual reflection. Incarcerated in isolation, they had no contact with fellow prisoners, minimal contact with prison officials and limited time out of their cells for the purpose of attending chapel and undertaking short daily exercise.

Based on the model set out in Philadelphia's Eastern State Penitentiary, the separate system was first introduced to Britain in Pentonville Prison, for male convicts, in 1842. Prisoners in Pentonville would be placed in separate confinement for eighteen months. Due to criticisms, this was reduced to twelve months and then to nine months in 1853. Cox and Marland have illuminated the difficulties of identifying and managing mental illness, especially alongside implementing this aspect of the carceral system. Several articles and their 2022 book each demonstrate that, while the separate system had many detractors from the time of its inception in the mid-nineteenth century, due to its association with cases of mental breakdown, its supporters pointed to this extreme form of separation as an indispensable step along the path to true reform. Cox and Marland's research explores the consequences of this upon provisions for, and the maintenance of, prisoner health.[28]

Joshua Jebb, Surveyor-General of Prisons and the architect of Pentonville Prison, wrote that the separation of prisoners was the bedrock of a sound prison system, as discipline could be formed and contaminating influences deprived.[29] In evidence sent to John G. Perry, Medical Inspector of Prisons, in 1854 the chaplain of Stafford County Gaol expressed his confidence in the separate system for women. He expressed confidence that young, first offenders could be saved from the ruination that came with association with the 'basest of their sex' under the old system. They could be more successfully encouraged to seek the retrieval of their character.[30] He stated his belief that many of the women in his care, even those of the worst character, came out of their period in separation possessed of better moral principles and a desire to achieve respectability.[31]

The separate system was established in female convict prisons, but from the outset prompted debate about the ability of women to withstand the full rigours of separation. In 1853 the Convict Prison Directorate issued instructions that women would spend four months in separate confinement, as opposed to the nine months specified for male convicts.[32] Officials working in the early female convict estate regularly reported upon the difficulties of containing some women in this way and the greater unsuitability of women to this system.[33] This acknowledgement of the potentially more adverse effects of separation upon women was also noted by officials in America's Virginia Penitentiary and actually led to directions that women received into the prison would not be subjected to initial months in separate confinement as male inmates were.[34] Florence Maybrick recalled in her memoir that in separate confinement, 'all individuality, all friendship, all things that make human beings attractive to one another are absent', describing how women would shriek loudly, tear their clothes and smash their cell windows when kept in such a condition.[35] There were also practical and logistical problems when confining women under the separate system.

A reading of the reports presented to the Visiting Justices of Westminster Prison reveals that there were not enough separate cells, and it was often the case that women were accommodated in dormitories. Officials regularly complained of persistent overcrowding and the resulting necessity to place prisoners in association, which undermined the separation of certain classes of prisoner, including first-time and habitual offenders, and rendered enforcing the rule of silence impossible.[36] This appears to have been particularly problematic in the case of women on account of the lack of space for their confinement, especially in mixed-sex institutions. Liverpool was designed based on the separate system when it opened in 1855, but officials regularly lamented the inability to fully implement the system due to overcrowding, especially in the female side of the prison.[37] Other prisons were adapted to implement the separate system, and parts of the prison were redesignated to increase the provision of separate cells. In addition, the women were in association for work and during chapel and exercise. Westminster's Matron reported to the

Contesting women's health in the prison system 43

Figure 1.1 Mothers with their children exercising at Tothill Fields Prison, c. 1860s.

Visiting Justices in 1869 that it was difficult to punish all infractions against the rule of silence. She stated, 'I feel it is contrary to human nature to suppose perfect silence is observed where so many women of the lowest class are in frequent association.' She continued that the only way to prevent communication would be for women to have separate pews in chapel and to never have more than ten women at a time exercising, but this would require at least three full-time officers to enforce it, which the prison did not have.[38]

Susan Willis Fletcher mused that 'no Home Secretary can absolutely govern the tongues of five or six hundred women', as they found ways to communicate through ventilators or even during chapel.[39] Women were considered to be naturally more sociable and thus they would feel more greatly the deprivation of conversation, which was posited as potentially harmful but also as a useful disciplinary tool. In 1851, officials in Hull Gaol were questioned about the effects of the separate system upon the inmates. Mrs Silvester, the matron in charge of the small number of female prisoners, provided a robust approval when she stated, 'I am fully convinced that nothing but the separate system will tend to prevent crime for at present they are not afraid of returning to gaol as they have sufficient food and congenial society.'[40] Despite stating that the separate system could not easily be surpassed, William Douglas Morrison, a chaplain in the prison system in the 1880s and 1890s, added that it was not effective in preparing prisoners for the duties of society.[41] This was perhaps a greater concern in the case of female prisoners if they were returning to homes and children, and is an issue to which the book returns in Chapter 3. However, the presence of mothers and babies posed logistical challenges to the separate system, as well as raising questions regarding the fundamental principle of silence that underpinned it.

Women in Westminster Prison worked in association but had to follow the rule of silence. Mothers in the prison's nursery were expected to follow the same rules. They were permitted to speak to their babies but not to communicate with each other, and only the prison children were allowed to talk to each other. Following their visit to the prison, journalists and social commentators Mayhew and Binny stated that 'even compared to the disciplinarian folly they had witnessed in their tour of the London prisons' they could scarcely believe that prison regulations could be carried to 'so wicked and unfeeling an extreme'. They added with consternation that even the sternest of observers must feel some compassion for the 'wretched mothers caressing the little things as if they were the only bit of all the black, blank world' that made life bearable to them.[42] The Gladstone Committee found that special consideration was needed in the treatment of female prisoners admitted with infants. At the time of the Committee in 1895 they were excluded from associated labour as they were caring for their babies, but their presence 'destroys discipline as they will talk, they cannot be punished'.[43] By the early twentieth century several larger prisons that contained women, including Holloway, Liverpool and Durham among others, established crèches where prison staff would care for the children of prisoners during the day so that they could go to work and be more subject to the ordinary prison discipline. Women would be allowed to visit the children through the day if they adhered to the prison rules.

Even after the relaxation of the separate system as the twentieth century progressed, pregnant women and new mothers were still locked in their cells for long periods of time, separated from their peers but given limited activity to occupy them. Barbara Roads served a sentence of one month in Holloway Prison during her pregnancy in the 1940s. She recalled having minimal interactions with the medical officer and spending up to twenty-three hours a day in her cell, pacing up and down due to the lack of meaningful occupation.[44] Women had long challenged the terms of the separate system. For some, this resulted in punishments such as a diet of bread and water or containment in a dark cell. For others their actions led to some amelioration or adaptation of the regime on the grounds of health.[45] Months after the crèche opened in Wormwood Scrubs Prison in 1896, the 350 women incarcerated in the prison broke the rule of silence to protest against the texture and colour of the official prison pinafore for the prison babies. Several women tore up their bed sheets to make white pinafores and the women in the laundry embroidered the names of the babies onto their clothes.[46] For many women, the prison babies brought a touch of something tender to what could be physically tough environments. The babies provided some prisoners with an opportunity to show care and to bond with the other women around them, including by making them clothes. For others, they were a painful reminder of their separation from their own children whom they had been forced to leave behind on the outside.

A delicate and worn-out constitution: women entering the prison system

Mary Size commented upon the diversity of the prisoners she encountered in her four decades in the prison service, 'each one was a problem carrying a badge of shame, heartbreak, unhappiness and frustration'.[47] In 1909 Dr Smalley, Medical Inspector of Prisons, reported that prisons were largely populated by 'the very poor, the very ignorant, the physical and mental weaklings, the unemployable and the unskilled, to say nothing of the drunkards'.[48] Sarah Amos summed up the plight of many women who entered prisons in the second half of the nineteenth century, stating, 'the crying children cling to the mother for food; the starving baby hangs at her breast, and almost drives her to theft. The hellish gin shop appeals more temptingly to the worn child-bearer, the weary char-woman, the cruelly abused wife.'[49]

For much of the period under examination here, the male breadwinner ideal, where the working husband provided for his dependent wife and children, was viewed as a source of familial and national stability. However, state policy took little account of the economic or social realities facing many families, and mothers were often castigated for the conditions in which they lived.[50] In her examination of early twentieth-century debates about child welfare, historian of maternity and motherhood Jane Lewis argued that working-class women posed more needs than the often middle-class reformers could address, namely those of poverty and poor living conditions.[51] Similarly, in her study of the history of women's prisons since the mid-nineteenth century, Zedner pointed to the dichotomy between the high moral standards expected of women and the paucity of moral powers they were believed to possess.[52] This was also something noted by prisoners themselves. Prisoner memoirs reveal complaints of having only coarse cloth and a very limited amount of soap to wash and note the difficulties of maintaining high personal standards and reclaiming respectability once lost in an environment that did not facilitate this.[53]

Liverpool's chaplain, James Nugent, stated that as many of the women he ministered to in the prison came from the lowest quarters of society, self-respect and morality were severely wanting and in their place was drunkenness and its associated vices, thus making prisons the 'best schools to study the weakness of poor human nature'.[54] This was a recurring lament identified in the records of several of England's prisons. Nugent regularly bemoaned the overcrowded nature of the female side of the prison and complained that it was owing to the number of women regularly recommitted to the prison for drink-related offences. He stated that many were scarcely thirty years of age but had been in and out of the prison fifty or sixty times. He cited one case of a thirty-one-year-old woman who had been in prison eighty-one times between 1855 and 1870 and had predominantly served sentences of between fourteen days and three months. He used her case as an example of the ineffective nature of short sentences, but to also complain of the cost morally and financially to society.[55] In 1854, Brixton's chaplain, John Henry Moran, claimed that 453 of the 664 women admitted during the year could trace the causes of their imprisonment to drink and keeping bad company.[56] Similarly, in 1856, Captain O'Brien, one of the Directors of Convict Prisons in charge of the female estate, consulted with the medical officer at Brixton and Miss Dyer, the Deputy Superintendent at Millbank, about the condition of the women in their prisons. Their reports acknowledged that some were deserving of pity, due to the impoverished conditions from which they had come, but almost half had either served previous prison sentences or were suspected to have been prostitutes and brothel keepers.[57] These were factors believed to have contributed to their poor health upon reception into prison.[58]

Henry Roome, Medical Officer in Parkhurst Prison, acknowledged in 1865 that placing a large number of women, many of whom were not in robust health when they entered prison, together 'under circumstances of a depressing character' with little occupation meant that it was to be expected that diseases arising from debility would occur.[59] In 1860, William Guy, Millbank's Medical Officer, noted the high proportion of women who had entered the prison as invalids. In that year alone, it had been deemed necessary to remove twenty-three women to Brixton's infirmary.[60] In 1868, Francis Archer, Liverpool's Medical Officer, reported that there had been an increase in the number of deaths in the prison in recent years, but hastened to add that this was not due to the spread of any disease or epidemic and was instead due to the circumstance of a larger number of persons 'of a delicate and worn-out constitution' being sent to the prison.[61] Despite the initial intention to send only healthy women to Parkhurst when it was made a women's prison in 1863, the medical officer commented upon the aged and debilitated condition of the women transferred there from Millbank.[62] Between 1853 and 1869, 138 women were moved to Brixton from either Millbank, Fulham Refuge or Parkhurst on medical grounds, including pregnancy cases.[63]

Quarterly returns made by Brixton to the Home Office provided brief notes on the condition in which women entered the prison. They have been used to glean a greater picture of the health of the prison population and to further understand laments by the prison's officials regarding the pressures that prisoner health posed to the institution. An average of 80 per cent of the women in the prison between 1853 and 1869 were deemed to be in 'good' health. However, the remaining 20 per cent were variously described as being in 'delicate' or 'bad' health. This included labelling them as 'feeble', 'not strong', 'weak-minded', 'insane' or 'invalids'. In some of the reports, up to 10 per cent of Brixton's total population were described as 'invalids' who not only required adaptations to the prison regime, such as a more substantial diet and an exemption from certain labour tasks, but actually required accommodation in the prison's infirmary, putting additional pressure on the infirmary which also had to accommodate other cases of illness as well as births and lying-in women.[64]

Prison authorities in Brixton, including the medical officer and the lady superintendent, repeatedly complained to the Convict Prison Directorate of the additional logistical pressures women in poor health could present, and also the disruption some of their number caused because they had not spent the requisite time in the probation stage of discipline, nor could they be subject to the full rigours of prison discipline on account of their health. One such example was in 1858 when Lady Superintendent Emma Martin reported that some of the women knew that they could not be subject to the strictest discipline and were thus 'deliberately defiant'.[65] Similarly, Rendle remarked in 1859 that 'the most troublesome prisoners ... are young women who know that their ill-health will shield them from punishment, however bad their conduct.'[66] The maternal body could also be a barrier to punitive treatment for infractions of the prison rules. A prisoner named Jones was transferred from Millbank to Brixton shortly after the latter's opening in 1853, as she was close to the date of her confinement. She was disruptive in the infirmary and refused to follow the rule of silence. She demanded a different bed and often argued with the matron. She threw a cloth cap made by the matron for her infant into the fire in the presence of other prisoners, but the prison authorities had limited recourse to means of punishment for these infractions.[67]

In addition to the maternal body posing physical challenges to the prison regime, the hundreds of mothers and their children who walked through the prison gates required adaptations to the prison both spatially and also in terms of the regime. During her correspondence with Nancy Astor, the first female Member of Parliament, in the 1920s, social reformer Dorothy Thain expressed frustration for the unwed or the poor working mother as there is 'only the workhouse or death, and when her trouble is over there is always the awful shame to endure.'⁶⁸ Historians of crime including Dobash and others have since gathered more evidence of the circumstances from which women came and found that the majority of the women convicted of theft had largely stolen clothes, food and household provisions such as coal.⁶⁹ Shortly after Westminster's redesignation in 1850, due to the large numbers of committals of women with babies and young children Governor Tracey asked permission from the Visiting Justices to adapt part of the prison into a nursery to tend to their 'peculiar treatment and wants'. An average of between twenty-five and thirty were committed each quarter, and Tracey added that he expected a considerable increase as the winter advanced.⁷⁰ The medical officer, John Lavies, reported that between January and March 1854 seventy-three young children, including very young infants, had been admitted to the prison with their mothers.⁷¹ Despite repeated concerns raised about the increase in the number of committals in the colder months, provision for the additional space and care required for these infants was not forthcoming from the Visiting Justices. Instead, their care and accommodation had to be managed by the prison staff, and put additional pressure on the prison's already overcrowded infirmary.

H. Waddington, one of Westminster's Visiting Justices, finally raised the difficulties this caused to the prison with the Home Secretary in 1855. However, his concern was largely couched in terms of the question of discipline more than that of health. He wrote that mothers having their children in prison with them 'interferes with prison discipline, encourages deception and causes trouble'. He further complained that prison was not a place to send these children just to relieve unions and parishes of their maintenance. He added that many mothers were practising a 'deception' by claiming that their infants were still at the breast or were misrepresenting their ages and condition in order to bring them into the prison. Waddington claimed that these actions were often motivated by women being aware of the 'indulgences' afforded to a breastfeeding mother and stated that it was difficult to ascertain a child's condition, owing to the 'sickly and feeble state' of many of those who entered the prison.⁷² Following the birth of her baby on 1 January 1888 in what appears to have been an Aston police station, Elizabeth Cheshire was transferred to Birmingham Prison on the morning of 3 January in order to be placed in the prison's infirmary. The medical officer, H. Manton, wrote to the Aston magistrate to complain that the workhouse would have been a more suitable place to care for Elizabeth and her baby than the prison, which was currently overcrowded.[73]

A recurring issue in debates about provisions in prison was the question of the conditions in which prisoners were contained and how they compared to conditions on the outside. The *Report of the Committee on the Dietaries of County and Borough Prisons*, published in 1864, stipulated that the prison diet was to be calculated with precision and set at a level just beyond the minimum limit at which 'loss of health and strength' might result.[74] However, the physical health of many of those who entered prisons meant this was difficult to quantify. In Brixton, prisoners placed in the infirmary and those convalescing, including new mothers, were given additional provisions to the ordinary prison diet, including cocoa, tea, bread, cheese, fish and eggs. This could be amended at the discretion of the medical officer. When they visited the infirmary in the early 1860s, Mayhew and Binny noted that it was 'plain the majority of the poor creatures fared more sumptuously under their punishment than they possibly could have done outside'.[75] The 'nursery breakfast' each morning was a pint of milk for each child and tea for the mothers.[76] The Middlesex magistrate Sir Peter Northall Laurie wrote to the Chairman of Westminster Prison's Visiting Justices in February 1864 about the women in the prison's nursery. Rather than commenting upon the recent adaptations that had been made to improve and expand provisions, he complained that 'a mother in your prison is practically a lady and far better off than an ordinary prisoner. I think if this could be altered you would stop some of these ladies making the prison a convenience.'[77]

The Holloway Discharged Prisoner's Aid Society was established in 1904. One of several branches attached to the central Discharged Prisoners' Aid Society, it was certified by the Prison Commission and subsidised by the Treasury, along with charitable donations. Agents from the Society visited women in Holloway and helped to make arrangements for them upon their release. The 'typical cases' detailed in their annual reports show the wide range of women they helped, but also reveal commonalities in terms of their living conditions on the outside and the obstacles they would face upon release. A woman with the initials F.C. was listed among these 'typical cases' in 1928. She was a first-time offender who had given birth in Holloway.

The Society helped to secure her a place in Dalmeny Hostel upon release, which had its own matron and staff to support mothers to find employment. She later wrote to them to state that 'life will be bright once again for me, and just when I thought life was not worth living' she had found support.[78] A report in 1929 stated that the worst part of the punishment for women was not the period of detention but the 'haunting dread of the future' without character, means or influence. This was a gulf the Discharged Prisoners' Aid Society sought to bridge, and one that was not properly considered or addressed by the criminal justice system for the mothers entering and leaving prison with children.[79]

Despite this chasm at policy level, this study has also found that female members of the prison staff acknowledged and, in some ways, attempted to address the specific issues facing women due to the conditions in which they lived on the outside, but had to do so within the boundaries of an often obstinate prison regime. Mary Size spoke of prison officials as custodians of the women who had been forcibly separated from their lives outside. She commented that in observing the different 'sorts and conditions' of women in prison she observed the importance of showing them kindness and interest, as the absence of 'gratitude and affection' earlier in life had contributed to their career of crime.[80] Size added that although using a prisoner's name instead of their number (which was based on their landing and cell number) was considered to undermine discipline, she found it was beneficial in managing and caring for the women.[81] Cicely McCall, a qualified psychiatric social worker, noted that professional social workers had years to train and craft their ability to interview and work with people facing complex conditions in life. However, when she entered employment in the prison system she found that prison officers were 'bundled into this difficult and responsible position with little specific training'.[82] McCall also wrote that when training at Aylesbury she had asked to see the records of some of the girls so as to better acquaint herself with their individual circumstances. However, the governor refused on the grounds that this could lead to prejudicial treatment. McCall lamented that it was astonishing that within the prison system there were still people in positions of power who believed that 'ignorance of facts makes for impartiality in treatment'.[83] While playing a part in shaping the history of penal policy, this debate, that equal treatment does not always lead to equal outcomes, is one that continues to permeate the criminal justice system today.

During an enquiry into the operation of the Penal Servitude Act of 1857, Millbank's Medical Officer, William Guy, was asked about how ill health among prisoners could be caused by grief and misfortune. He replied that women's domestic ties were often closer than those of male prisoners and thus were more broken down by imprisonment.[84] In their enquiry into conditions in English prisons in the early twentieth century, ex-prisoners Hobhouse and Brockway found evidence to suggest that women felt more deeply the deprivation of normal conversation as, for some, it was 'the one relaxation in life' and the pain of separation was made more acute due to the separation from their children.[85] However, such acknowledgements were rarely considered when deciding upon the imposition of prison policy.

Communication was not only limited among those incarcerated: the regulation of contact extended to a prisoner's family beyond the prison walls. Social and political commentator Sarah Amos was active in writing about the fraught position of women in prison, lamenting that there was not adequate opportunity to speak about the difficulties facing female prisoners. She highlighted the specific plight of mothers who were confined in prison with no way of knowing if anyone was looking after their children and their home.[86] Letters were restricted to one every six months, and as a prisoner progressed through the disciplinary stages they could gradually earn more regular opportunities to write to loved ones. Although they were entitled to a limited number of letters and visits, many women in prison received neither, even when they had family on the outside. Of the 288 female prisoners sampled in Johnston's study, 142 of whom were mothers, only 10 per cent received a visit and 30 per cent received a letter during their incarceration. This limited contact meant that women often found it difficult to obtain news of their children and this could have severe ramifications on their prison experience. Maria Cain had received no news of her children during her sentence and was anxious to gain some from a fellow prisoner recently admitted who lived in her neighbourhood, who informed Maria that one of her children had died.[87]

The isolation and separation from their families could have a severe impact on the mental health of women in prison. In June

1854 a woman described as a 'feeble invalid' was transferred from Millbank Prison to be placed in Brixton's larger infirmary. She later received word of her daughter's death and could get no news about her son. In April 1855, the medical officer detailed how she began having delusions that the prison was keeping her children from her, and she claimed to hear them crying out. By June, her conduct in the infirmary had become so violent and difficult to manage that she had to be physically restrained. Her removal to Fisherton Asylum upon the recommendation of the medical officer was approved by the Home Office in July.[88]

Walking the line: managing health and discipline

Within Britain's criminal justice history, several protagonists have shaped the experiences of the people who have served sentences in the country's penal institutions. The administration of the prison system has been debated, decided and directed by the Home Office, the Prison Directorate, local magistrates and others who designed prison policy. This policy has then been staunchly defended and ruminated over, rigidly administered, criticised and adapted by those who have worked in prisons on a daily basis, including by governors, medical officers, matrons, lady superintendents and prison warders. It is to those who were placed in charge of confining England's female prisoners that this chapter now turns to further explore their importance in shaping health experiences behind bars.

Following the establishment of the Convict Prison Directorate in 1850, convict prisons employed doctors who worked full time in their respective institution. Prior to the nationalisation of prisons in 1877, a doctor would visit local prisons during the week to check on the health of inmates. The Prisons Act 1865 stipulated that an infirmary would be established in every prison and that all inmates would have a statutory weekly examination. Prison medical officers determined a prisoner's fitness for work and subjugation to the prison regime, including certifying them as fit or unfit for labour, dietary punishment and restraint. Wiener labelled this decision-making process a form of 'moral categorisation' that involved the interpretation of behaviour as well as the identification of ill health.[89] The prison doctor's statutory duty to distinguish between those fit and unfit for prison labour and punishment was a difficult one and, Watson argued, facilitated the production of knowledge and debates about categories of mental behaviour that were unique to the prison setting.[90]

In his evidence to the Carnarvon Committee in 1863 regarding the role of the medical officer, William Guy, Medical Officer of Millbank between 1859 and 1869, stated his belief in their role of promoting the discipline of the prison but not interfering with it.[91] The medical officer at Dartmoor, a male prison, wrote in 1878 of the anxiety that none but a prison medical officer could understand of having in their charge everything relating to the health of the prison, including ventilation, diet, work and punishment. He commented that the latter in particular was the source of great anxiety and careful consideration, as the doctor had to regard the convict's health and yet not screen prisoners from or interfere with the duties and prerogatives of discipline.[92] However, this line between discipline, punishment and the maintenance of physical and mental health was blurred, and subject to shifting parameters across the period under examination here.

Davie argued that it was both practical and crucial for prison doctors to establish objective criteria to reflect upon the distinct nature and extent of physical and mental disabilities among prison inmates. This was not only to decide upon their fitness to undergo the full rigours of the regime, but to also pre-empt any challenges to their diagnoses from other quarters of the prison hierarchy.[93] Edward Parker, Liverpool's Medical Officer, reported to the Visiting Justices of the difficulties of exercising the discretionary powers invested in him, due to the need to avoid imposition upon penal authority on the one hand, and undue punishment on the other. Parker added that 'whenever there has been doubt in my mind, I have not hesitated to decide in favour of the prisoner'.[94] However, several prisoners across the period recalled feeling that the doctor was more on the side of the system than of the patient.

Dr Mary Gordon lamented that during her service in the prison estate the prisoner had no right to their own confidence as 'the doctor may take it away and may give it to the Governor, the police or the court'. In turn, when discussing the medical care offered to prisoners, Gordon made a key distinction that could impact upon medical treatment and health in prisons, namely, that 'the prisoner does not consult the doctor, the state pays the doctor and consults him about the prisoner'.[95] Susan Willis Fletcher captured how decision making on the part of prisoners, warder and doctors could have a serious impact on prisoners' health, observing that 'the cunning may deceive even a very clever physician while the really sick and suffering may possibly, if under a hard warder, be neglected'.[96] A woman serving a sentence in Aylesbury in the 1920s reported that the medical officer was 'very unsympathetic' to the needs of prisoners. Instead, their primary concern was to ensure that the women remained subject to the prison regime, which involved 'seeing how much you can stand without dying'.[97]

Some medical officers viewed part of their role as not only providing medical care to those who needed it but also identifying instances where they did not. Prisons were unique sites in this sense, as prison doctors did not only need to examine prisoners to ascertain if and what treatment they needed. There was an additional layer, wherein doctors deliberated over the motives of prisoners in seeking treatment. Samuel Rogers, Birmingham's Medical Officer, reported in 1854 that he was pleased to report that cases of serious illness were low. He added that around one third of cases that came before him were 'of a very trifling nature that no complaint would have been made had not the facility of obtaining medical assistance been constantly present'. He continued that some prisoners reported themselves sick in the hopes of obtaining a better diet and some exemption from labour, as well as from a desire to 'create an incident in the day by being visited by the surgeon'.[98] Arthur Griffiths, the Deputy Governor of Millbank between 1872 and 1874, bemoaned the specific difficulties the authorities faced when making these judgements in the case of female prisoners. He stated that some women maintained 'an unbroken warfare with authority', adding, 'it is often difficult to draw the line between madness and outrageous conduct'.[99] Research into the early female convict estate has demonstrated the difficulties faced by prison doctors when deciding upon the appropriate treatment of inmates, including balancing the management of behaviour and the maintenance of health.[100]

In addition to the medical officer, several other members of the prison staff were required to walk this line and attempt the balancing act between discipline and prisoner health, notably the female warders and officers who were responsible for their confinement on a daily basis. Following their visit to Brixton, Mayhew and Binny commented that one of the main peculiarities of the prison was that the majority of officials were women. Even though the chaplain, medical officer and steward were men, Mayhew and Binny were at pains to point out the novelty of having women, especially the Superintendent, Emma Martin, in positions where they were invested with powers of governance. They mused that observing the maintenance of discipline and order was more interesting when it was the work of 'those whom the world generally considers to be ill-adapted for government'.[101]

Following a visit to Newgate Prison in 1813, Elizabeth Fry began her work to reform conditions for female prisoners in 1816. The initial aims of the Association for the Improvement of the Females at Newgate were to provide practical support such as clothing and employment alongside the teaching of good habits in sobriety, industry and knowledge of the Holy Scriptures. A distinguishing characteristic of Fry's work was the emphasis she placed on the importance of gaining the cooperation of inmates if true reform were to be achieved.[102] The Gaol Act 1823 stipulated that female prisoners had to be supervised by women warders. Female warders would also be present when female prisoners were visited by the governor or the medical officer. This was in contrast to practices in some American prisons such as Virginia Penitentiary, which accommodated male and female convicts but where they were not entirely separated until 1931. It was also not until the 1880s that women in Virginia were supervised by female warders instead of the previous practice of having all-male guards. Coulson's historical study of the experiences of women in American prisons identified several cases of women becoming pregnant and giving birth years into their prison sentences throughout much of the nineteenth century, further illuminating the lack of proper consideration in confining women as well as potential abuses carried out within the prison by either male convicts or male guards and authorities.[103] Although this study has identified no evidence of similar cases of women becoming pregnant during their sentence in England, it does acknowledge that the nature of research into prison history means that we rely heavily upon records created by those in charge of prison rather than by those incarcerated within, which makes the unearthing of potential abuses committed against prisoners difficult if not impossible.

As well as answering criticisms by herself and others in the late eighteenth and early nineteenth century of the moral and physical dangers posed to women who were imprisoned and managed by men, Fry also believed that the women who found themselves in prison were 'persons of an abandoned character'. Thus, to place them under the care of men was injurious to both parties. Instead, they required female officers who exercised authority alongside providing a constant example of feminine propriety and virtue.[104] Zedner argued that this placed higher expectations upon female members of the prison staff than their male counterparts, as they were expected to be 'guardians of their sex'.[105]

Later in the nineteenth century, during debates about the efficacy of prison discipline, Arthur Griffiths, then an Inspector of Prisons, commented in 1894 that female prisoners were more troublesome because they could not be so firmly governed. He continued, 'they require humouring, a lighter hand, the tact women can command while seeking to persuade'.[106] Elizabeth Little, Matron of Strangeways Prison, and Jane Taylor Gee, Matron of Liverpool, both advocated regimes based on more kindness and engagement with prisoners in their evidence to the Departmental Committee on Prisons in 1895.[107] However, reconciling their duties of locking and unlocking, watching and reporting alongside the expectation that they provide a moral example was a particular difficulty facing female warders.

In her article about the intersection of gender with debates about the role of prison officers, Johnston argued that female warders were often regarded as lower in status and not as worthy of the task of reformation as middle-class reformers and Lady Visitors.[108] Despite this, high expectations were placed upon these women. Emma Martin, Brixton's Lady Superintendent, expatiated on the role that her subordinate officers played in providing a good moral example to the women in their care.[109] Historical studies, including those of Zedner and Dobash et al., have since respectively argued that this additional layer of morality prompted greater intolerance of infractions of the prison rules among female inmates.[110] However, the current study has identified evidence to suggest that in some cases it also led to the paradox of female staff feeling constrained between the bounds of the institution and the desire to show humanity to those in their charge. This reinforces an ambiguity identified by Brown and Clare in their study of prisoner memoirs, namely that prison regimes placed staff in a predicament between power and powerlessness.[111] This study has explored this contradiction further in relation to those staffing the female prison estate, who were invested with the full weight of a powerful prison regime but sometimes struggled to enact it when faced with the daily realities of prison life. In addition, prison warders could play a crucial role in the decision-making processes that dictated the health and disciplinary experiences of women, especially mothers, in prison.

Susan Willis Fletcher's account of her time in Westminster Prison in the late nineteenth century explored the importance of the character and disposition of the prison warders in shaping the experiences of the women in their charge. When recalling those she encountered, Fletcher mused that warders could be either very kind or very cruel, without breaking the prison rules.[112] Florence Maybrick similarly spoke of the importance of how female warders responded to the health of those in their charge. She described hearing women shrieking, tearing their clothing and bedding and smashing the furniture in their cells at night. Some prisoners rang their bell to alert the attention of the warder on duty. In many cases, these instances were met with little sympathy on the part of warders.[113] Cicely McCall spoke of the 'dictatorial pettiness' of some warders when attending to the day-to-day running of the prison and the need for prisoners to ask warders for any kind of medical or sanitary provision, which they sometimes faced difficulty in obtaining.[114] In some cases, warders played a crucial role in the decision-making process when it came to prisoners having access to medical care. Maria Clarkson complained to the Governor of Westminster Prison in 1853 about her treatment by warder Charlotte Howe. She had sent for a quantity of salt to rub onto Maria's lips to 'ascertain whether she was in a fit or pretending to be labouring under one' before calling for the medical officer. This was not the first instance of Howe being reported for her treatment of prisoners, a previous report having been made by the matron in May 1852. Following Maria's case, the governor resolved that warders should not use such tests in cases of suspected illness and instead should apply to the proper officer for assistance.[115]

Prisons were populated by a diverse range of women, bringing with them varied lived experiences which had led them to the gates of the prison. Although prison directors, inspectors and governors directed the terms under which prisoners would be incarcerated, it was female matrons, superintendents and warders who were tasked with enacting these policies on a day-to-day basis. Female warders came from a range of backgrounds, including domestic service and shop work. Some had families, including children, but many were either single or widowed. Debates about the staffing of prisons often placed higher importance on the morality and temperament of female warders than that of their male counterparts. In addition, their living arrangements were often more constrained. By 1911 it was a requirement that all female officers should live in the prison or in quarters assigned by the prison.[116] Hobhouse and Brockway noted that male warders were more likely to go home to their families after their day working in the prison estate but female warders were far less likely to have family lives.[117] Similarly, following her visit to women's prisons in the mid-nineteenth century, Mary Carpenter wrote of the long hours prison officers worked and the toll the role could take on them, which impacted upon their ability to closely watch and correct prisoner behaviour.[118]

In addition to the impact that the logistics of the job, such as hours and living conditions, could have on prison staff, others spoke of feeling ill prepared or trained to confine and care for the women in their charge and of their frustrations with aspects of the system in which they worked. This was particularly evident in terms of the question of caring for prisoner health and mothers. Mary Size recalled the first time she was placed on hospital duty and having to sit by the bed of a woman who had attempted suicide. She stated that prison rules meant she was not allowed to talk to the woman and instead had to sit in silence for what she termed 'the longest and dreariest four hours I had ever known'.[119] Training schools for prison officers were introduced following the Gladstone Committee of 1895. Between 1898 and 1907, 338 female officers undertook the four months of training required to become a permanent officer, this training for women largely taking place in Liverpool or Manchester before being moved to Holloway in 1911.[120] However, prison staff were often not trained in the care of the babies and young children who lived for varying periods of their lives within the confines of England's penal institutions. This could have an impact on the care they received. Betsy Jones, a warder in Westminster Prison, was fined in 1850 for 'want of feeling' towards the children in the nursery, as she had failed to provide them with their milk allowance on time.

Betsy claimed in her defence that she had previously worked in Coldbath Fields and had not been in charge of the care of infants before, and that she was not yet fully acquainted with the requirements of this part of her duty.[121] Betsy was dismissed in September 1851 when she was found to be in breach of the prison rules, as she had talked with a prisoner and allowed her to do some knitting.[122]

In addition to instances where female warders were ill equipped to enact the rules of the institutions in which they worked, the current study has uncovered cases where they were unwilling to do so. In her observations on the female prison staff, Maybrick described instances of warders showing kindness to the women in spite of the regime. She argued that this was evidence that for some their heart could emerge from 'its official shell'.[123] A reading of cases where female prison warders were brought before the Visiting Justices of their respective prisons for breaking the rules associated with their position makes clear that these rules were adapted on a daily basis. In several cases, these rule breaks were to do with warders breaking the rule of silence or attempting to relax the limitation of communication in some way. For some this resulted in warnings, fines and even dismissals. The Matron of Westminster Prison reported warder Harriet Stevens for several infractions in the prison nursery. These included allowing a prisoner to share some of her child's clothes with another prisoner and allowing and partaking in 'familiar conversation' in the nursery. Harriet had been fined previously for similar infractions and was dismissed in October 1850.[124] Others gave up their positions. For example, Rachael Townsend was one of the warders moved from Coldbath Fields Prison to Westminster Prison in September 1850 when the latter became a prison for women and juvenile males. Among the list of officers, she was described as one of the longest serving, having been in the prison service for over seven years. In October, Rachael went before the Visiting Justices of Westminster to tender her resignation, stating she 'declined to conform' to the rules of the prison's regime.[125]

A long-standing debate within the history of women's prisons has surrounded the consideration, or lack thereof, of the distinctions required within the women's system, from the physical buildings to the regimes enacted therein. A key element of this has been the appointment of women to positions of greater power within prisons such as governor and medical officer. In mixed prisons, lady superintendents or matrons would be placed in charge of the female portion of the prison but they were subordinate to the male governor. Even in Holloway, England's largest female prison, the positions of governor and medical officer were occupied by men, something that drew increasing criticism. Sarah Amos commented in 1898 that women prisoners often already felt a 'deep sense of injury' when they entered prison. Some had been led into crime by men, others were victims of a drunken and dissolute society and when they entered prison they were condemned, inspected and governed by men, which was a state 'womanhood must resent'.[126] The need to increase the number of female warders and to have more women in positions where they could oversee the management of women's prisons was among the recommendations made by the 1895 *Report of the Departmental Committee on Prisons*.[127]

Officials including Mary Gordon, Mary Size and Cicely McCall criticised the marks and stages that characterised the prison system and instead advocated for regimes that aimed not to entirely subjugate women but to provide them with a sense of agency for when they left prison. They argued that female members of staff in positions of greater influence would be more likely to achieve this. However, the appointment of women to positions of greater power in the prison hierarchy was not without resistance. Mary Gordon's appointment as an inspector of prisons in 1908 was met with opposition, despite the fact that women had been appointed to inspectorate positions in other sectors. For example, in 1904 the appointment of a female Inspector of Girls' Schools was believed to be necessary, as she would notice matters connected to 'domestic management that may escape the notice of a man'. Similarly, women had been increasingly appointed as inspectors of factories to minister to the needs of factory girls.[128] Despite Gordon's being a qualified doctor, Sir Evelyn Ruggles-Brise, the Chairman of the Prison Directorate, opposed her appointment. Her support of the suffragettes, discovered following a raid of the Women's Social and Political Union offices in 1914, compounded the disapproval of her position. Gordon served in military hospitals abroad during the First World War but was reappointed by the Prison Commission at the war's end.[129] When she requested an increase in her salary in 1919 a Home Office reply labelled her appointment as a 'sop to feminism', continuing that any increase in wages would be yet another unwarranted concession.[130]

In 1913 Reginald McKenna, Home Secretary, received a letter from Ida Smedley, Secretary of the Federation of University Women, regarding the staffing of women's prisons and the fact that the higher administrative offices in women's prisons were filled by men. The Federation members argued that a woman in power would be better placed to understand the needs of women prisoners and asked that, when vacancies appeared in these offices, suitable women be considered for the roles.[131] In response to this letter, McKenna stated that although the positions of governor and medical officer were occupied by men in Holloway and Aylesbury, the immediate control of female prisoners was entrusted to matrons.[132] However, there were continued debates about this issue. Dr Selina Fox was appointed to be Lady Superintendent and Deputy Medical Officer of Aylesbury Prison and Borstal in 1914. She became the first female prison governor in 1916. This position was subsequently taken up by Lilian Barker in 1923, before she later became the first woman to be an assistant prison commissioner in 1935.

The end of the First World War brought with it renewed debates about the staffing and conditions in women's prisons. At a conference organised by the Penal Reform League in June 1917, one ex-prisoner complained of the lack of attention to the specific needs of women during menstruation. She spoke of the embarrassment suffered by women when provisions were not readily available and the fact that male governors, doctors and chaplains could come into cells with no notice.[133] In June 1918 Ruggles-Brise wrote to the Home Office regarding the 'great difficulty arising in carrying out medical examinations' in female prison establishments. He attributed this in part to the prevalence of venereal diseases, but also to the growing disinclination among female prisoners and the press, in response to campaigns from different groups, for women to be medically examined by male doctors. Dr John Hall Morton was Governor and Medical Officer of Holloway Prison, but in response to this correspondence two female doctors, Dr Moss Rougvie and Dr Edith Hudgell, were appointed as deputy medical officers.[134]

In 1921 an article in the *Daily Herald* posed the question 'why should a man rule the castle?' in relation to the question of Holloway's next governor upon the retirement of the current post holder.[135] The Women's Freedom League wrote to the Prison Commission regarding the matter, stating that they were continuing an argument made by the suffragettes following their imprisonment in Holloway before the war. The League's petition used the fact that there were women magistrates and women medical inspectors as further justification of the need for women governors in prison.[136] It was announced that the position would be filled by Mr Shortt, who was already a medical officer in the service, but that there would be two lady superintendents to take daily charge of the disciplinary side of the prison and the hospital respectively. In response, Florence Underwood, Secretary of the Women's Freedom League, wrote to the *Manchester Guardian* to state with consternation, 'surely if a woman is needed anywhere, it is in control of a women's prison?', adding that penal reform held little prospect for women for so long as the highest offices were reserved for men.[137]

Mary Size, who had entered the prison service in 1906 and spent over four decades in the service as a warder, a school mistress and a lady superintendent, was appointed Deputy Governor of Holloway Prison in 1927. However, it was not until 1945 that Dr Charity Taylor became the first female governor of Holloway Prison, the largest women's prison of its time. She had been Deputy Medical Officer since 1942. In 1959 Taylor was appointed as Assistant Director and Inspector of Prisons for Women. During her time as Holloway's Governor, Taylor instituted several reforms to the prison's regime, notably in terms of the classes offered to instruct women and offer them more meaningful employment opportunities. She also made notable changes to the prison dress, including, along with several other prisons in 1949, introducing more practical maternity dresses, and allowed prisoners to buy make-up and hair products at the prison canteen as part of her attempts to foster the pride, self-respect and agency so long advocated for by officials working in women's prisons.[138] In 1946 Taylor appeared at the Conference of Women's Organisations alongside Teresa Billington-Greig, the first suffragette imprisoned in Holloway during the campaign for the right to vote, who later went on to help create the Women's Freedom League. Billington-Greig spoke of Taylor's concern with improving provisions for female prisoners and praised her commitment to humanising the prison system to allow women to 'retain their dignity' while behind bars.[139]

Conclusion

In August 1855, Joshua Jebb declared that the different establishments in the female convict estate would be 'components of the same system', wherein the progression of prisoners through the classifications, from the reflection of their separate confinement to the reclamation of respectability by their release, would 'work smoothly and well'.[140] A recent study of the early convict estate concluded that the challenges of reconciling health and discipline prompted modifications and negotiations of the terms of their incarceration by the women themselves, as well as by those tasked with their custody. In addition, this balancing act played a crucial role in the decision to rethink the arrangements in place for the incarceration of female prisoners when Brixton was closed for women in 1869.[141] This chapter has revealed that in the century that followed the aims set out by Jebb, the containment and care of women and their children continually challenged the principles of uniformity and deterrence underpinning England's penal system. Rather than producing the smooth system envisaged by Jebb, the application of central components of the penal regime, from accommodation to the rule of separation, required constant negotiation. To weave together the complexities of imprisoning mothers and children introduced in this chapter, the book now turns to examine how prisons and those who administered them, at all levels of the hierarchy, attempted to negotiate the perennial difficulties posed by the maintenance of their health.

Notes

1. Mary Carpenter, *Our convicts, Vol. II* (London: Longman, 1864), p. 204.
2. Phyllis Jo Baunach, *Mothers in prison* (New York: Transaction Publishers, first published 1983, this edition 2020), p. 1.
3. Rachel Bennett, 'Bad for the health of the body, worse for the health of the mind: Female responses to imprisonment in England, 1853–1869', *Social History of Medicine*, 34:2 (2021), 532–552, https://doi.org/10.1093/shm/hkz066.
4. Report of the Directors of Convict Prisons for the year 1864 (London: 1865), p. 13.

5 Report of the Directors of Convict Prisons for the year 1865 (London: 1866), p. 10.
6 Report of the Directors of Convict Prisons for the year 1869 (London: 1870), p. 369.
7 Lucia Zedner, *Women, crime and custody in Victorian England* (Oxford: Oxford University Press, 1991), p. 131.
8 Zedner, *Women, crime and custody*, p. 137.
9 Hull History Centre [hereafter HHC], TCGL, Draft Reports for the Gaol Committee 1856–57.
10 Zedner, *Women, crime and custody*, p. 1.
11 Martin J. Wiener, *Reconstructing the criminal: Culture, law and policy in England, 1830–1914* (Cambridge: Cambridge University Press, 1990), p. 309; Zedner, *Women, crime and custody*, pp. 100, 202.
12 Zedner, *Women, crime and custody*, p. 156.
13 Lucia Zedner, 'Wayward sisters: The prison for women', in Norval Morris and David J. Rothman (eds.) *The Oxford history of the prison: The practice of punishment in Western society* (Oxford: Oxford University Press, 1995), pp. 329–361, p. 341.
14 Helen Johnston, 'Gendered prison work: Female prison officers in the local prison system, 1877–1939', *Howard Journal of Criminal Justice*, 53:2 (2014), 193–212, https://doi.org/10.1111/hojo.12043, p. 195.
15 Stephen Hobhouse and A. Fenner Brockway, *English prisons today: Being the report of the Prison System Enquiry Committee* (London: Longmans, Green and Co., 1922), p. 336.
16 Johnston, 'Gendered prison work', p. 195.
17 Paul Rock, *Reconstructing a women's prison: The Holloway Redevelopment Project, 1968–88* (Oxford: Oxford University Press, 1996), p. 120.
18 Johnston, 'Gendered prison work', pp. 196–197.
19 Rachel E. Bennett, *Capital punishment and the criminal corpse in Scotland, 1740–1834* (London: Palgrave Macmillan, 2018).
20 Michel Foucault, *Discipline and punish: The birth of the prison* (London: Allen Lane, 1977).
21 Wiener, *Reconstructing the criminal*, p. 103.
22 Victor Bailey, *The rise and fall of the rehabilitative ideal, 1895–1970* (Abingdon: Routledge, 2019), p. 16.
23 Report of the Directors of Convict Prisons for the year 1856 (London: 1857), p. 338.
24 Bill Forsythe, 'Women prisoners and women's penal officials 1840–1921', *British Journal of Criminology*, 33:4 (1993), 525–540, https://doi.org/10.1093/oxfordjournals.bjc.a048357, p. 530.
25 Forsythe, 'Women prisoners and women's penal officials', pp. 527–528.

26 Bennett, 'Bad for the health of the body'.
27 Hilary Marland, '"Close confinement tells very much upon a man": Prison memoirs, insanity and the late nineteenth- and early twentieth-century prison', *Journal of the History of Medicine and Allied Sciences*, 74:3 (2019), 267–291, https://doi.org/10.1093/jhmas/jrz027, p. 267.
28 Catherine Cox and Hilary Marland, '"He must die or go mad in this place": Prisoners, insanity, and the Pentonville Model Prison experiment, 1842–1852', *Bulletin of the History of Medicine*, 92:1 (2018), 78–109, https://doi.org/10.1353/bhm.2018.0004, p. 81. See also Catherine Cox and Hilary Marland, 'Broken minds and beaten bodies: Cultures of harm and the management of mental illness in mid- to late nineteenth-century English and Irish prisons', *Social History of Medicine*, 31:4 (2018), 688–710, https://doi.org/10.1093/shmhky038; Catherine Cox and Hilary Marland, *Disorder contained: Mental breakdown and the modern prison in England and Ireland, 1840–1900* (Cambridge: Cambridge University Press, 2022).
29 Joshua Jebb, *Modern prisons: Their construction and ventilation* (London: John Weale, 1844), p. 6.
30 Nineteenth Report of the Inspectors appointed under the provisions of the act 5 & 6 Will. IV c.38 to visit the different prisons of Great Britain (London: 1854), pp. 107–108.
31 Nineteenth Report of the Inspectors, pp. 107–108.
32 Report of the Directors of Convict Prisons for the year 1853 (London: 1854), p. 308.
33 Bennett, 'Bad for the health of the body'.
34 Hilary L. Coulson, '"In the care of the supposed powerful state": Women and children in the Virginia Penitentiary, 1800–1883', in Erica Rhodes Hayden and Theresa R. Jach (eds), *Incarcerated women: A history of struggles, oppression, and resistance in American prisons* (London: Lexington Books, 2017), pp. 17–36, p. 23.
35 Florence Elizabeth Chandler Maybrick, *Mrs Maybrick's own story: My fifteen lost years* (London: Funk and Wagnalls Company, 1905), pp. 67, 86.
36 London Metropolitan Archives [hereafter LMA], WA/G/008 Minute Book of the Visiting Justices, November 1855–November 1857, 22 December 1855.
37 Liverpool Record Office [hereafter LRO], 347 MAG/1/2/2, Minutes of the Visiting Justices 1870–1878, 28 July 1870.
38 LMA, WA/G/013, Minute Book of the Visiting Justices for the House of Correction, Westminster [hereafter Minute Book], May 1868–April 1871, 3 July 1869.

39 Susan Willis Fletcher, *Twelve months in an English prison* (New York: Charles T. Dillingham, 1884), p. 331.
40 HHC, TCGL 15 Gaol Committee Report, 1851.
41 William Douglas Morrison, *Crime and its causes* (London: Swan Sonnenschein & Co., 1891), p. 216.
42 Henry Mayhew and John Binny, *The criminal prisons of London and scenes of prison life* (London: Griffin, Bohn and Company, 1862), pp. 474, 475.
43 Report from the Departmental Committee on Prisons (London, 1895), p. 32.
44 Kathleen Lonsdale et al., with introduction by Ethel Mannin, *Some account of life in Holloway Prison for women* (London: Prison Medical Reform Council, 1943), p. 22.
45 Bennett, 'Bad for the health of the body'.
46 Caitlin Davies, *Bad girls: A history of rebels and renegades* (London: John Murray, 2018), p. 268.
47 Mary Size, *Prisons I have known* (London: George Allen & Unwin, 1957), p. 95.
48 Hobhouse and Brockway, *English prisons today*, p. 7.
49 Sarah Amos, 'The prison treatment of women', *Contemporary Review*, 73 (1898), 803–813, p. 804.
50 Jane Lewis, 'The working-class wife and mother and state intervention, 1870–1918', in Jane Lewis (ed.), *Labour and love: Women's experience of home and family 1850–1940* (Oxford: Basil Blackwell, 1986), pp. 99–120, p. 100.
51 Jane Lewis, *The politics of motherhood: Child and maternal welfare in England, 1900–1939* (London: Croom Helm, 1980), p. 61.
52 Zedner, *Women, crime and custody*, p. 42.
53 For examples of such complaints see Maybrick, *Mrs Maybrick's own story*, p. 180; Lonsdale, *Some account of life in Holloway Prison*, pp. 8–9.
54 LRO, 347 MAG 1/2/2, Minutes of Visiting Justices 1870–1878, 26 October 1871.
55 LRO, 347 MAG 1/2/2, Minutes of Visiting Justices 1870–1878, 28 July 1870.
56 Report of the Directors of Convict Prisons for the year 1854 (London: 1855), p. 390.
57 First Report from the Select Committee on Transportation together with the minutes of evidence and appendix (London: 1856), p. 68.
58 An extensive survey of the economic and social profiles of women suspected of prostitution in the Victorian period found that poverty was the principal cause for their entry into prostitution. See Judith

R. Walkowitz, *Prostitution and Victorian society: Women, class and the state* (Cambridge: Cambridge University Press, 1980), pp. 14–19.
59 Report of the Directors of Convict Prisons for the year 1865 (London: 1866), p. 254.
60 Report of the Directors of Convict Prisons for the year 1860 (London: 1861), p. 72.
61 LRO, 347 JUS 4/1/2, Minute Book 1864–1870, 30 October 1868.
62 The National Archives, Kew [hereafter TNA], PCOM 2/164, Millbank Book of Questions and Suggestions 1855–1863, 6 February 1863.
63 These figures were compiled using returns made in the Reports of the Directors of Convict Prisons between 1853 and 1869.
64 The study consulted the returns made in September of each year. Records for Brixton were included in the returns from December 1855, therefore the figures cover the period from September 1856 to September 1869. See: TNA, HO 8/129, Quarterly returns of prisoners in hulks and convict prisons, September 1856; HO 8/133, September 1857; HO 8/137, September 1858; HO 8/141, September 1859; HO 8/145, September 1860; HO 8/149, September 1861; HO 8/153, September 1862; HO 8/157, September 1863; HO 8/161, September 1864; HO 8/165, September 1865; HO 8/169, September 1866; HO 8/173, September 1867; HO 8/177, September 1868; HO 8/181, September 1869.
65 Report of the Directors of Convict Prisons for the year 1858 (London: 1859), p. 311.
66 Report of the Directors of Convict Prisons for the year 1859 (London: 1860), p. 273.
67 *Female life in prison, by a prison matron, Vol. II* (London: Hurst and Blackett Publishers, 1862), p. 200.
68 Ginger Frost, *Illegitimacy in English law and society 1860–1930* (Manchester: Manchester University Press, 2016), p. 49.
69 Russell P. Dobash, R. Emerson Dobash and Sue Gutteridge, *The imprisonment of women* (Oxford: Basil Blackwell, 1986), p. 90.
70 LMA, WA/G/006, Minute Book, September 1850–December 1852, 9 November 1850.
71 LMA, WA/G/006, Minute Book, September 1850–December 1852, 1 April 1854.
72 LMA, WA/G/008, Minute Book, November 1855–1857, 9 February 1855.
73 Library of Birmingham [hereafter LB], PS/B/4/5/1/1, Birmingham Petty Sessions, 1878–1892.
74 Helen Johnston (ed.), *Punishment and control in historical perspective* (Houndmills: Palgrave Macmillan, 2008), p. 184.

75 Mayhew and Binny, *The criminal prisons of London*, p. 185.
76 Mayhew and Binny, *The criminal prisons of London*, p. 191.
77 LMA, WA/G/011, Minute Book, November 1862–October 1865, 6 February 1864.
78 Modern Records Centre, University of Warwick [hereafter MRC], MSS/67/4/24/8, Holloway Discharged Prisoners' Aid Society Report, 1928.
79 MRC, MSS/67/4/24/9, Holloway Discharged Prisoners' Aid Society Report, 1929.
80 Size, *Prisons I have known*, p. 63.
81 Size, *Prisons I have known*, p. 68.
82 Cicely McCall, *They always come back* (London: Methven & Co., 1938), p. 19.
83 McCall, *They always come back*, p. 46.
84 Report of the Commissioners appointed to inquire into the operation of the acts relating to transportation and penal servitude (London: 1863), p. 246.
85 Hobhouse and Brockway, *English prisons today*, p. 345.
86 Amos, 'The prison treatment of women', p. 807.
87 Helen Johnston, 'Imprisoned mothers in Victorian England, 1853–1900: Motherhood, identity and the convict prison', *Criminology & Criminal Justice*, 19:2 (2019), 215–231, https://doi.org/10.1177/1748895818757833, p. 13.
88 Report of the Directors of Convict Prisons for the year 1855 (London: 1856), p. 297.
89 Wiener, *Reconstructing the Criminal*, pp. 122, 126.
90 Stephen Watson, 'Malingerers, the "weak-minded" criminal and the "moral imbecile": How the English prison medical officer became an expert in mental deficiency, 1880–1930', in Michael Clark and Catherine Crawford (eds), *Legal medicine in history* (Cambridge: Cambridge University Press, 1994), pp. 223–241, p. 224.
91 Report of the Select Committee of the House of Lords on Gaol Discipline (London: 1863), pp. 399–400.
92 Anne Hardy, 'Development of the prison medical service, 1774–1895', in Richard Creese, W.F. Bynum and J. Bearn (eds), *The Health of Prisoners* (Atlanta: Rodopi, 1995), pp. 59–82, p. 75.
93 Neil Davie, *Tracing the criminal: The rise of scientific criminology in Britain, 1860–1918* (Oxford: The Bardwell Press, 2005), p. 71.
94 LRO, MAG 1/2/2, Minutes of Visiting Justices 1870–1878, 28 October 1870.
95 Mary Gordon, *Penal discipline* (New York: George Routledge & Sons, 1922), p. 234.

96 Fletcher, *Twelve months in an English prison*, p. 330.
 97 Hobhouse and Brockway, *English prisons today*, p. 259.
 98 LB, QS/B/23/3, Birmingham Quarter Sessions, October 1854–June 1859, 18 October 1854.
 99 Arthur Griffiths, *Memorials of Millbank and chapters in prison history* (London: Chapman and Hall, 1884), p. 199, p. 208.
100 Bennett, 'Bad for the health of the body'.
101 Mayhew and Binny, *The criminal prisons of London*, p. 178.
102 For further details of Fry's beliefs about the treatment of female prisoners see Elizabeth Fry, *Observations on the visiting, superintendence and government of female prisoners* (London: John and Arthur Arch, 1827).
103 Coulson, '"In the care of the supposed powerful state"', pp. 17–36.
104 Fry, *Observations on the visiting*, pp. 26, 30.
105 Zedner, *Women, crime and custody*, p. 121.
106 Arthur Griffiths, *Secrets of the prison house*, *Vol. 1* (London: Chapman and Hall, 1894), p. 41.
107 Forsythe, 'Women prisoners and women's penal officials', p. 534.
108 Johnston, 'Gendered prison work', p. 194.
109 Report of the Directors of Convict Prisons for the year 1853 (London: 1854), p. 311. Elizabeth Fry was an early proponent of the belief that women required more feminine moral guidance. See Fry, *Observations on the visiting*.
110 Zedner, *Women, crime and custody*, pp. 209–213; Dobash et al., *Imprisonment of women*, pp. 84–88.
111 Alyson Brown and Emma Clare, 'A history of experience: Exploring prisoners' accounts of incarceration', in Clive Emsley (ed.), *The persistent prison: Problems, images and alternatives* (London: Francis Boutle, 2005), pp. 49–73, p. 67.
112 Fletcher, *Twelve months in an English prison*, p. 329.
113 Maybrick, *Mrs Maybrick's own story*, p. 87.
114 McCall, *They always come back*, p. 110.
115 LMA, WA/G/006, Minute Book, September 1850–December 1852, 8 May 1852, 29 October 1853.
116 Johnston, 'Gendered prison work', p. 198.
117 Hobhouse and Brockway, *English prisons today*, p. 379.
118 Carpenter, *Our convicts*, Vol. II, p. 215.
119 Size, *Prisons I have known*, p. 19.
120 Johnston, 'Gendered prison work', p. 200.
121 LMA, WA/G/006, Minute Book, September 1850–December 1852, 16 November 1850.
122 LMA, WA/G/006, Minute Book, September 1850–December 1852, 27 September 1851.

123 Maybrick, *Mrs Maybrick's own story*, p. 87.
124 LMA, WA/G/006, Minute Book, September 1850–December 1852, 26 October 1850.
125 LMA, WA/G/006, Minute Book, September 1850–December 1852, 12 October 1850.
126 Amos, 'The prison treatment of women', p. 807.
127 Report of the Departmental Committee on Prisons (London: 1895).
128 Deborah Cheney, 'Dr Mary Louisa Gordon (1861–1941): A feminist approach in prison', *Feminist Legal Studies*, 18:2 (2010), 115–136, https://doi.org/10.1007/s10691-010-9151-4, p. 118.
129 Clive Emsley, *Crime and society in twentieth-century England* (London: Routledge, 2011), p. 210.
130 Cheney, 'Dr Mary Louisa Gordon', p. 117.
131 TNA, HO 45/24643, Prisons and Prisoners: Prison Governors and Medical Officers, appointment of women (1913–1938), letter from Ida Smedley to Reginald McKenna, 25 February 1913.
132 TNA, HO 45/24643, Prisons and Prisoners: Prison Governors and Medical Officers, …, letter from Under Secretary of State to Ida Smedley, 23 April 1913.
133 Joe Sim, *Medical power in prisons: The Prison Medical Service in England 1774–1989* (Milton Keynes: Open University Press, 1990), p. 149.
134 TNA, HO 45/19977, Prisons and Prisoners: Women Medical Officers at Holloway and Aylesbury Prisons (1918–20), letter from Evelyn Ruggles-Brise to Under Secretary of State, 19 June 1918.
135 'Women's gaol governor', *Daily Herald* (29 July 1921), p. 3.
136 TNA, HO 45/24643, Prisons and Prisoners: Prison Governors and Medical Officers, …, Minutes of the Prison Commission, 26 July 1921.
137 'Letter from Florence Underwood', *Manchester Guardian* (1 August 1921), p. 4.
138 For details of the introduction of maternity dresses in several prisons see TNA, PCOM 9/1443, Women prisoners: Introduction of maternity dresses.
139 Davies, *Bad girls*, p. 166.
140 TNA, PCOM 2/164, Millbank Book of Questions and Suggestions 1855–1863, 12 August 1855.
141 Bennett, 'Bad for the health of the body', p. 552.

2

Maternity care in prison

Upon its inception in the mid-nineteenth century, the modern prison system was intended to regulate the prisoner in body and in mind. Every hour of the daily lives of the incarcerated population was governed by a set of officially sanctioned rules intended to uphold the strictest possible discipline. For much of the nineteenth and first half of the twentieth century, prisons were often fortress-like structures, intended to appear imposing to those who stepped through their gates. The system was subject to intense and lengthy debates and enquiries which led to the production of reams of reports and recommendations for its effective administration. However, the specific requirements for the confinement and care of the women who entered the system pregnant and gave birth in one of its institutions largely remained a notable chasm within the official discourse shaping penal policy. Instead, prison staff had to negotiate the terms of their incarceration within physical spaces not intended for their accommodation and as part of obdurate regimes not designed with their health needs in mind.

For much of the period under examination, identifying pregnancy was often difficult, and even framing what was meant by the maternal body and maternity care was complex. Some women chose to conceal their pregnancy or were not even aware of it themselves. This chapter also exposes the sparse consideration given to prison births at policy level, despite the fact that they were a regular feature of life in women's prisons. One significant consequence of this was the imprisonment of heavily pregnant women in separate confinement and in conditions where the limiting of association and communication was pervasive but potentially posed a danger to health.

A substantial part of this chapter is dedicated to examining a major enquiry into maternity care in English prisons. Led by Adeline Marie Russell, the Duchess of Bedford, the enquiry was carried out in Holloway Prison, the largest female prison in the country. It was prompted by an intensification of debates about health care in prisons as well as specific provisions for women, and coincided with broader debates about the appointment of more female staff to positions of greater power in prisons. The enquiry was the first of its kind to place maternity care at its centre and this chapter demonstrates that it marked a watershed in the history of the women's prison estate.

Provisions for maternity care in prisons

Women giving birth or caring for very young infants often appeared in the backgrounds of the testimonies of ex-prisoners and staff alike, and were discussed as an everyday feature of life in women's prisons. Their frequency varied from prison to prison and across the period under examination. Some prisons only ever accommodated a small number of women and may have only witnessed a couple of births in a year. However, in others births could be a monthly if not weekly occurrence. Some women spent a large proportion of their pregnancy in prison, others only a matter of weeks, due to the short nature of their sentence, while in some cases women entered only days before they gave birth. This was clearly demonstrated in a table of prison births between February 1852 and February 1854 compiled by the Medical Officer in Westminster Prison. Margaret Carey had been in the prison for almost eight months before she gave birth; however, Joanna Courier and Margaret Edwards each gave birth the day after their admission into the prison.[1] The prison occasionally had time to assess prisoners, in other cases the prison authorities would only become aware of an impending birth when it began.

In 1851 John Lavies, Medical Officer of Westminster Prison, reported to the Visiting Justices on the need for a greater number of beds in the infirmary and more officers to attend the prisoners, as the number of births and lying-in women meant that between ten and thirteen beds would be constantly required.[2] In the second half of the nineteenth century there were regularly in excess of twenty births per year in the prison, sometimes up to four in a month. The reports to the Visiting Justices demonstrate that there was also an average of between twenty and thirty children at any one time who had been committed with their mothers for varying sentence lengths. By the 1930s it appears that the number of births had slightly decreased, likely due to the decreased female prison population. Thirty-two births were recorded in the matron's journal between 1933 and 1937.[3]

In Liverpool's Walton Gaol there were an average of twenty births annually in the second half of the nineteenth century. A reading of the reports made by the prison's governor, medical officer and chaplain to the Visiting Justices reveals repeated laments about the number of women in the prison who either were pregnant or brought young infants into the prison with them. This was believed to be particularly exacerbated by the harsher winter conditions and often meant that the number of women equalled, and sometimes surpassed, the number of male prisoners, and in this sense made Liverpool unique in terms of mixed-sex prisons. Officials repeatedly complained of a lack of space to accommodate these women and their children, of an inability to confine them according to the prison regime and of the fact that many of them were serving very short sentences but were notorious recidivists who returned to the prison gates time and again. In his first report to the Visiting Justices in October 1874, the chaplain, David Morris, conflated the issues of drunkenness, venereal disease and pregnancy when complaining of the crowded nature of the prison. He described it as being used as both a lying-in hospital and a 'kind of lock hospital', including by mothers bringing in young infants. He detailed the case of a twenty-eight-year-old woman who had been in the prison thirty-five times, sometimes pregnant, and each time brought her young children in with her and posed logistical as well as disciplinary difficulties for the prison officials.[4]

By the 1920s there were an average of thirty to forty births annually across the eighteen prisons in England and Wales that accommodated women. However, this varied from prison to prison. In the early twentieth century Holloway usually witnessed between ten and twenty births annually. Some smaller local prisons or local prisons with a small number of female prisoners may have had only one or no births in a year. For example, between March 1922 and March 1924 there were forty births in the women's prison estate. Holloway accounted for thirteen of these, followed by Newcastle and Aylesbury Borstal with four each, three in each of Durham, Birmingham, Leeds and Winchester and one or two births each in other prisons. Some smaller prisons, including Hull and Portsmouth, recorded no births in those two years. In the same period twenty-seven women were discharged on account of their pregnancy, as was sometimes the practice if a woman's expected date of confinement coincided with their release date, so as to avoid her being detained beyond the expiration of her sentence.[5]

By the early twentieth century, when a woman entered prison and pregnancy was identified the medical officer was required to complete a report. This report included details of the name, the offence committed and length of the prisoner's sentence, as well as information about the stage of her pregnancy and the date her confinement was likely to take place. The report would be forwarded to the Home Secretary only if it was probable that the woman's date of confinement was likely to mean she would be detained beyond the original term of her imprisonment.[6] This practice is further discussed in Chapter 4. Interestingly, Bristol, which had an average female population of 195, witnessed no births in the two years between 1922 and 1924, but its medical officer did recommend the discharge of three women on account of their advanced pregnancy.[7] This reinforced the argument that prisons had to be prepared to confine women in an advanced stage of pregnancy even if they did not give birth behind bars. The disparity in the numbers of births in prisons and the differences in the sizes of their female populations were also reflected in the provisions some prisons made for caring for these women and their infants.

Prisons of the mid-nineteenth century were built and modified to enact the penal regimes established at the outset of the modern prison system. They included separate cells, chapels, exercise yards, punishment cells and variously included laundries, bakeries, associated workrooms and space to accommodate members of the prison staff. They also included infirmaries and, later, hospitals and, in the case of prisons containing women, spaces for the accommodation of mothers and their children. However, the size of these spaces and the provisions within varied across different prisons. When women entered prison pregnant, they were predominantly placed into cellular confinement along with the hundreds of women around them. In cases of advanced pregnancy women could be placed two or three to a larger cell at the discretion of the medical officer, with the intention that the other women could raise the alarm if they needed to gain the attention of the staff on duty.

For much of the second half of the nineteenth century the majority of women remained accommodated in their cells until their expected date of confinement, at which point they would be placed in the infirmary and spend a short period lying in. In some prison infirmaries there would be a room designated for births and beds reserved for lying-in women. In several prisons this was a room that had been converted from a cell or a warder's quarters. Chapter 1 explored the pressures facing some of the larger local prisons which accommodated women in the second half of the nineteenth century, including Liverpool and Westminster, and how officials regularly reported that the number of women entering prison either pregnant or with young infants exacerbated these pressures. Sections of the infirmaries in these prisons were permanently designated for women in an advanced stage of pregnancy, who required closer monitoring, and women who had recently given birth.

Alongside the laments over the pressures mothers and infants could place upon penal institutions, being under the close supervision of a doctor was held up as an example of the benefits to pregnant women of a certain class. Although this is an area further discussed in Chapter 4, it is beneficial to highlight one such example here, as it illuminates not only debates about the condition of women upon arrival in prison, but also reveals the perceived importance of the prison infirmary in caring for the plight of some of the women who entered prisons. In July 1890 *The Lancet* reported upon the case of prisoner E.G., who was serving two months in Canterbury Prison. Her sentence commenced on 10 April and she was eight months pregnant. On 13 May she was delivered of a male child. However, during the labour she complained of an intense headache which did not cease when the child was born. Five hours after the birth she had an epileptic fit. In the space of the twenty-four hours thereafter she had twenty-seven seizures. The doctor gave her hourly drop doses of nitro-glycerine until the fits first relaxed in their violence and then ceased. Reflecting upon the case, the medical officer and the matron pointed to the fact that the woman had received quick access to treatment which she would not have had access to on the outside. They took pains to highlight that being in the prison infirmary meant she was monitored around the clock, and that the prison environment and having a place in the infirmary for some days after the birth had allowed her the time and care to recover prior to her release with her child on 10 June.[8]

When it was opened for female convicts in 1853, Brixton's building was adapted to provide greater space for the infirmary, which was larger than those of other prisons for women at the time. A recent study has found that Brixton's infirmary was quickly put under pressure, due to the health needs of the women entering the prison. James Rendle, the medical officer, regularly reported overcrowding and the difficulties of caring adequately for the health needs of the women, who often entered the prison in ill health and could not be subject to the ordinary discipline of the institution.[9] Cases of pregnancy and new mothers were a distinct group of prisoners who required accommodation in Brixton's infirmary, in some cases being transferred to the prison from other penal institutions for that express purpose. Between 1853 and 1869 138 women were moved to Brixton from Millbank, Fulham Refuge or Parkhurst on medical grounds. Of these 138 cases, 22 women had been removed from Millbank due to pregnancy, so they could give birth in Brixton's infirmary, which was better equipped to accommodate lying-in women.[10]

By the early twentieth century, some of the larger prisons containing women had specific landings for the accommodation of cases requiring greater medical supervision and care, including pregnant women. In Holloway, if pregnancy was identified the woman was placed on the A2 or B2 observation landing. However, the cells on these landings were also used for cases of mental illness, epilepsy and tuberculosis. It was then the practice in most prisons to move the women to the prison infirmary in the final month of their pregnancy, although this study has found evidence that this was not consistently done, due to logistical pressures such as space and availability of adequate staff in the infirmary, as well as uncertainties about a woman's expected due date.

In the second half of the nineteenth century, following a period of lying in, women who had recently given birth, or those who entered the prison with young infants, would be placed in the prison nursery. Similar to infirmaries, the provisions in place for nurseries varied in different prisons. The nurseries in which young infants would spend the first months of their lives were labelled by journalists

Henry Mayhew and John Binny as the most distinguishing features of women's prisons. They described scenes that are at odds with the more common imagery of the imposing, fortress-like prisons built and modified in the mid-nineteenth century, of children clinging to their mother's skirts, of 'toleration and true wisdom, if not goodness'.[11]

At the turn of the twentieth century, prison nurseries were replaced with crèches in prisons including Wormwood Scrubs, Liverpool, Birmingham and Holloway. After the birth of their baby and a few days of recovery in the prison hospital, mothers would be placed back into cellular confinement. In Holloway the C1 landing was reserved for these women, but the cells in which mothers would spend the first weeks and months with their babies were described as being 'cold, dark and draughty'.[12] With the establishment of prison crèches it was intended that children in the prison would receive greater care from a dedicated member of the prison staff during the day, before being accommodated with their mothers in their cells at night. Debates about the importance of these crèches and their role in the imprisonment and care of mothers are further explored in Chapter 3.

Despite the fact that the hospital was a place for the reception of the sick, it was also intended that it would be subject to a strict set of rules in line with the broader discipline of the prison. Ex-prisoners spoke of a lack of privacy in the hospital and of rules dictating their behaviour within. Constance Lytton described how prisoners in the hospital were not allowed to lie in their beds unless they were so ill as to be undressed and in bed. Instead, they had to sit in the chair beside the bed.[13] Joan Henry described a ward in Holloway's hospital which contained eleven iron bedsteads, linoleum-covered floors and large windows. Adjoining it was the matron's office, and at its entrance was a large door with a grille through which she was aware of eyes constantly observing, even if no one entered or spoke to the women inside.[14] However, as with other aspects of the running of prisons explored in this study, implementation of the prison rules was adapted in practice. In turn, the treatment of women, including those who were pregnant and who gave birth, was shaped by the other prisoners and the staff around them. Kathleen Lonsdale recalled spending time in the prison hospital during her imprisonment in 1943. She remarked that some of the officers on

Figure 2.1 The nursery, Holloway Prison, c. early twentieth century.

duty were kind to those who were sick and went 'beyond their duty to supply the deficiencies' of the system when caring for the health of prisoners. However, others were not.[15]

In addition to the physical spaces within prisons that were set apart for childbirth and for the accommodation of mothers and their children, the prison regime also played a major role in shaping their experiences. This began when women walked through the prison gates and became subject to an initial reception process. Cicely McCall summed up this process when she recalled that 'kindliness, cleanliness and a deadly scepticism' were what the new admission found when she arrived in prison.[16] Miss Whyte, the Matron in Holloway, described how the women would be given a bath and checked for verminous conditions such as head lice. Their possessions were confiscated, and they would change into the prison-issued clothing.[17] Women would then be placed in small, cubicle-style reception cells where, in the larger prisons especially, they could wait for hours for the medical officer to arrive to carry out examinations of the new arrivals.

Medical examinations upon entry into a prison were brief and often perfunctory in nature. Pat Collins recorded 'seeing the doctor' as an almost literal description of medical examinations upon entry into prison.[18] Kathleen Lonsdale recalled her medical examination on her entry into Holloway Prison in 1943. She stated that a nurse examined her hair, asked if her periods were regular and if she had children. A female doctor then checked her chest with a stethoscope but did not remove her blouse to do so. She continued that if a woman 'wished to conceal a state of pregnancy, she could so quite easily' under the circumstances she observed. On the basis of this examination Lonsdale was deemed fit for work and allocated her landing.[19] Joan Henry spoke of becoming accustomed to the question 'are you all right?' from the medical officer, the matron and the officers on duty and of the 'correct replies' expected unless you were 'dying on your feet'.[20]

In many cases of pregnancy, it was up to the women themselves to disclose their condition when they entered prison, especially in the early stages, if they themselves were even aware of it. Even in the early twentieth century, identifying pregnancy and then estimating the due date was 'hit and miss'. For many women, they did not know for sure that they were pregnant until the baby started moving at sixteen to eighteen weeks.[21] In addition, relying on their menstrual cycles to identify pregnancy could be unreliable, as many of the women entering prisons were in ill health and were malnourished, which could have an impact on menstruation and its regularity. Some pregnant women asked to consult a prison doctor about their condition, but were afforded little consideration. One such case was that of Phyllis Ward.

Phyllis Ward served a seven-week sentence in Holloway, commencing at the beginning of January 1919. Upon her release on 22 February she went to a Church Army home for shelter. Sister Bryant, who ran the home, immediately asked Phyllis if she was pregnant and recommended sending her to Marylebone Infirmary on account of her having a weak heart. Phyllis gave birth to a stillborn child on 13 March. She told the doctor in the infirmary that she had not initially regarded the cessation of menstruation as a sure sign of pregnancy, as she was often irregular. However, shortly after entering Holloway she noticed that she was short of breath when climbing the stairs and felt weak. Phyllis recalled 'booking' to see the medical officer and asking him about her condition. She claimed that he had examined her breasts but not her abdomen or vagina and told her she was not pregnant. She had also spent the final week of her sentence in the prison hospital due to a heavy cough, but again her pregnancy remained undetected. The Medical Superintendent at Marylebone Infirmary reported to the Prison Commission regarding her case, stating that her child had been born about three weeks before her full term and that anti-syphilitic treatment had also been given. He added that there were multiple signs of pregnancy, including the dark pigmentation of the areola and clear signs when carrying out an abdominal examination, and stated that it was difficult to explain how these signs had been missed in the prison. Holloway's Medical Officer was asked to report on the case and replied that although multiple members of staff could recall Phyllis being in the hospital, they had not suspected pregnancy and would not have given a negative diagnosis of such without thorough examination.[22]

In Phyllis's case, the brief nature of her medical examination upon entry into prison and the fact that the prison doctor did not thoroughly examine her even after she expressed her belief that she was pregnant meant that she remained subject to the ordinary prison discipline, despite being in an advanced stage of pregnancy. However, some women deliberately concealed their condition and it remained undetected, especially if they were serving relatively short sentences. As a result, they received no maternity care or adaptation to the prison regime at all. Others were either unaware of their condition or successfully concealed it until the birth of their child. In January 1870, Mary Ann Shaw was admitted to Wakefield Prison and was placed in an infirmary cell as she was suffering from a venereal disease. The matron suspected she was pregnant, but Mary had denied it and there was no further medical examination. However, another prisoner was in the cell that had recently been vacated by Mary Ann, when she felt something in the corner of the bed. This was called to the attention of the matron who found it to be the body of a female infant. Mary Ann was examined and confessed to having given birth to the child on 14 February. She claimed that the child was born in the early hours of the morning but had lived for only ten minutes. She feared punishment, and so hid the child's body in the bed.[23]

This study has identified a few other cases similar to Mary's throughout the second half of the nineteenth century at several prisons. In some cases, it was not prison staff who noticed signs of ill health or pregnancy in women, but their fellow inmates. Ellen Evans reported her fellow prisoner Ellen Stammers in Westminster in 1874 for showing signs of recently having given birth when they were working together. When questioned, Stammers admitted that she had been delivered of a child at eleven o'clock the previous evening, and the child's body was found wrapped in a blanket in her hammock. The child's body was examined, and although there were no signs of violence the lungs had been thoroughly inflated, showing that the child had lived for a short time. Ellen was twenty years old and described as having 'not a friend in the world'. The coroner returned a verdict of 'found dead' and Ellen avoided further punishment.[24] Cases such as these, and several others like them, offer perhaps the starkest demonstration of the isolation women in prison could face, an isolation exacerbated for pregnant women facing a life-altering moment without family or friends. They demonstrate a theme running throughout this study, namely the physical closeness but detached nature of prison life in which serious health conditions remained undetected despite a key principle of prisons at this time being the close surveillance of their inmates.

A refinement of cruelty? Prison regimes for pregnant women

Following their reception into prison, women would commence their sentence and be subject to a set of prison rules by which they had to strictly abide, and regulations that would heavily dictate every hour of their day. The chapter now turns to two major areas of these regimes that shaped the health experiences of mothers in prison, namely the prison diet and the terms under which they were confined. As part of their role in deciding if the prisoner's body or mind was likely to be injured by the discipline in the prison, medical officers could adapt a prisoner's diet. In the case of pregnant women and new mothers, medical officers could direct that they be given additional milk, tea, cocoa, sugar, bread and fish and meat. However, adaptations to their diet differed across this period and within different institutions; and in addition to being inconsistent, they were also subject to scrutiny on the part of prison authorities and observers, and steeped in debates regarding the role of the prison diet within the broader aims of the penal system and the need to maintain health but not pose a better prospect than provisions on the outside.

In Brixton the diet was adapted, following the opening of the prison in 1853, to offer greater provision for women undertaking more strenuous labour, notably working in the laundry, and for convalescents, which included women in the infirmary, those in an advanced stage of pregnancy and those who had recently given birth. They were given additional rations of bread and, on occasion, a half ounce of cheese. The 'nursery breakfast' consisted of a pint of milk for each child and tea for each mother in place of the cocoa served as part of the ordinary diet. In the infirmary the prisoners could be served pieces of boiled cod if they had been placed on a fish diet by the medical officer, and some were also given eggs, batter pudding or rice-milk to rebuild their strength or to aid in the recovery from illness.[25] Dietary information discussed at the Birmingham Petty Sessions in 1878 stated that the diet for all prisoners was predominantly comprised of bread, potatoes, suet pudding and gruel. After nine months, cocoa was given at breakfast instead of gruel. However, the medical officer had the ability to order items such as bacon, butter, cake, eggs, fruit, vegetables, jam, milk, poultry and even wine in cases where they deemed it necessary to ensure the health of the prisoner.[26]

Zedner argued that there was some acknowledgement during official enquiries, such as the Royal Commission on the Penal Servitude Acts in 1863, that a sufficient prison diet was considered essential for women, as it was feared that their reproductive system could be damaged by prolonged privation of food.[27] In his 1863 report, John Lavies, Westminster's Medical Officer, argued that an insufficient diet could potentially affect the menstrual system, observing that 'women under imprisonment for long terms are very apt to lose the healthy performance of functions peculiar to their sex', due to the rigours of the prison system, including being subject to the prison diet for long and repeated periods.[28] However, these acknowledgements were not translated into official policy and this study has found limited evidence of specific consideration at policy level of the dietary needs of pregnant women, those who had recently given birth and those breastfeeding children. Instead, as with other aspects of medical care in prison, the administration of the prison diet for these women was subject to variation based upon questions of health and discipline within individual institutions, daily decision-making processes shaped by the proclivities of staff regarding prisoner welfare and the availability of resources.

In the case of pregnant women, decisions were also influenced by the need to consider the health of the unborn child while balancing the woman's status as a prisoner. In response to repeated entreaties regarding the number of women in Westminster Prison and the disruption to the regime and logistical pressures posed by those giving birth or bringing in children, the Middlesex magistrate Sir Peter Laurie wrote to the Visiting Justices in February 1854. When commenting upon the special arrangements for the accommodation of women and children, including additions to their diet, their reception into the infirmary where necessary and the care afforded to the children by the prison staff and the medical officer, he stated that 'a mother in your prison is practically a lady', as a means to rebuff calls for greater provision.[29]

In 1943 a Miss Dorothy Borup wrote to her local Member of Parliament, Dr Haden Guest, to complain of the condition of her friend who was confined in Holloway Prison. This included her imprisonment in cellular confinement and elements of the regime. Dorothy stated that the food was inadequate and that pregnant women could become so hungry that they ate crusts of bread from the ground. In addition, it was only after their sixth month of pregnancy that women would be given an additional half pint of milk and some dry bread.[30] In response to this enquiry, the governor and medical officer compiled a report to the Home Office in which they stated that as soon as pregnancy was established a prisoner was located on the maternity landing and received extra food and milk, which increased at different stages of pregnancy; from the fifth month of pregnancy, it was an extra half pint of milk, from the seventh month it was an extra pint. Additional provisions of vegetables as well as milk and cocoa could be ordered by the medical officer following 'any reasonable complaint of hunger'.[31] Dr Guest visited

Holloway and, following his report back to the Home Secretary on his inspection of the kitchen, hospital and cellular accommodation, it was concluded that Miss Borup's account was 'far from accurate'.[32]

Despite this seeming vindication, correspondence between the governor and the Home Secretary reveals a long-standing issue in debates about prisoner health, but one that was further complicated when considering the case of pregnant women. The governor wrote of the Ministry of Health campaign that was ongoing at the time to persuade expectant mothers to drink more milk. The Ministry of Food was providing milk at a reduced price to women as soon as their pregnancy was established, which it stated was commonly around three months. He stated that this had likely evoked the criticism the prison system was facing. He added that it was difficult to justify the policy of providing women in prison with less milk, and only at a more advanced stage of pregnancy. Even among those who readily accepted the principle that prison food is 'not meant to provide an optimum diet, but the minimum necessary for the maintenance of health', he mused, would it likely be accepted that a more generous policy ought to be adopted in the case of pregnant women, where not only the health of the mother but also that of the child was involved. He continued that in such cases 'generalisations about the principles of prison treatment may be thought inapplicable'.[33]

Despite some modifications to the separate system within the female convict estate, the principle that association and communication between prisoners should be limited and carefully regulated remained a pervasive one into the early twentieth century. Ex-prisoners described experiences of desolation and isolation in tomb-like cells where they marked their day with the passing of footsteps, and a brief visit from the chaplain broke the silence.[34] Observers of the realities of prison life described the 'wicked and unfeeling' rules that were intended to prevent even the mothers in prison nurseries from finding some small semblance of human interaction within these obdurate regimes.[35] However, what garnered more debate and shock for some was the practice of locking up pregnant women in their cells for hours at a time, sometimes up to twenty-three hours in a day. Following debates about the practicalities of this in the case of the sick or those who required medical attention, in 1906 Birmingham's Winson Green Prison reissued its rules and regulations to all prison staff. Originally dated 1860, they placed particular reinforcement on the rule directing that every prisoner in separate confinement would be supplied with a means of communicating at any time with an officer, especially those who might require closer observation.[36] However, the study has uncovered examples of women crying out for help from officers on duty across this period, and of these cries going unheard, not responded to in time, being denigrated as attempts at malingering or seeking to break the monotony of cellular confinement or simply being ignored.

Hobhouse and Brockway lamented the practice of confining sick people alone in their cells for long periods of time. They stated their hope that highlighting this practice would 'strike every ordinary humane person as monstrous' and lead to a rethinking of how people in prison spent their time.[37] For pregnant women, the feelings of isolation and helplessness were already heightened due to their facing the prospect of giving birth in prison. They were exacerbated further still when facing up to twenty-three hours in a day alone in a cell with limited contact, prompting stress and psychological anxiety, especially for those nearing the date of their confinement. Kathleen Lonsdale labelled the practice of confining pregnant women for the same hours as the rest of the prison population as 'a refinement of cruelty that one can only ascribe to lack of imagination on the part of those who are responsible for it'.[38]

Although some prisons implemented the practice of incarcerating pregnant women two or three to a shared dormitory-like cell to ensure that they could call out in an emergency, it was not universally applied. It was also dependent upon individual staff members, the availability of adequate space and the correct identification of a prisoner's stage of pregnancy and expected due date. For many women, they remained in isolation. Some women suffered miscarriages or went into premature labour alone in their cells with no medical assistance. Lonsdale's fellow contributor to the Prison Medical Reform Council's account of medical care in Holloway, Vera Mayhew, spoke of the impact of confining pregnant women in isolation upon the hundreds of women locked in cells around them, physically close but unable to offer any support or assistance when it was required. She recalled often hearing the sound of the emergency bell go unheeded. She wrote of the case of a young girl whose cries throughout the night had become more distressed, alerting the attention of the whole landing who rang their bells in desperation to call for help. However, no one arrived until the following morning, when it was discovered that she had given birth in her cell.[39] Although in this case mother and child were eventually examined and recovered from their ordeal, there were others where the outcome was not the same.

On 20 August 1918 twenty-eight-year-old May McCririck entered Holloway Prison to begin her sentence of six months' imprisonment. Like every prisoner to pass through the gates, May was subject to a brief medical examination as part of the reception process. She was found to be in the early stages of pregnancy and thus the medical officer recommended that she be placed on the 'B2' landing, reserved for prisoners believed to require additional observation. May, like all of the women incarcerated in Holloway, was locked in her cell for hours at a time, physically close but relatively isolated from the hundreds of women and prison staff around her. On the night of 9 February 1919, around seven months into her pregnancy, she went into premature labour. She rang the emergency bell in her cell to alert the attention of the officer on duty. Upon hearing her cries, the women in the cells next door joined in her calls for help. However, they went unanswered, and May gave birth to her son alone in the darkness of her prison cell. May described how he neither moved nor cried, so she 'wrapped the child up in a sheet and put it under the bed'. It was not until their morning rounds, some hours later, that a prison officer discovered May and sent for one of the prison doctors. The child was believed to have died during or immediately after the birth, and thus a coroner's inquest was deemed to be unnecessary. May was moved to the prison hospital to recover, where she spent the remainder of her sentence until she was released on 26 February.[40] Sadly, May's story was not an isolated incident. Instead, this study has found other cases where similar circumstances prompted equally tragic experiences for women in prison. However, May's case was among those held up as a testimony of the inadequacies of the prison system for mothers and was used to call for a shift in how the country confined and cared for maternity cases.

A record of the greatest public value? The Duchess of Bedford's 1919 enquiry

In March 1919 a landmark enquiry was carried out in Holloway Prison. Chaired by Adeline Marie Russell, the Duchess of Bedford and a notable penal reformer in the early twentieth century, the enquiry was the first of its kind to focus exclusively on the health needs of women and their babies in prison and offered extensive recommendations regarding the provisions for maternity care. The ensuing report was labelled by the Prison Commission as a record of the 'greatest public value'.[41] At the time of the enquiry Holloway was the largest women's prison in England and conditions behind its turreted gates had become increasingly visible to the public, due to the imprisonment there of several suffragettes, debates about the appointment of more female staff to positions of greater power in the prison system and an intensification of scrutiny regarding health in prisons in the wake of the First World War. The enquiry highlighted several cases, including that of May McCririck, to make recommendations regarding the conditions in which pregnant women were imprisoned, the arrangements in place for childbirth and the availability of specially trained staff, notably midwives.

At the time of the enquiry several cases had been reported upon in the press and raised with the Prison Commission regarding the provisions for health and sanitation in women's prisons. One such example was the allegations raised by Sister Grace of the Home at Highbury Park for women who had recently left prison, with Sir Evelyn Ruggles-Brise, Chairman of the Prison Commission. She wrote of women arriving at the Home with lice and venereal diseases, despite some of them having certificates stating that they were free from such diseases. Sister Grace made specific mention of the condition of Edith May Southgate when she arrived from Holloway on 25 November 1918, describing her as being 'in a shocking state', her flesh raw owing to the lack of proper sanitary towels despite asking for them in the prison. It took over a week for her skin to heal.[42]

In response to these allegations, and the broader interest in health in prisons at the time, Ruggles-Brise wrote to the Duchess of Bedford expressing the need for an independent enquiry to be made into conditions in Holloway. He wrote of the difficulties of administering the prison estate during the war and the issue of the continuing shortage of medical staff to attend to the excessive number of cases requiring medical care and attention. He assured her that all records would be placed at the disposal of the committee and that they could invite witnesses to give evidence as they might think necessary, including interviewing the prison's staff.[43] The committee entrusted to carry out the enquiry consisted of the Duchess of Bedford as Chair, Miss Burrell and Miss Blunt, both Lady Visitors at Holloway, Mrs Gilbert Samuel, Chairman of the Prison Reform Committee in connection with the Joint Parliamentary Advisory Council, and Dr Ada Whitlock, a Lady Inspector of the Reformatory and Industrial School Department.

Adeline Russell was selected to chair the committee as she was a notable reformer who had led several campaigns aimed at the moral and occupational improvement of women's lives. She had been closely involved with the Associated Workers League, which was concerned with the well-being of women at work. In 1900, she became the president of the National Lady Visitors' Association. The Lady Visitors visited women in prison and sought to educate them and to help them prepare for life after their imprisonment. Russell also regularly visited Aylesbury's Inebriate Reformatory after its opening in 1902 and the borstal wing of Aylesbury Prison, which opened in 1908.[44] Prior to the outbreak of the First World War she had criticised the conditions in which Royalist prisoners in Portugal were being kept. Reporting upon her involvement, the *Illustrated London News* stated that Russell had a 'special qualification for criticising the management of prisons' as, for many years past, she had taken a special interest in the matter.[45]

In addition to her interest in prisoner welfare, the Duchess of Bedford was also involved in several other areas pertaining to the well-being of women. The National Society for the Prevention of Infant Mortality was founded in 1912. Its Honorary Secretary, Jeanette Halford, is credited with the initial promotion of the idea of a National Baby Week to advise mothers in matters of infant care. In February 1917 the renamed National League for Healthy Maternity and Child Welfare organised a meeting presided over by Adeline Russell to discuss plans for the event, which was held in July. Exhibitions during the event included information on lifestyle, hygiene, diseases, alcoholism and the importance of health visitors. Linda Bryder argues that, despite the health politics of the time often blaming mothers for their perceived inadequacies, the event also acknowledged the social and economic factors which shaped the lives of many working- and lower-class women. Bryder concluded that the women who led the event seized the opportunity presented by it to promote maternal, as well as infant, interests and well-being.[46]

Following their brief medical examination upon entry into prison, the health experiences of pregnant women were shaped not only by the medical officer but also by female warders, who were not medically trained, infirmary and hospital staff and even their fellow prisoners. In the early twentieth century women were generally unlikely to receive any antenatal care and would call in a midwife or a doctor only during labour.[47] However, there were increasing debates about the availability of staff within prisons to care for the health needs of female prisoners, including mothers and their children. These debates were not only bound up in the question of the state's responsibility to these women and their children, who were deemed to be innocents in the eyes of the law, but were also aimed at avoiding public censure of the system in cases of poor or inadequate care.

One particular aspect of the prison regime which the committee highlighted as problematic for prisoner health was the placing of women in separate confinement. They pointed to the experiences of women including May McCririck and several others to state unequivocally that no cases of advanced pregnancy or those where there might be complications during pregnancy should be isolated in a cell for long periods of time. They stressed that isolation in these circumstances was especially liable to produce nervous depression and took no account of the danger posed by sudden confinement. In addition, their report stated that it ought not to be assumed that a pregnant woman would always complain of labour pains in time for help to be summoned. It stressed that, apart from the fact that a woman might deliberately conceal the fact that she was in labour, it was possible for delivery to occur unexpectedly. It spoke of additional complications, such as the mother collapsing or haemorrhaging after the birth and the possibility that she could die before assistance arrived. Furthermore, the report pointed to the potential dangers for the child if the mother gave birth in a cell. It could fall head first onto the floor or drown in the commode if the mother was sitting there. The child could also be strangled by the umbilical cord. The committee also warned that prisons rarely considered the possibility that the mother might not know how to care for the infant, or might not want to care for it or even to preserve the life of the child.[48]

The committee recommended that the current remand side of the prison hospital instead be used for the reception of all prisoners in an advanced stage of pregnancy and for women who had recently given birth, to spend time convalescing. They recommended that the adjoining room could be used as a lying-in ward and the additional hospital cells could be repurposed for cases requiring special attention, where cell doors would be replaced by curtains. In his response to the committee following receipt of their reports, Ruggles-Brise gave assurances that the arrangements in place for the care of pregnant women would be considered and there were changes made to their accommodation and the staffing arrangements for their care, as detailed below. However, there was one area of contention that reveals the continued difficulties posed when attempting to balance punitive considerations with those of health. In answer to the recommendation of placing all maternity cases in the present remand side of the hospital, he replied that the Commissioners could not accept this suggestion, as it would seriously conflict with the 'all important principle that there should be an absolute segregation of convicted and un-convicted cases'.[49] However, he acceded that there was a need for more specific consideration of the needs of maternity cases. An area believed to be crucial in this respect was the prison staff.

Dr Walker, Medical Officer of Holloway, told the Gladstone Committee in 1895 that women who gave birth in the prison infirmary were attended to by female infirmary warders, one of whom had experience of working in a London hospital, but advocated for greater provision in this area as it was inconsistent.[50] Correspondence between the Treasury and the Home Secretary in 1914 debated the provision of trained nursing staff in prisons. Although the outbreak of the First World War halted the debate, it was renewed in its wake. In this sense there were parallels with practices outside, as training provision for nurses more broadly was expanded after the conclusion of the war. Prisons offered a unique site to stage discussions around nursing and the training of nurses. At the time, Holloway was the first prison to have trained nurses as part of the staff, which included a hospital superintendent and twelve trained nurses. When the Prison Nursing Service was established in 1928, the position of hospital superintendent was superseded by nursing matron-in-chief, who would be based in Holloway but visited other women's prisons.[51] However, at the time of the debates immediately before and after the war, the small number of hospital patients in some of the smaller prisons meant that the employment of nursing staff was not deemed to be necessary. There were also cases that required specialist medical treatment that the medical officer deemed could not be carried out by the ordinary prison staff. In such cases the governor could authorise the engagement of the services of outside practitioners.[52] This was due to instructions issued by the Treasury in 1884 which authorised the bringing in of trained nurses from outside in cases where it was deemed 'absolutely necessary'. It appears that some maternity cases fell within this remit, as correspondence in July 1919 remarked that in prisons such as Holloway the sheer numbers of pregnancy cases and venereal disease meant that it was currently necessary to use such provision, pending the employment of more trained hospital staff.[53]

A long-running tension in the prison system has been the balancing of maintaining prisoner health and managing the discipline of the institution. It was often the case that it fell to prison staff to navigate the boundaries between the two. The enquiry found that the nursing staff's duties were not wholly devoted to nursing and the care of prisoner health, as they were expected to carry out other disciplinary duties. In addition, despite certain categories of prisoners being identified as requiring closer supervision, and perhaps ready access to medical assistance, for large parts of their time in prison they were largely under the charge of prison officers with little or no medical training.

The medical staff in Holloway at the time of the enquiry in 1919 consisted of three male doctors and one female doctor who were responsible for administering medical treatment and overseeing the prison's hospital. However, the nursing in the hospital was done by wardresses who were not trained nurses. There had been only one certified midwife among the staff, who had resigned and had not been replaced at the time of the enquiry. The committee found it somewhat difficult to give exact figures for the number of cases dealt with, but according to the records for the year beginning March 1918 and ending March 1919 the number of remand cases found to be pregnant was about 110 and a total of 120 convicted women had entered the prison pregnant. The number of births in the prison during the previous three years was fifty, an average of about sixteen per annum. Of these fifty confinements, forty were full term and in two of these cases the child was stillborn. Ten of the confinements were premature, the babies being born at between six and eight and a half months; in five of these cases the child lived and in five they died.[54] The committee identified twenty cases of pregnancy under treatment in the hospital on the days of their visits, including four cases complicated by haemorrhaging, three cases of mothers with a venereal disease, one of a woman with epilepsy and three women under observation for mental illness.[55] The committee stressed that specialised medical treatment was even more essential in these instances and used the case of seventeen-year-old Ellen Sullivan to illustrate the dangers of having inadequate maternity staff to attend cases of pregnancy and childbirth.

Ellen was a remand prisoner in Holloway and was almost seven months pregnant when she was placed in a hospital cell in January 1919 after she began to vomit violently. The medical officer had decided to place her in one of the ordinary hospital cells instead of the hospital ward where several prisoners would be in the same room – a common practice to try to separate younger, first offenders from older prisoners whenever possible., The impact of punitive considerations upon decisions about prisoner health is a recurring theme in the present study, and Ellen's case would demonstrate the potential consequences of such choices. The committee also noted that there were bells in the hospital cells, but they were placed close to the door and thus were separated from the bed by the whole length of the cell, which again exacerbated the isolation many pregnant women experienced, an isolation made more acute as they neared the time of their due date. During the night of 17 January Ellen was attended by a young, inexperienced wardress who was not a trained nurse and who was responsible for patrolling the two floors of the hospital. On her rounds she suspected something was wrong when she observed Ellen through the cell door. She woke up the day hospital officer who slept on the upper floor to ask for assistance, but by the time she returned, Ellen was found to have given birth. The baby had fallen onto the floor during labour and the umbilical cord had been ruptured. When the officer discovered this, she sent for one of the prison doctors and a midwife from outside, which was sometimes the practice when no midwives were employed within women's prisons. However, the child died before they arrived. When the doctor and midwife arrived Ellen delivered the placenta, after which they left her in the care of a member of the hospital staff who was not a trained midwife. Ellen died the following day. Her death was found to have been caused by traces of diabetes and severe kidney disease and due to her premature confinement. However, the coroner was at pains to conclude that Ellen's death and that of her child had not been caused by a lack of adequate care, despite the delay in the arrival of a midwife and the doctor.[56]

When interviewing Dr Forward, the medical officer, the committee ascertained that nursing in the hospital was done by older and more experienced wardresses, who had built up considerable experience with sickness in the prison but were not trained nurses. They were assisted by younger wardresses who were placed on hospital duty, as in the case of Ellen Sullivan. Dr Forward stated that he had found it difficult to get reliable wardresses for the hospital staff, as when older members of staff left, others did not want to be placed on nursing duties due to the added worry and responsibility of the work, there being no compensating advantage in terms of salary or other benefits. He reported that efforts had been made to recruit more experienced hospital staff but without much success, attributing this in part to the shortage of medical practitioners generally in war time, and to the recent influenza epidemic.[57]

In their report to the Prison Commission, the committee stated their firm conviction that the lack of proper provision for nursing the sick and caring for maternity cases marked a 'serious defect in the prison administration'. They continued that it was unfair to the prison doctors, who had to try to manage prisoners' health in such conditions and who could never 'feel free' from the weight of obligation resting upon them, and to the hospital staff, who had to undertake heavy responsibilities for which they had not been trained. However, a crucial point made in their report, and one that speaks directly to a key theme running throughout this study, was that prisoners, 'whatever their delinquencies', were entitled to proper care while in the charge of the state.[58]

The committee strongly recommended that a fully trained and experienced nurse should be appointed as matron in charge of both sides of the hospital, the remand and the convicted, and should have a fully trained staff of nurses under her charge. They added that the hospital should never be left without a trained nurse in charge and that its staff should include nurses with special experience of mental and venereal cases.[59] They also recommended the appointment of at least two members of staff with a certificate from the Central Midwives Board. Furthermore, they advocated for an increase in the number of prison officers more broadly to facilitate the demarcation of duties that would help to avoid officers having to constantly shift from one landing to another and would allow officers to be assigned with responsibility for particular branches of work.[60]

In the months following the report, a fully trained nurse with a certificate from the Central Midwives Board was placed in charge of the 'B2' observation cases and was to accompany prison doctors visiting the complaining sick. She would also be responsible for administering any medicines on the wings at the hours when they were due, replacing the practice where this responsibility was assigned to an officer.[61] Two nurses certified by the Central Midwives Board and nurses with experience in treating venereal disease and mental illness were appointed by June 1919. In addition, with a view to encouraging nursing staff to undergo the necessary training to acquire the Certificate of the Central Midwives Board, the Prison Commission successfully petitioned the Treasury to allow an additional fee to be paid in each midwifery case attended to by a prison officer holding this qualification. They pointed to the benefits to both the women themselves and, crucially, their babies, for whose health the state had a responsibility to care.[62] In the 1930s every nurse in Holloway was also a qualified midwife, and other women's prisons were gradually appointing qualified midwives to their staff.[63]

Despite some of the recommendations of the committee being translated into practical change, the standard of medical care and health in prisons continued to garner commentary and debate. Reflecting upon the changes that had occurred during her career in the prison service, which spanned over four decades, Mary Size labelled the 'skilled pre-natal care of expectant mothers, and the excellent training they received in child welfare' as perhaps the most vital developments of all.[64] Following the establishment of the Prison Nursing Service in 1928, members of the Advisory Committee visited Holloway in March of that year. They spoke to several of the women in the prison hospital and reported that several expressed appreciation for the care they received and the care given to their babies.[65] Amid debates about the practice of having women give birth in prisons, which intensified in the post-war period, the standard of maternity care available in prison hospitals was used in its defence. In response to a petition to end the practice in 1949, Home Secretary Chuter Ede stated that he was not prepared to take steps to force all women to go to an outside hospital for the birth of their baby, as the hospital in Holloway was fully equipped to provide the necessary care in maternity cases. This included having a full nursing staff, including full-time midwives whom expectant prisoners had come to know and trust.[66]

By the late 1940s pregnant women in Holloway attended a monthly antenatal clinic which was held in the prison.[67] Provisions for this were further developed amid debates about the number of women who would end their prison sentences and return to homes where they were believed to be ill equipped to properly care for their home and children. Chapter 3 will examine how courses in mothercraft, domesticity and home management were introduced, or provisions for them expanded, in several women's prisons in the wake of the Second World War. Several such courses were taught by external practitioners including doctors, nurses, health visitors and state-certified midwives, as well as by external reformers. Joan Henry, who served an eight-month sentence in Holloway and then in Askham Grange in the early 1950s, was fairly critical of the health and sanitary provisions for women in prison. However, she recalled that she was 'quite impressed' by the care given to the mothers and their children.[68]

Despite improvements in some aspects of the provisions for mothers and their children, these changes did not address all of the issues raised by the enquiry of 1919, or indeed those which had posed significant challenges to the prison system since its inception in the nineteenth century. Some changes were not as immediate as others and were not implemented on a consistent basis, and were subject to policy shifts and changing prison personnel. In addition, certain practices, beliefs and inadequacies remained and had serious health implications for mothers. Pregnant women and new mothers were still being locked in their cells for several hours at a time, often from the late afternoon of one day until the following morning. In spite of the increase in maternity staff, pregnancy cases still went undetected. Cicely McCall described a case in the early 1930s where a paid domestic servant in the nurses' quarters gave birth, but none of the qualified nurses or midwives in Holloway had suspected her condition.[69] Other women continued to suffer the isolation and anxiety of cellular confinement during advanced pregnancy and gave birth alone in their cells, crying out for help that did not arrive.

Conclusion

When they walked into prison, women entered an environment that was intended to be physically imposing and rigidly governed. For women who commenced their sentences pregnant, there was an added layer of uncertainty and isolation. For the staff charged with their custody and care, they posed significant challenges to systems and spaces that were not designed with their confinement in mind. At the outset of the modern penal system, prison buildings were modified to incorporate infirmaries, nurseries and, later, crèches for the reception of mothers and babies. Prisoners and staff each played roles in adapting the rules regulating the running of prisons so as to address the daily realities of prison life. Some made the argument that the prison environment was a safer place for the birth of their child than the conditions many women left behind on the outside. For others it was a place of suffering and heartbreak. The extent to which the terms of their incarceration caused ill health in mothers, the anxiety caused by the prospect of premature labour or isolation in a prison cell, and the impact of the deaths of babies upon their mothers and the other women, while often not easy to ascertain for all women, are starkly demonstrated in the cases illuminated here. What is clear is that placing pregnant women in separate confinement exacerbated their isolation and often left little room for support or reassurance at a life-altering moment.

The enquiry of 1919 was a landmark, due to its illumination of an issue that had previously been largely unaddressed within official prison policy, namely the specific provisions required for the care of pregnant women and those giving birth. It led to some practical improvements to maternity care provisions in women's prisons and made other long-standing issues more visible both within and beyond the higher echelons of the prison system administration. However, its significance in the history of women in prison in England is that it provides an early history of some of the fundamental questions that continued to emerge in reviews, debates, enquiries and policy shifts that have occurred in the century since, namely those centred on the questions of whether prisons were appropriate places for maternity cases and, if so, how the safe custody of mothers and their babies could be ensured.[70]

Notes

1 LMA, WA/G/006, Minute Book, September 1850–December 1852, 1 February 1854.
2 LMA, WA/G/006, Minute Book, September 1850–December 1852, 25 January 1851.
3 LMA, CLA/003/ME/01/001, Matron's Journal 27 December 1933–23 November 1937.
4 LRO, 347 MAG 1/2/2, Minutes of the Visiting Justices 1870–1878, 29 October 1874.
5 These figures were collated from Home Office records. See TNA, HO 144/3982, Prisons and Prisoners: Childbirth in prison. Memorandum on existing practice and the arguments for temporary removal 1924.
6 The study has not found any of the reports completed by medical officers. However, for a blank copy of the report that would have been completed in these cases see TNA, HO 144/3982, Prisons and Prisoners: Childbirth in prison.
7 These figures were collated from Home Office records. See TNA, HO 144/3982, Prisons and Prisoners: Childbirth in prison.
8 'Notes, short comments and answers to correspondents', *The Lancet*, Vol. 135 (1890), pp. 833–834.
9 Rachel Bennett, 'Bad for the health of the body, worse for the health of the mind: Female responses to imprisonment in England, 1853–1869', *Social History of Medicine*, 34:2 (2021), 532–552, https://doi.org/10.1093/shm/hkz066.
10 Bennett, 'Bad for the health of the body'.
11 Henry Mayhew and John Binny, *The criminal prisons of London and scenes of prison life* (London: Griffin, Bohn and Company, 1862), pp. 190–191.
12 TNA, PCOM 7/40, Report of committee presided over by Adeline, Duchess of Bedford to inquire into various matters concerning Holloway Prison, May 1919, p. 21.

13 Constance Lytton and Jane Warton, *Prisons and prisoners: Some personal experiences* (London: William Heinemann, 1914), p. 102.
14 Joan Henry, *Women in prison* (London: White Lion Publishers, first published 1952, this edition 1973), pp. 52, 56.
15 Kathleen Lonsdale et al., with introduction by Ethel Mannin, *Some account of life in Holloway Prison for women* (London: Prison Medical Reform Council, 1943), p. 13.
16 Cicely McCall, *They always come back* (London: Methven & Co., 1938), p. 13.
17 TNA, PCOM 7/40, Report of committee presided over by Adeline, Duchess of Bedford, p. 11.
18 Lonsdale, *Some account of life in Holloway Prison*, p. 17.
19 Lonsdale, *Some account of life in Holloway Prison*, p. 6.
20 Henry, *Women in prison*, p. 54.
21 Tania McIntosh, *A social history of maternity and childbirth: Key themes in maternity care* (Abingdon: Routledge, 2012), p. 38.
22 TNA, PCOM 7/40, Report of committee presided over by Adeline, Duchess of Bedford: Appendix of pregnancy cases.
23 'Extraordinary case of concealment of birth in a prison', *Dundee Courier* (4 March 1870), p. 2.
24 'Birth in a prison', *London Evening Standard* (4 April 1874), p. 3.
25 Mayhew and Binny, *The criminal prisons of London*, pp. 185–191.
26 LB, PS/B/4/5/1/1, Birmingham Petty Sessions 1878–1892, 15 July 1878.
27 Lucia Zedner, *Women, crime and custody in Victorian England* (Oxford: Oxford University Press, 1991), p. 115.
28 LMA, WA/G/011, Minute Book, October 1862–1865, 15 February 1863.
29 LMA, WA/G/011, Minute Book, October 1862–1865, 7 February 1864.
30 TNA, HO 45/23653, Prisons and Prisoners: Report on the Conditions in Holloway. Treatment of Pregnant Prisoners (1940–49), letter from Miss Dorothy Borup to Dr Haden Guest MP, 2 June 1943.
31 TNA, HO 45/23653, Prisons and Prisoners: Report on the Conditions in Holloway. …, Observations by the Governor and Medical Officer of Holloway, 18 June 1943.
32 TNA, HO 45/23653, Prisons and Prisoners: Report on the Conditions in Holloway. …, letter from Herbert Morrison to Dr Haden Guest MP, 26 June 1943.
33 TNA, HO 45/23653, Prisons and Prisoners: Report on the Conditions in Holloway. …, Holloway Prison conditions for pregnant prisoners, 19 June 1943.
34 Susan Willis Fletcher, *Twelve months in an English prison* (New York: Charles T. Dillingham, 1884), p. 323.
35 Mayhew and Binny, *The criminal prisons of London*, p. 474.

36 LB, PS/B/4/5/1/2, Birmingham Petty Sessions 1896–1906, 7 February 1906.
37 Stephen Hobhouse and A. Fenner Brockway, *English prisons today: Being the report of the Prison System Enquiry Committee* (London: Longmans, Green and Co., 1922), p. 269.
38 Lonsdale, *Some account of life in Holloway Prison*, p. 14.
39 Lonsdale, *Some account of life in Holloway Prison*, p. 19.
40 TNA, PCOM 7/40, Report of committee presided over by Adeline, Duchess of Bedford, Appendix of cases.
41 TNA, PCOM 7/40, Holloway Prison: Duchess of Bedford's Committee of Enquiry into Various Matters 1919, letter from Sir Evelyn Ruggles-Brise to Adeline, Duchess of Bedford, 5 June 1919.
42 TNA, PCOM 7/40, Holloway Prison: Duchess of Bedford's Committee …, letter from Sister Grace of the Home at Highbury Park to Sir Evelyn Ruggles-Brise, 20 February 1919.
43 TNA, PCOM 7/40, Holloway Prison: Duchess of Bedford's Committee …, letter from Sir Evelyn Ruggles-Brise to the Duchess of Bedford, 25 February 1919.
44 Bill Forsythe, 'Russell, Adeline Mary, Duchess of Bedford (1852–1920)', *Oxford Dictionary of National Biography*, 2004.
45 'Duchess of Bedford', *Illustrated London News* (3 May 1913), p. 33.
46 Linda Bryder, 'Mobilising mothers: The 1917 National Baby Week', *Medical History*, 63:1 (2019), 2–23, https://doi.org/10.1017/mdh.2018.60, p. 15.
47 McIntosh, *A social history of maternity and childbirth*, p. 38.
48 TNA, PCOM 7/40, Report of committee presided over by Adeline, Duchess of Bedford, pp. 23–24.
49 TNA, PCOM 7/40, Holloway Prison: Duchess of Bedford's Committee …, letter from Sir Evelyn Ruggles-Brise to Adeline, Duchess of Bedford, 5 June 1919.
50 Report from the Departmental Committee on Prisons (London: 1895), p. 184.
51 Mary Size, *Prisons I have known* (London: George Allen & Unwin, 1957), p. 91.
52 Hobhouse and Brockway, *English prisons today*, p. 272.
53 TNA, HO T1/12409, Staffing of the prison service: Improvement of arrangements for medical care of prisoners, 1919. Letter to the Treasury dated 2 July 1919.
54 TNA, PCOM 7/40, Report of committee presided over by Adeline, Duchess of Bedford, p. 20.
55 TNA, PCOM 7/40, Report of committee presided over by Adeline, Duchess of Bedford, p. 21.

56 TNA, PCOM 7/40, Report of committee presided over by Adeline, Duchess of Bedford, Appendix of cases.
57 TNA, PCOM 7/40, Report of committee presided over by Adeline, Duchess of Bedford, p. 41.
58 TNA, PCOM 7/40, Report of committee presided over by Adeline, Duchess of Bedford, p. 44.
59 TNA, PCOM 7/40, Report of committee presided over by Adeline, Duchess of Bedford, p. 44.
60 TNA, PCOM 7/40, Report of committee presided over by Adeline, Duchess of Bedford, pp. 62–64.
61 TNA, PCOM 7/40, Holloway Prison: Duchess of Bedford's Committee … Suggested alterations in the present nursing staff scheme at Holloway Prison, 4 August 1920.
62 TNA, HO 45/10429/A53867, Nursing Staff in the Prison Service 1892–1919, letter from Sir Evelyn Ruggles-Brise to the Home Secretary, 18 June 1919.
63 McCall, *They always come back*, p. 97.
64 Size, *Prisons I have known*, p. 125.
65 National Justice Museum, Nottingham, Prison Nursing Advisory Committee reports on prison visits, 1928–1954, 19 March 1928.
66 TNA, HO 45/23580, Birth of children in prison 1924–1949, letter from J. Chuter Ede to Michael Young, 19 December 1949.
67 TNA, PCOM 9/1435, Women convicted of child neglect: Investigations in prisons 1946–1950.
68 Henry, *Women in prison*, p. 84.
69 McCall, *They always come back*, p. 97.
70 For a more detailed analysis of how the 1919 enquiry can be situated within broader policy debates surrounding maternity care in women's prisons see Rachel Bennett, 'Maternity care reform in English prisons: A century of unanswered concerns', *History & Policy* (2019).

3

Mothering in a carceral space

In her 1864 work *Our Convicts*, educational and penal reformer Mary Carpenter wrote at length about the incalculable benefit of a good mother's influence upon her child's development. However, she warned, 'no one can estimate the evil which is caused to society, both directly and indirectly, by a wicked one'.[1] When the modern prison system was created in the mid-nineteenth century, motherhood had emerged as a dominant social construct and concern in Victorian England, with the question of what made a 'good mother' prompting debate and scrutiny within medical, social and government discourse. Using the prison as its setting, this chapter advances our understanding of the shifting views about, and expectations placed upon, mothers between the mid-nineteenth and the mid-twentieth century. It uncovers the efforts made to educate female prisoners in domesticity and mothercraft and to use this instruction as a reformative tool.

Throughout this period, women, particularly mothers, who committed crimes were subject to especial censure. Female criminality was believed to be symptomatic of a woman's lack of domesticity and their straying beyond the bounds of ideal femininity, but was also posited as a threat to the fabric of family life. The opening section of this chapter explores debates about using prison as a place to address these issues. Zedner highlighted the contradictions with regard to how broader societal views about female criminals impacted upon their treatment in prison, and stated that 'women were described as being both incapable of moral judgement and yet at the same time as morally degraded, as being shameless and yet desperate for self-respect'.[2] Late nineteenth- and early twentieth-century periodicals and commentaries on crime, its causes and its suppression were saturated with tales of fallen women, and of children as the collateral damage of their mother's moral and criminal degradation.³ However, this chapter demonstrates that it was not until the turn of the twentieth century that these laments about the undomesticated female offender translated into more determined efforts to use a prison sentence as an opportunity to train women to be 'good' wives and, especially, mothers. Initially, these efforts were largely driven by individual members of staff within women's prisons and by Lady Visitors, who sought to offer instruction to and influence on their imprisoned sisters. They were shaped by the experiences of staff attempting to contain and care for the women under their charge.

The efforts to educate and train mothers in prison became more centrally driven in the decade following the end of the Second World War. Motherhood was idealised to lure women back from the workplace to the home, but mothers were also subject to intense scrutiny. They were believed to be culpable in creating the social evil that was the 'problem family' who lived in cramped and unsanitary conditions and who produced unhealthy and ill-educated children. However, there were more determined efforts which posited education as an important tool in combating these issues. Using the unique setting of a prison enables the chapter to highlight how this education was shaped and delivered to women deemed to be in particular need of it. Courses in mothercraft were established in all women's prisons and for women in some mixed-sex prisons in the early 1950s and were delivered on a more consistent basis than ever before. Although their organisation differed slightly in each prison, the composition and teaching of the classes were the result of a sharing of ideas, experiences and best practice between prison officials, charities and organisations such as the National Society for the Prevention of Cruelty to Children (NSPCC) and the Women's Voluntary Services (WVS) and, crucially, the Ministry of Health and local health authorities, including health visitors and the newly expanded maternity and child welfare services. Thus, the prison offers a previously underexplored setting in which to further the significant body of work which has charted the medicalisation and regulation of child-rearing in the twentieth century.

This chapter charts a discernible increase in acknowledgements in prison and medical rhetoric that greater education, particularly in mothercraft, during a prison sentence provided an opportunity for more practical and, in some cases, more medically focused intervention. This was intended to achieve lasting rehabilitation and reintegration into the community. However, it is vital to acknowledge that the mothers who found themselves on the wrong side of the law continued to face moral condemnation for their perceived maternal shortcomings throughout this period. Despite the greater provision for practical and, to an extent, health training in mothercraft and domesticity after the turn of the twentieth century, the question of morality remained pervasive in the mid-twentieth century and beyond.

Raising their nature and habits? Prison education for women

'No person will deny the importance attached to the character and conduct of a woman.'[4] This was a principle at the heart of the work of nineteenth-century Quaker Elizabeth Fry. Now regarded as one of Britain's most eminent penal reformers, in the early nineteenth century Fry was a pioneer in advocating for the specific needs of women in prison. She believed that the helpless, depraved, afflicted and ignorant women she encountered in Newgate Prison had 'the greatest claim to the compassion of their own sex'. Fry argued that the superintendence of women over female inmates would not only be a check on the abuses she highlighted, but would also exert a moral influence over their fallen sisters.[5] Prison authorities, including governors, commentators and reformers, lamented that female respectability, once lost, was very difficult to reclaim. Despite this, there were arguments, ignited by Fry and continued by female prison officials in her wake, that women in prison could potentially be more malleable to reform than their male counterparts if kindness was shown alongside firmness. Emma Martin, Brixton's Lady Superintendent, remarked in 1853 that it was necessary for female officers, as far as their 'carrying out strict discipline would allow', to show kindness and provide a good moral example to the women in their care.[6]

In her study of the Victorian period, Zedner argued that female prisoners were subject to closer surveillance than their male counterparts, with moral standards more rigorously reinforced.[7] The primary responsibility for this fell most heavily upon the shoulders of staff and, to some extent, Lady Visitors. Dobash et al. argued that a consequence of this greater management for the purpose of moral reclamation was the more rigorous enforcement of discipline upon female convicts.[8] While acknowledging the important role of male beliefs about respectability in shaping penal systems for women, Forsythe countered that the difference in treatment based upon sex was less pronounced than Zedner had suggested, and refuted the assertion made by Dobash et al. that female prisoners were punished with greater severity and frequency than their male counterparts.[9] Recent exploration of the female convict estate in the 1850s and 1860s has questioned how notions of ideal femininity impacted upon debates about the management of health and discipline. This research found that certain infractions of the rules, such as the use of immoral language or displaying fits of temper, were particularly lamented as being unfeminine and were thus believed to require greater censure.[10] The present chapter strengthens this scholarship by examining the interconnections between the management of female behaviour in prison and the preparation of women in prison for motherhood through training in domesticity and mothercraft.

By ending up in prison at all, pregnant women and those with young children were already believed to have negated their role as mothers. However, prison sentences were posited as potential opportunities to inculcate in these 'bad' mothers the traits and skills required of a 'good' one. Journalists and social commentators Henry Mayhew and John Binny, reflecting upon their visits to London's prisons in the mid-nineteenth century, claimed to observe a difference between the women in the various prison nurseries and the other inmates. They stated that the women in the nursery 'do not glory in their shame as some others do', and added that their being new mothers meant their hearts were not entirely withered and thus they still felt the degradation of their position,[11] the implication being that they were more malleable to, and eager to achieve, reform. Arthur Griffiths, former Deputy Governor of Millbank Prison and a prison administrator, expressed a similar sentiment in 1903 when he argued that in Wormwood Scrubs the 'prison mothers are generally a pattern to their sex'. He continued that there were 'no incentives to neglect of offspring, no drink, no masterful men, no temptation to thieve or go astray, their better feelings, their purer maternal instincts have full play'.[12] Despite their importance in revealing beliefs about the potential for motherhood to be a tool of reform, we must question the extent to which acknowledgements such as these shaped the labour, education and training undertaken by female prisoners across this period.

Following their period in separate confinement, male convicts were sent to public works prisons to undertake forms of outdoor labour.[13] While demanding, this physical exertion was believed to be advantageous, as it offered a change in environment and employment. However, outdoor labour was deemed unsuitable for female convicts. Instead, their prison labour predominantly consisted of needlework, making clothes for male prisons and working in the prison laundry. The laundry was viewed as a beneficial form of labour as it allowed some degree of physical exertion, particularly for the more robust women, yet it was also deemed a monotonous task. The laundry at Brixton did the washing for Brixton, Millbank and Pentonville. The women also made prison uniforms, shirts and other linens to meet external orders. In local prisons including Westminster, Stafford, Bristol and Worcester the majority of the women worked in silent association in the 'knitting room' or in laundries with specially built 'washing cells' that were separated by high wooden partitions to prevent communication. In Westminster's Tothill Fields Prison in the late nineteenth century mothers in the nursery had a pound and a half of oakum to pick in the course of a day. When their children were over the age of eight months they worked in the associated workroom and their babies were cared for by other mothers in the nursery.[14] They would be expected to pick about two-thirds of the usual allocation of oakum.[15]

Foster Rogers, Assistant Chaplain in Westminster Prison, complained in 1850 that female prisoners needed more opportunities to learn about domestic order and cleanliness, skills which he believed to be at the heart of the 'decencies of life'.[16] William Douglas Morrison, Assistant Chaplain at Wakefield and Wandsworth Prisons in the 1880s, echoed this sentiment and added that for women with children the 'duties of maternity' could mitigate against their criminal tendencies, as they promoted the unselfish natural feminine instincts.[17] Prison officers and doctors repeatedly complained to the Prison Commission about the lack of suitable labour options for women and the dangers posed to their health by remaining in the same sedentary conditions for the duration of their sentence.[18] In addition, the prison environment itself was the physical antithesis of the ideal middle-class feminine space, although it may have been an improvement upon the conditions women from the poorest communities faced outside. Florence Maybrick, a middle-class observer, bemoaned that prison sentences did not encourage reform nor offer the chance to 'raise the nature or habits', and that she herself had to work hard to maintain a regime of unyielding personal neatness and civility in an environment that facilitated neither.[19] Prison labour for women also attracted external criticism, particularly by the late nineteenth and early twentieth century. In 1898, Sarah Amos, a political activist, penal reformer and Superintendent of the Working Women's College in London, criticised what she viewed as the drudgery of prison labour for women, such as doing the prison washing and making mail bags. She labelled this type of work as a false idea of economy, as it did not offer any useful training for women. Instead, she advocated teaching a woman to make her home healthier and happier, which would make her return to it upon release a more welcome one.[20]

With the creation of the modern prison system in the mid-nineteenth century, prisons were adapted for the reception of women and, in some cases, modified to incorporate a distinct group of prisoners, namely pregnant women and mothers with young infants who were either born during their sentence or accompanied them into prison. In September 1850 it was decided by the Inspectors of Prisons to remove all the adult male prisoners in Westminster Prison to Coldbath Fields Prison so as to provide much-needed additional accommodation for female prisoners in the former. The governor, A.F. Tracey, reported to the Visiting Justices that the resulting large number of committals of women with infants, which was anticipated to increase further with the onset of winter, with its seasonal unemployment and harsher living conditions for the poor, rendered it paramount to make arrangements to ensure their 'peculiar treatment and wants' were met. After conferring with the prison's doctor, he was granted permission and funding to make extensive adaptations to part of the prison's ground floor, which included making ample space for a nursery wherein 'health and proper cleanliness' could be better maintained.[21] When Brixton became England's first female convict prison in 1853, a nursery was built to house mothers and their children, described as 'the most touching portion of the female convict prison'. The mothers in the nursery cared for their babies, made them clothes and were regularly visited by the chaplain, who brought toys for the children.[22] In these spaces, women were encouraged to care for their child with some instruction from female members of staff, the chaplain and Lady Visitors. However, formal instruction was very limited, and taking care of their infants had to be done as part of a strictly regulated regime with little room for individual choice or initiative. It was not until the very late nineteenth and the early twentieth century that more concerted efforts were made, driven from within and outside of the prison system, to offer organised courses in domestic crafts and mothercraft.

In 1895 Herbert Gladstone chaired a committee of enquiry into the operation of the prison system. The ensuing report recommended a renewed focus on reformation, following three decades during which prison policies were characterised by severity, uniformity and economy. The report stated that it should be the object of the prison authorities to 'humanise the prisoners, to prevent them from feeling that the state merely chains them for a certain period and cares nothing about them'.[23] In his evaluation of penal policy in England and Wales, Bailey argued that the Gladstone Committee marked a notable shift in emphasising the rehabilitative role of prisons in the two decades prior to the outbreak of the First World War. Notable legislation, including the Prison Act 1898, the Inebriates Act 1898, the Prevention of Crime Act 1908 and the Mental Deficiency Act 1913 established arrangements for the extended training of prisoners and the abolition of labour deemed to have little reformatory function, and provided for the segregation and distinct treatment of habitual drunkards, recidivists and the mentally ill.[24] Although much of this was ultimately ineffective in properly addressing the issues intended, it provides useful context to the efforts being made in relation to domesticity and motherhood in prisons.[25]

A problem repeatedly highlighted in evidence to the committee had troubled prison authorities for decades, namely deciding upon appropriate occupations for female prisoners. In her evidence, Jane Taylor Gee, the Matron at Liverpool Prison, summed up this issue when she complained that the limited labour options and educational opportunities available meant 'the women do not feel they are doing anything good'.[26] By the turn of the twentieth century, these broader debates about reforming prison education prompted a rethinking of the educational needs of mothers in prison in particular.

For centuries, mothers were believed to know instinctively how to raise their children with the help and experience of extended family. However, by the early twentieth century, infant welfare reformers, doctors and policy makers stressed that child-rearing in a modern society required mothers to be instructed in scientific methods of childcare. This education, it was argued, needed to begin in schools and continue in newly established 'Schools for Mothers'.[27] Historians of motherhood and maternity care, including Davin, Lewis and Dwork, have detailed the extensive efforts made in Britain to offer this advice and instruction to mothers by local authorities and voluntary organisations in the early twentieth century, at a time when high infant mortality rates were of critical concern. They have demonstrated how child health and child-rearing took a more prominent place in public discussion and were framed as a national issue as well as a moral duty for mothers.[28]

Ross identified that the period between 1870 and 1918 saw the flourishing of the belief that mothers were responsible to the state and were expected to turn out children reared in specific ways prescribed by medical professionals.[29] This period also witnessed the rise of the modern eugenics movement in Britain, which espoused that social position was determined by individual inherited qualities such as mental ability, susceptibility to sickness and predisposition to immorality. Although overtly eugenic responses were rejected by policy makers in Britain, Tania McIntosh found that the interaction between these ideals and the prominent question of public health influenced attempts to regulate certain aspects of motherhood, particularly among women from the poor and working classes.[30] When discussing the links drawn by prison officials, eugenicists and criminologists in the late nineteenth and early twentieth century between habitual inebriety, recidivism and feeble-mindedness, Zedner argued that these tendencies were labelled as both a cause of crime and a symptom of a pathological condition of physical and mental degeneracy among female prisoners.[31] The danger believed to be posed by these deficiencies was increasingly extended to include the children of these women. Combined with the rethinking of prison education prompted by the findings of the Gladstone Committee and the ever-increasing momentum of the infant welfare movement, these concerns drove efforts to offer better education in domesticity and mothercraft to women in prison and coalesced in 1904 when prison policy responded directly to this much broader national issue.

The 1904 Report of the Inter-Departmental Committee on Physical Deterioration examined overcrowding, infant mortality, conditions of factory employment, alcoholism and parental ignorance as causes of high infant mortality. It drew attention to the low living standards of the urban poor and placed particular blame upon younger women, who were believed to possess a diminished level of maternal skill than even their own mothers before them, or perhaps had never had the proper opportunity to learn these skills. Mothers were accused of having no knowledge of how to treat their children's ailments and of lacking the skills to provide a healthy home environment for their families.[32] Certainly a crucial pillar of the broader health politics of the early twentieth century, the report's findings also added weight to ever-increasing calls for a more diverse, and medically driven, educational programme to be offered to women in prison.

The *British Medical Journal* (*BMJ*) reported upon an experiment in penal reform that was carried out with female prisoners in Portsmouth Prison in January 1904. Charlotte Smith-Rossie, an honorary lecturer for the Hampshire County Council, had been given permission by the prison to initiate a course of fortnightly lectures on sanitary subjects. The women who maintained the highest standard of behaviour and adherence to the prison rules were selected as students. Smith-Rossie commented that she had heard about a similar course being tried in Wormwood Scrubs Prison, but pointed out that there was a vast difference between training prisoners in a penal establishment like Wormwood Scrubs, and in a local prison like Portsmouth, where the women were mainly serving short sentences for very minor crimes. She claimed that these women, perhaps due to the petty nature of their criminality, were more responsive to teaching about the 'dignity of housekeeping and the efficient discharge of the duties of wife and mother'. Lectures and practical demonstrations on nursing, the care of children and domestic hygiene were reportedly well received by the women. In addition to their aim of offering training in domestic science, Smith-Rossie argued that the lectures offered a crucial 'safeguard against the outbursts of hysteria to which women in prison are particularly subject'.[33] Her comments provide further evidence of the recognition by the early twentieth century that the monotony of prison life posed serious dangers to the health of prisoners but was also counterproductive to reform. Due to the early success of the course, the *BMJ* called for the Home Office to develop similar classes on a more regular basis in the prison system, instead of leaving their organisation to the private enterprise of individual volunteers. In their report for the year ending March 1904, the Prison Commissioners detailed a similar scheme which had been initiated in Holloway and marked a 'new departure' in prison education. The women in the prison were given a series of lectures on subjects including health, nursing and sanitation in the home by a group of voluntary Lady Visitors. They reportedly enjoyed early success with the women, who viewed the lectures as not only 'a reward for good conduct, but also a source of useful instruction'. The scheme was subsequently extended to several larger provincial prisons.[34] By 1909, there were 257 lectures on subjects including hygiene in the home and child welfare delivered across the year in the forty-three prisons containing women. In the final month of their sentence women were given a book entitled *A Happy Home and How to Keep It* to study before their release.[35] In addition, the same year saw the opening of a new crèche in Holloway. The *Illustrated London News* reported how mothers would keep their babies with them in their cells during the night but at 8.30 in the morning would take them to the crèche, where they would be cared for by a wardress while their mothers worked in the workroom. It was noted that if the mother's conduct was satisfactory she would be allowed to see her baby and take the child out to exercise in the prison yard in the afternoon.[36]

The outbreak of the First World War and its aftermath had a profound impact on the fabric of British society. The capital and human resources required to fight the Great War reinforced concerns that had been repeatedly raised about the health of the nation since the late nineteenth century. The condition of children, which had been at the centre of these health politics, was a subject raised again in relation to the war effort. Children represented the nation's future – it was upon their feet that 'the race marches on' – yet they were believed to be facing perils comparable to those faced by the men at the front.[37] These comments were made to *The Times* by Lord Rhondda, President of the Local Government Board and Chair of the Council of National Baby Week. This national event was held during the first week of July 1917 and comprised a series of exhibitions, films and lectures on subjects ranging from lifestyle, hygiene and health visitors to the impact of parental alcoholism upon the home. Trudi Tate has argued that, for those who believed the best way to improve infant health was through better food and medical care, Baby Week was a 'nuisance' that promoted the pro-natalist idea that mothers required supervision in order to be better, while failing to address the impact of broader socio-economic factors upon child health.[38] However, following a deeper exploration of the organisation and running of the event, particularly in London, Linda Bryder countered that those who led the campaign did not seek to blame mothers but, rather, crafted a carefully orchestrated event intended to harness the wartime circumstances to achieve reform of maternal and child welfare policy.[39] Some of the key figures involved in its organisation were also important figures in other areas of social reform impacting upon the lives of women, notably Adeline Russell, Duchess of Bedford, who was later to chair the 1919 enquiry in Holloway.

A theme to emerge during National Baby Week was one that had long been debated in relation to the prison population, namely the impact of parental alcohol consumption upon children. Children born to female drunkards were believed to face the dual disadvantage of being at greater risk of being born with poor physical and mental efficacy, making them more liable to fall under the influence of drink themselves, and of suffering from a lack of proper care, due to their mother's reliance on alcohol.[40] In their report for the year 1917, the Prison Commissioners praised the greater restrictions placed upon the licensing and drinking of alcohol owing to the wartime circumstances and drew a direct correlation with the decrease in the number of prisoners serving sentences for offences including neglect and cruelty to children. They made particular note of comments made by Holloway's Governor and the chaplains in several prisons including Bristol, Newcastle and Plymouth, who noted not only a decrease in the number of women in their prisons but also an improvement in their behaviour and malleability to reform and a 'greater interest both in their homes and themselves' which could be harnessed.[41] Despite the limited resources in prisons and the lack of a comprehensive policy to govern prison education, there was an evident desire on the part of some prison authorities and penal reformers to nurture this interest among female prisoners through training in domesticity and mothercraft. The 1920s and 1930s witnessed further efforts to develop the education and training opportunities offered to women in prison. They were primarily driven by female prison officials and philanthropists and reformers. Ladies from the Brabazon Society, initially established in 1882 to provide classes in crafts such as knitting and embroidery to the less able-bodied inmates of workhouses, offered classes in needlework to the women in Holloway. Similarly, three female teachers from Dudley High School gave lessons in handicrafts and school teaching to the younger women in Birmingham Prison. In March 1922 the Prison Commissioners praised their efforts and stated their conviction that voluntary visitors were an essential feature of 'any system which has for its object the rehabilitation of a social failure'.[42] In the autumn of 1922 the Prison Commission developed a scheme in collaboration with the Adult Education Committee wherein each local prison would be allocated an education adviser who would work with the governor to frame the educational curriculum in their respective prison and would help to obtain the services of voluntary teachers. When discussing the need for a 'new departure' in the standard of prison education, the Commissioners lamented the 'peculiar difficulty of restoring women to ordinary standards of life and conduct once they have become accustomed to prison surroundings'.[43] The issue of restoring female respectability, once a woman had been tainted by association with the criminal justice system, was not a new conundrum but, by the early twentieth century, education was increasingly viewed as the means to achieve this.

Chapter 1 demonstrated that the treatment of prisoners by staff, and their views of the women under their charge, varied considerably. Despite this, between the mid-nineteenth and mid-twentieth century, efforts to educate women in prison were largely driven and shaped by a sense of shared responsibility among those female members of staff who sought to adapt the daily monotony of the prison routine and to use education as a means of reforming the behaviour of the women they supervised. When Lilian Barker took up the position of Governor of Aylesbury Borstal for girls in 1923, she secured the services of a trained handicrafts teacher and introduced embroidery, leatherwork and dressmaking into the education offered to all of the girls in the institution.[44] Following her appointment as Assistant Prison Commissioner in 1935, Barker continued to espouse a more humane model of prison reform with education at its centre. In 1938 she addressed the annual meeting of the HDPAS to talk about the benefits of offering the women in Holloway more advanced training in needlework, cookery and dressmaking. She argued that it made the women more efficient domestically and also, with the help and advice of the Society, more attractive to potential employers.[45]

Mary Size, prison officer, school mistress and Lady Superintendent in Manchester, Liverpool and Leeds Prisons and Aylesbury Borstal before being appointed Deputy Governor of Holloway in 1927, also implemented initiatives and improvements during her four decades of service in the women's prison estate. Her memoir *Prisons I have known*, published after her retirement in 1957, offers a detailed insight into the realities of daily prison life and a valuable means of exploring the role members of staff played in shaping the experiences of female prisoners. Throughout her career, Size reiterated that she believed education to be the keynote of reform. She recalled how the implementation of more classes in handicrafts, home care, cookery and gardening had helped to create a healthier atmosphere in prisons, as these greater educational opportunities marked a shift away from the harsh discipline that had bred hatred and distrust and had resulted in poor behaviour. Instead, she recalled, these classes, taught by members of the prison staff as well as by external voluntary visitors, fostered a sense of cooperation 'between official and prisoner and between woman and woman'.[46]

Women who gave birth in prison and those who brought infants in with them were believed to require greater guidance and education during their prison sentences. Reflecting upon her thirteen-year tenure serving as Holloway's deputy governor, Mary Size considered the advancements made in offering training in child welfare and management to the mothers who gave birth during their sentence as 'perhaps the most vital developments' in the prison's curriculum.[47] Cicely McCall, who worked as an officer in both Holloway and Aylesbury in the 1930s, praised the efforts of the staff to offer instruction in childcare to the women who had babies in prison. However, she complained that opportunities to properly teach the women subjects such as sickness, hygiene and mothercraft were wasted by the prison authorities. She further regretted that there were no lectures or classes for the hundreds of women in prison who had children outside.[48] When liaising with a local branch of the NSPCC regarding the introduction of lectures on mothercraft to women in Durham Prison in 1945, the governor, R.F. Owens, lamented that the women in his charge 'had the most elementary ideas, if any at all, of their responsibilities as mothers or of how to tend their children'. He also bemoaned the fact that they had not been given an opportunity to learn these things until they came into the 'official care' of the prison.[49] However, the mid-twentieth century, especially the post-war decade, witnessed the introduction of a more comprehensive and centrally driven programme of courses on mothercraft into several women's prisons in England. They were intended to redress the perceived inadequacies in prison education, especially for mothers, but were also a response to the broader societal concern about the 'bad' mother and the danger she posed to the fabric of family life.

A new departure: mothercraft in the mid-twentieth century

During the Second World War, women had been called upon to step into several types of employment, previously reserved for men, to contribute to the war effort on the home front. In its wake, there were concerns that the traditional family unit would collapse in the face of such rapid change, and efforts were made to 'lure women back from the workplace to the home'.[50] Ann Dally described the thirty years following the Second World War as 'an age of idealisation of motherhood', and marked the period as one in which society emphasised the importance of the family and the need for children to be under the constant care of their mothers but, at the same time, took limited steps to help mothers adapt to a fast-changing world.[51] However, more recently, Laura King has explored how children were conceptualised as future citizens in the mid-twentieth century to provide justification for greater spending on improving child welfare.[52] During the war there were shortages in staff and provisions in prisons. Recounting their imprisonment in Holloway in the early 1940s, a group of conscientious objectors, including Kathleen Lonsdale, highlighted shortages in everything from clothes to nutritious food, and detailed the poor sanitary provisions and medical care for women in prison.[53] These concerns were compounded by the difficulties women's prisons faced when accommodating the rising number of female prisoners, and led to calls for greater resources to tackle these issues.

In April 1945 the Prison Commission reported that the population in women's prisons was at a point 'well above danger level' and could no longer be ignored. It had risen from a pre-war figure of around 700 to 1,701 in April 1945. Particular concerns arose about the appropriate classification and accommodation of the women, due to the increased numbers. In Manchester and Birmingham each cell was at double capacity, and in the latter it was reported that 'all women, however unwilling or unsuitable, were sleeping in association'. In Cardiff and Exeter, prisoners had to be accommodated in the workrooms, meaning that proper classification and supervision was difficult. One reason that was dwelled upon to explain the increased female prison population was the number of women serving sentences for child neglect. In 1913, 731 women were sentenced to a term of imprisonment for cruelty to children. This figure had decreased markedly, to 120, by 1938.[54] Although the exact reasons for this are not fully clear, the reduction was most likely due to a combination of improved child welfare services and the introduction of the Children and Young Persons Act in 1933, which consolidated previous child cruelty legislation and introduced supervision orders for children deemed to be at risk of cruelty or neglect.

In the post-war period cases of child neglect rose sharply again, with 1,239 women convicted for child neglect in 1944, of whom 578 were sent to prison for varying terms.[55] The impact was widely felt in the women's prison estate, which was already under-resourced due to the impact of the war. In 1948, an article in the *BMJ* noted the dangers to health posed by overpopulation in women's prisons due to the continuing rise in sentences for child neglect. However, it noted the poor home conditions from which the majority of these women came, both to partly explain the increase and also to highlight the poor opportunities for redressing these issues. The article stated with consternation that 'it does look as though the housing situation in the country generally is reflected in its gaols'.[56] Debates about the impact of environmental circumstance in cases of child neglect is something to which this chapter returns later.

Taylor and Rogaly argued that the emergence of concerns about the 'problem family' in the immediate post-war years were prompted by the belief that widespread deprivation among families no longer existed. Instead, the causes of poverty were individualised and efforts to combat it were targeted at certain families who were designated as 'problem' families.[57] Welshman situated the 'problem' family of the mid-twentieth century within a broader chronological examination of successive reinventions of the 'underclass' idea since the 1880s, from the 'social residuum' notion of the nineteenth century to the 'social problem group' idea propagated in the early twentieth century.[58] Taylor and Rogaly identified similar continuities with earlier debates and highlighted how the 'problem family' posed a means for the Eugenics Society to reinvent itself following the decline of the respectability of eugenic theories in the late 1940s.[59] Within this evolution of the concept of the 'underclass', women from the poorer classes, especially mothers, often took centre stage. In her study of the stigmatisation of poor and working-class mothers in this period, Pat Starkey demonstrated how the image of the feckless mother meant that explanations for her plight were hinged on personal failings, as opposed to environmental circumstances.[60] For mothers in prison, they had long been deemed to be 'bad' mothers for ending up there at all, and their crimes were believed, at least at a policy level, to stem primarily from immorality, as opposed to poverty. However, crucially, the mid-twentieth century saw greater acknowledgement of the impact of poor housing and environmental circumstance as contributory factors to female imprisonment.

In their exploration of conditions in English prisons in 1922, Hobhouse and Brockway commented that women imprisoned for cruelty to children were often highly strung, with fraught nerves and tempers that had given way under an accumulation of 'repeated child-bearing and crowded miserable housing'.[61] Mary Steel, who had worked in both Birmingham and Holloway Prisons in the mid-twentieth century, echoed these sentiments when asking the question 'what makes a mother a failure?' She asserted that it was a combination of low intelligence, an unfortunate childhood, bad housing and a growing sense of irresponsibility among younger women.[62] When criticising the use of short prison sentences to punish mothers convicted of neglect, Lady Allen of Hurtwood, a child welfare advocate who served as a liaison officer with UNICEF after the Second World War, commented that it was recognised that a high proportion of the women in prison for child neglect 'are probably of low intelligence' and that the majority faced economic and housing difficulties.⁶³ In their report for 1955, the HDPAS also pointed to the problem of women marrying men 'of low intelligence and far weaker character' who were wholly inadequate in their roles as husbands and fathers, and how this negated the woman's ability to be a good wife and mother.⁶⁴

In December 1946 a meeting was held to discuss the problem of mothers being sent to prison for child neglect. Attendees included Dr Charity Taylor, Holloway's Governor, Miss Perrott, a psychiatric social worker who had visited and interviewed women in Holloway, Dr Methven and Miss Mellanby, both from the Prison Commission (the latter being responsible for the women's estate), Muriel Glyn-Jones, Woman Inspector of the Home Office's Children's Branch and Miss Goode, from the Home Office's Probation Branch. It was decided that a thorough examination would be carried out to identify the primary reasons why women ended up in Holloway for child neglect. This investigation was conducted over the course of two years and involved carrying out interviews with eighty-nine women during their sentence. The ensuing report was submitted to the Prison Commission in June 1949. It stated that all of the women had between one and eight children, with the majority having between one and five children at home at the time of their conviction. It was found that sixty of the women had no previous convictions but nine had served previous sentences for child neglect. The report pointed to the issue of the majority of the mothers themselves having had a poor education and lacking opportunities to establish a respectable social life, and stated that at least thirty of their number had grown up in neglectful homes, arguing that the neglect of their children stemmed from absence of knowledge and experience, as opposed to the intentional commission of cruelty.⁶⁵

The marital status of the women was also discussed to illustrate their home life. Of the eighty-nine interviewees, forty-five were married, eleven were cohabiting, nineteen were separated or divorced, five were widows and nine were single. Of the fifty-six women living with men, thirty-seven stated that they were in 'unhappy relationships' and spoke of regularly being ill-treated by their partners, which made them 'lose interest' in their homes and children. In addition, thirty of the married women admitted to being pregnant before they got married. Having to 'hurriedly set up home' was believed to have placed them at a disadvantage from the start.[66] Thus there was a discernible shift away from the nineteenth-century tendency to view the 'bad' or neglectful mother as a moral problem alone. Instead, there was some acknowledgement of the difficulties women faced when trying to maintain hearth and home, particularly those from the poorest or most marginalised backgrounds. For the women behind bars, particularly the new mothers, their prison sentence was believed to be an opportunity for intervention which would come in the form of practical, medical and demonstrative education. In response to the report, the training offered to women in Holloway was expanded to include more classes on home management and the care of infants, which were delivered by hospital staff and by visiting health and educational professionals.

Following their introduction in Holloway, courses in mothercraft were expanded and introduced into several other women's prisons in England in the early 1950s (Figure 3.1). Attendance was compulsory for all women committed for child neglect and all expectant mothers, but women were also able to volunteer to attend. Although they differed slightly in composition in different prisons, the courses involved a notable sharing of ideas, experiences and good practice by prison officials, organisations such as the NSPCC and the WVS and also, crucially, by the Ministry of Health, local medical authorities, including health visitors and local maternity and child welfare services. The classes were taught by a variety of professionals, including health visitors, nurses, midwives and local education authorities. They garnered favourable feedback from officials and prisoners alike. The Countess of Radnor visited Holloway as part of the Prison Nursing Advisory Committee in May 1951. When she was shown the prison's hospital by the matron-in-chief, the Countess reported that she was greatly impressed by the arrangements for new mothers, especially the large percentage of babies being breastfed. She remarked that the support and encouragement of this was 'a particularly valuable achievement' for the prison hospital.[67] Despite offering several criticisms of the conditions and regime in Holloway, Joan Henry remarked, 'I was quite impressed by the care given to the mothers and their children'. Expectant mothers attended classes in childcare and were given the instruction and materials to make

Figure 3.1 Women in a mothercraft class at Exeter Prison, c. 1960s.

clothes for their infants.[68] They were also among the women who attended weekly evening classes, introduced in 1952, which covered subjects including cookery, embroidery, home making, childcare, handicrafts, shorthand and country dancing.[69]

Dr Winifred Kane was the Senior Assistant Medical Officer for Maternity and Child Welfare for the City of Manchester and, in 1951, had been elected the Manchester Paediatric Club's President. She was also a voluntary visitor at Manchester Prison and had built up a good relationship with Miss D. Wilson, the deputy governor. When advocating for classes in mothercraft to be introduced into the prison, Dr Kane informed Miss Wilson of the work being done in the city by health visitors going into Mayfield House, a place provided under the stipulations of the National Assistance Act 1948 for mothers with young children to go to get advice and guidance on nursing their infants. The classes began in Manchester Prison in January 1951 and initially consisted of ten lectures lasting around fifty minutes each, with an additional ten minutes for questions. The group sizes were between ten and fifteen prisoners at a time.

The lectures were given by Miss Lamb, a qualified health visitor. She had been selected by Miss Gowing, Manchester's Superintendent Health Visitor, as she had a wealth of experience in providing talks at her local child welfare centre and ran a 'Mothers' Club' in the evenings. Mr Hare, Governor of Manchester Prison, agreed to provide Miss Lamb with a domestic science room, which had a kitchen containing a sink, a gas cooker and a water supply, to teach the classes. Demonstration materials were provided by the Local Health Authority. Miss Lamb and Deputy Governor Wilson reported back to Dr Kane and made suggestions for the adaptation of the course moving forward. A.E. Girling, Public Health Nursing Officer, attributed the early success of the course to the establishment of a successful partnership between prison officials, the local health services and the women themselves. For its second iteration the course was adapted and extended to thirteen lectures. It was intended that each lecture would offer instruction in a specific subject and would be complete in itself, which was believed to be important due to the often transient nature of the female prison population as several of the women were serving only short sentences that would not last the duration of the full course.

The course included lectures on a woman's health needs during pregnancy, preparation for labour, antenatal care including information on diet, exercise and hygiene, breastfeeding and the care of the breasts before and after birth. There were also lectures on clothing and bathing babies, appropriate bedding and cots for infants, suitable toys and the importance of routine for babies as well as simple first aid in the home. The lectures were intended to offer as much practical instruction as possible to the women so that they could emulate it in their own homes, although the achievability of this varied depending upon the conditions to which the women would return following their release. This was an issue repeatedly raised by organisations such as the HDPAS and the WVS, who stressed the importance of supporting women to put their training in prison into practice outside. This support was both material, helping them to obtain things like furniture, bedding and clothing to improve their home conditions, and also sought to encourage women to use the local health and maternity services in the community.

In addition to practical instruction in domesticity and mothercraft, there were also lectures on the development of the foetus, a description of labour and the importance of post-natal examinations. The lectures were taught by Dr Brache, from Manchester's Maternity and Child Welfare staff, and Deputy Governor Wilson commented that having the doctor take these lectures helped the women to gain a greater understanding of what she termed the 'how and why' of certain aspects of motherhood.[70] It is highly likely that these areas were taught in more depth to some women in prison than to many outside who had limited opportunities to acquire certain knowledge of the 'how and why' before they commenced their mothering journey. The teaching of these parts of the course by a doctor, while intended to provide women in prison with more practical information of what to expect during labour and their post-natal care, can also be situated within the broader professionalisation and medicalisation of maternity care in the late 1940s and 1950s.

When speaking in Liverpool in February 1945 on the rise of convictions for child neglect, Lady Allen of Hurtwood stated that 'before joining in the clamour for harsher and longer prison sentences for parents who ill-treat their children, we should do well to pause and consider the consequences'. These consequences included the further dislocation of families and the permanent removal of children from their parents. Lady Allen advocated committing parents and children under a probation order to cottage homes where, under the supervision of skilled workers, they would gain practical instruction in caring for their home and understanding their children, and would be restored a sense of responsibility. She asserted that a rehabilitative scheme of this kind would be more constructive than joining 'the cry for filling the already crowded prisons'.[71] These suggestions certainly provided further voice to the mid-twentieth-century view that women often needed help, as opposed to censure alone, to help them to be 'good' mothers. Although the scheme described by Lady Allen was never fully adopted to replace short prison sentences for mothers, aspects of this idea, namely to provide a more homely physical space in which to educate women in domesticity, were implemented to some extent in the teaching of mothercraft in prison.

In February 1952 an experiment was initiated in Birmingham Prison to train the women serving sentences for child neglect in domesticity and mothercraft. Within the grounds of the prison there was a red-brick house set apart from the main prison building, which had previously been used as officers' quarters. It was adapted to offer more home-like accommodation for the women undertaking the course. It had bedrooms and a well-fitted sitting room and kitchen. No doors were locked in the house, but outside of teaching hours the women would be supervised by a prison officer. The scheme offered an intensive course in home management and the care of children. Its syllabus and running were organised in collaboration with the City of Birmingham Education Authority, the Public Health Authority and the Children's Committee. The classes were taught by several health and educational professionals, including health visitors, teachers and a psychiatric social worker. Twelve women at a time took part in the course and were transferred in from various prisons across the country. They qualified for a place if they had been convicted of child neglect, were pregnant, were deemed eligible to live in a hostel-style environment rather than under the stricter conditions in the main part of the prison and they had long enough left on their sentence to complete the course. In its first year there were five iterations of the course, which lasted for two months, and sixty women took part.

Throughout the year reports were sent back to the Prison Commissioners about the progress of the course, including case histories of the participants. In their report of 1952, the Commissioners synthesised some of the similarities identified in cases of child neglect, including poor home conditions. However, they argued that this was not always the result of poverty and instead was due to wasteful and unintelligent spending, slovenly habits, unhappy marital relationships and the low mentality and poor physique of the mothers. Most of the women were described as having no knowledge of home management and the proper care of children when they began the course. However, the Commissioners praised the fact that the teachers had not been discouraged by the 'appalling degree of ignorance and idleness with which they have been confronted'. Instead, they had shown a real sense of vocation and zeal to awaken in the women a desire to learn.[72]

A large part of the course focused upon the training in mothercraft. Lectures offered instruction in antenatal care, preparing the home for a baby, breastfeeding and weaning, bathing a baby, hygiene in the home and the prevention of infection. They detailed the specific developmental needs of infants and children between the ages of one and five years. Lectures were also given to provide women with information about the public health services available to them on the outside and advice on how to access them.[73] When writing about the early progress of the course in Birmingham, Mary Steel, one of the teachers, remarked that 'this is the first time that it has officially been recognised that depriving a bad mother of her liberty does not automatically make her into a good one'.[74] At the Women's Public Health Officers' Association Superintendents Group Meeting in March 1953 Mrs Potter, the Health Visitor and Organiser for Health Education for the Birmingham Health Department, spoke about the mothercraft training in the city's prison. She stated that, in addition to the more demonstrative practical training, the course placed emphasis on the emotional stress faced by mothers and offered advice on how to work through it.[75] A key part of this was offering them instruction on home care, budget management and diet and nutrition as well as handicrafts such as making curtains and flower decorations. There was a big common room, which was used to teach the housecraft lectures, and there were two smaller rooms used to provide shorter talks with smaller groups or individual mothers. Mary Steel remarked that, in teaching the courses in this way, 'slowly it became clear that the women were getting their first glimpse of what a home could really mean'. She added that, in taking pride in their communal living space, 'they were closer to serenity than they had ever been'.[76]

Printed reports and accounts of the courses overwhelmingly adopted this positive tone. The women who took part were repeatedly described as relishing the opportunity to be a part of them. However, it is important to acknowledge that these accounts were often written by strong advocates for these courses, who sought to reinforce their necessity to other members of the prison hierarchy. In addition, some of the women on the courses may have embraced them as providing a means to escape the monotony of prison life. As discussed previously, the want of meaningful occupation for women in prison was something bemoaned by prisoners and staff alike throughout the period under examination here. There was some resentment among those not given the chance to undertake the classes in domesticity and mothercraft. Following the first series of classes in

Birmingham, it was reported that there had been some bad feeling between the 'privileged' women chosen to attend the course and other prisoners who considered those convicted of child neglect to be a worse class of prisoner undeserving of special treatment. Joan Henry, when recalling her own time spent in prison, commented that any crimes committed against children generally garnered loathing among fellow prisoners.[77] There were instances of the women who were on the course in Birmingham being targeted for especial censure when working in the main part of the prison. The prison officers had some success in easing these tensions when they allowed the meals cooked as part of the domestic course to be sent over to the women in the main part of the prison.[78]

The overall success of the mothercraft courses, particularly in Manchester, Birmingham and Holloway, prompted the sharing of expertise and good practices between other prisons that accommodated women and their local health and education authorities in the early 1950s. In response to an enquiry made by Dr G. Lilico, the Principal Medical Officer for the Ministry of Health based in Newcastle, regarding mothercraft training in Durham Prison, Dr Ian McCracken, the County Medical Officer of Health in Durham, informed him that the lectures had been organised by the County Education Department in consultation with the Prison Commissioners, notably Miss Mellanby. The lectures were taught by a Mrs Hall, who had qualifications in domestic science and cookery from the University of Durham's Institute of Education, and Mrs Hutchinson, a state registered nurse and state certified midwife.[79] In March 1953 Dr Herbert, from the Welsh Board of Visitors, informed the Home Office that Dr Greenwood Wilson, a doctor in Cardiff who had connections with the medical officer in the city's prison, was interested in the recent reports of the success of the courses in mothercraft in some of the English prisons. He stated that he was interested in providing similar lectures in Cardiff Prison.[80]

Prison aftercare: the last and vital chapter in a long story

Although they were optimistic about the reformative potential of these courses in mothercraft and home care upon the women who completed them, several quarters of the prison hierarchy acknowledged that 'the real trial awaits them when they return to cope with the conditions that defeated them before'.[81] The issue of women returning to poor home conditions and to husbands of a low moral character upon the expiration of their prison sentence had long been lamented by prison officials, discharged prisoners' aid organisations and charities. James Nugent, chaplain to Liverpool Prison in the second half of the nineteenth century, repeatedly complained to the Visiting Justices about the large numbers of women in the prison and the problem of short sentences, and thus the very limited opportunity to enact any true reform, in contributing to high levels of recidivism. In April 1870 he reported that he had interviewed some of the women not yet hardened in their criminality who expressed a real desire to abandon their life of vice but who had quickly fallen back into old criminal habits by bitter necessity, due to their poor home circumstances.[82] As detailed further in Chapter 1, Nugent and many other prison officials and penal reformers had used such testimony to reinforce their argument for the need for refuges to be set up to receive women from prison and provide an intermediate period between incarceration and reintegration into society, allowing time for the good resolutions they had made in the prison to manifest and to counter the harsh realities facing women when they returned to their old lives.

In her study *The Politics of Motherhood*, Jane Lewis provided a detailed exploration of the problem of class in relation to child and maternal welfare services and offering education and training to mothers. Lewis argued that women of all social classes wanted advice in raising their children, but working-class women posed more complex needs than their instructors could fully meet. She found that by the 1930s poverty and unsanitary conditions, as opposed to the inadequacies of individual mothers alone, were acknowledged by medical professionals as being causes of infant mortality and poor health. However, policy makers still believed that mothers, if instructed properly, could manage adequately, despite their circumstances.[83] There was evidence of comparable acknowledgements among those working in the prison system. Cicely McCall, a qualified psychiatric social worker, recalled that during her tenure as a prison officer she had often lamented that, despite observations of the plight of the women in prison, 'golden opportunities for the beginnings of constructive social work' were not taken.[84] The disparity in the aims and efforts to bring about reform during a prison sentence and the means to sustain this thereafter endured throughout much of the period under investigation here. They also featured heavily in debates about the role played by prison aftercare organisations.

A reading of the 'typical cases' included in the HDPAS's annual reports throughout the first half of the twentieth century demonstrates that, although the women helped by the Society varied widely in terms of their age, the crimes they had committed, marital status and social background, there were recurring commonalities in the domestic situations of married women with children who found themselves on the wrong side of the law. They faced overcrowded and poor housing conditions, debt and the difficulty of having to work to supplement the family income but being unable to afford suitable childcare. By the late 1940s and early 1950s, discussions about the provision for mothercraft and homecraft training in prisons increasingly included more serious consideration about these issues and how to ensure the effectiveness of the courses beyond the prison gates.

In his address to the HDPAS's annual meeting in 1951, the Reverend Hugh Smith, Chaplain Inspector to the Prison Commission, talked about the concerted efforts being made to take a more individualised approach to the education of prisoners. However, he stated that this was not the complete answer and that prison aftercare organisations had a key role to play in bridging the gulf between prison training and its exercising outside, especially in the case of women. He continued, 'real after-care should not be considered merely a charitable extra tacked on'. Instead, it should be the final stage of reformative treatment, the 'last and vital chapter of a long story'.[85] In the post-war period the WVS established their After-Care Scheme, wherein a 'Friend' would be appointed to any woman who requested one upon release from Holloway Prison. They would offer the women advice on gaining employment and would help those with children to access the services of their local health visitors. Following the establishment of the mothercraft training courses in Birmingham Prison the WVS After-Care Scheme was extended to the women held in the prison. In addition, the Discharged Prisoners' Aid Society's (DPAS) welfare officer interviewed each woman who took part in the course to try to make arrangements for her release and put her in contact with her local DPAS branch.[86] In 1954 Dr

Charity Taylor, Holloway's Governor, commended the ongoing cooperation between the WVS and the Holloway branch of the DPAS, and their success in identifying the needs of the women before their release and making suitable arrangements to meet them in the community.[87]

Prisons without bars

In May 1932 the results of a government enquiry into the problem of persistent offending were presented to the House of Commons by the Home Secretary, Herbert Samuel. He stated that, although 86 per cent of women received into prisons since 1930 were repeat offenders, the great majority of them were a nuisance to society rather than a danger to it. The report concluded that 'prison buildings of the fortress type are unnecessary for the purposes of security and the effects of such buildings on women seem to be in many respects worse than on men'. Therefore, he recommended exploring ways to reform the women's prison estate to avoid 'the complete loss of self-respect' which women frequently suffered as a result of imprisonment.[88] In 1937 plans were drawn up to begin the conversion of Askham Grange, a manor house in Yorkshire, into a non-security prison for women, but were shelved due to the outbreak of the Second World War. However, the issue was revisited in 1946 and in November of that year Askham Grange was opened for the reception of its first female inmates.

Mary Size was recalled from her retirement to serve as the prison's governor. She described Askham Grange's opening as 'a revolutionary moment in prison reform', as it accommodated up to sixty women in dormitories instead of cells where they would 'live together as a family and behave in every way as a decent family should'.[89] Recalling her time in Askham Grange, 'the prison without bars', in the early 1950s, Joan Henry noted how the women ate their meals together around a table instead of alone in their cells as they did in other prisons. She added that Governor Size and the other officers treated her 'more like a person than a number'.[90] Training in cookery and housewifery began in March 1947; officers were employed who had been trained in technical schools before the war and the Local

Education Authority assisted in preparing the syllabus. The women would complete a twelve-week course and take an examination at the end.[91] In 1951 the West Riding Education Authority appointed an additional handicrafts teacher to teach embroidery, quilting and hemstitching. Mrs McMahon, a qualified dressmaking teacher, taught the classes and prepared the women to take the London City and Guilds examinations. All the candidates passed in the first year and some went on to work in dressmaking upon release.[92]

Special arrangements were also made to accommodate mothers and their babies in Askham Grange, where they were housed in dormitories that were part of the prison's hospital. In addition, Sister Bissell was appointed as the Nursing Sister to play a lead role in caring for their specific needs. She organised an infant welfare class, first aid lessons and a personal hygiene course. In the infant welfare lectures the women were given the same instruction as that given at welfare clinics outside. Other women who were mothers with children outside joined the classes, and the babies born to the women in the prison were used as living examples of how to feed, clothe and care for infants.[93]

Following the early success of Askham Grange, the Prison Commissioners decided to open a second regional training prison for women at Hill Hall, near Epping, Essex in October 1952. Hill Hall was a large country house surrounded with extensive grounds and, like Askham Grange, it could house up to sixty women in dormitory-style accommodation. Its opening was part of an initiative to establish more open prisons for men and women, the result, the Commissioners explained, of recognition of the benefits of individualisation in the treatment of offenders and its rehabilitative potential.[94] In the same year two additional open prisons for men were opened at Grendon Hall in Buckinghamshire and in Dover, Kent.[95] The opening of these prisons and the adaptation of the obdurate and heavily regulated regimes that had long prevailed in England's penal institutions demonstrates some recognition on the part of the highest prison authorities of the benefits of custodial differentiation, something that those who worked within the daily realities of prison life, such as Mary Gordon, Cicely McCall and Mary Size, had long since recognised in their efforts to use education to improve the lives of the women in their care during their time in prison and beyond it.

Conclusion

A key theme running throughout this book is that notions of ideal domesticity and femininity were so often at variance with the realities of prison life, from the management of female prisoner health and behaviour to the conditions under which women were accommodated, their prison dress and the labour they were expected to perform during their sentence. Despite this, prisons for women were expected to morally reclaim their inmates and prepare them for release back into respectable society. While there was no shortage of official discourse castigating the 'bad' mothers who populated prisons and the dangers they were believed to pose to hearth, home and child, prison regimes offered little opportunity for them to become 'good' ones. Instead, efforts to provide mothers in prison with education and training in childcare and home management were largely driven by the individual efforts of female prison officials and external reformers for much of this period. It was not until the early twentieth century, when affairs of the home were increasingly believed to be matters that required state intervention, due to concerns about national efficiency and child health, that there was more central recognition among the prison hierarchy of the benefits of initiating more regular classes in domestic science and mothercraft.

The introduction of more comprehensive courses in mothercraft to women in prison in the mid-twentieth century was a major step in the history of motherhood in prison. They were a response to the laments about 'problem families' in newspapers, medical discourse and government debates, wherein mothers in prison were held up as cautionary tales of the dangers of not properly educating 'bad' mothers to be good ones. However, these courses also marked a shift away from attempts to reclaim women through religious and moral instruction alone, and towards acknowledgement that prison was a space for medical, as well as penal, intervention. Furthermore, they can be contextualised within the broader contemporary discussions about educating, incentivising and medicalising motherhood occurring outside of the prison walls in post-war Britain. Their content was reflective of the increasing contemporary acknowledgement, particularly among those who worked in the women's prison estate on a daily basis, that imprisoning a 'bad' mother did not necessarily make her into a good one upon release, and they sought to address the difficulties women faced in the home, whether through impoverished conditions, stress or lack of educative opportunities to learn how to be a mother. Considerations of how penal policies transcended the prison walls and affected families on the outside developed further in the second half of the twentieth century and, within debates about the treatment of mothers in prison, attention was increasingly diverted towards considerations of their children's needs on the outside. These discussions are ongoing in debates about the broader societal and familial consequences of maternal incarceration today.

Notes

1 Mary Carpenter, *Our convicts*, *Vol. II* (London: Longman, 1864), p. 205.
2 Lucia Zedner, *Women, crime and custody in Victorian England* (Oxford: Oxford University Press, 1991), p. 186.
3 Select examples include James Devon, *The criminal and the community* (London: J. Lane, 1912). Devon, the Medical Officer of Glasgow Prison and a prison administrator in Scotland, worried that daughters in particular suffered from their mothers' neglect and that when this was added to their bad examples it could have a severe effect upon girls. Mary Carpenter criticised the practice of having children and juveniles in prisons and used the fear of moral contagion as part of her promotion of reformatory schools. See Carpenter, *Our convicts, Vol. II*.
4 Elizabeth Fry, *Observations on the visiting, superintendence and government of female prisoners* (Norwich: S. Wilkin, 1827), p. 3.
5 Fry, *Observations on the visiting*, p. 3.
6 Report of the Directors of Convict Prisons for the year 1853 (London: 1854), p. 311.
7 Lucia Zedner, *Women, crime and custody in Victorian England* (Oxford: Oxford University Press, 1991).
8 Russell P. Dobash, R. Emerson Dobash and Sue Gutteridge, *The imprisonment of women* (Oxford: Basil Blackwell, 1986), p. 86.
9 Bill Forsythe, 'Women prisoners and women's penal officials 1840–1921', *British Journal of Criminology*, 33:4 (1993), 525–540, https://doi.org/10.1093/oxfordjournals.bjc.a048357, pp. 527–528.
10 Rachel Bennett, 'Bad for the health of the body, worse for the health of the mind: Female responses to imprisonment in England, 1853–1869', *Social*

History of Medicine, 34:2 (2021), 532–552, https://doi.org/10.1093/shm/hkz066.
11 Henry Mayhew and John Binny, *The criminal prisons of London and scenes of prison life* (London: 1862), p. 475.
12 Major Arthur Griffiths, 'In Wormwood Scrubs', in George Sims (ed.), *Living London: its work and its play, its humour and its pathos, its sights and its scenes*, Vol. III (London: Cassell and Company, 1903), pp. 126–131, p. 127.
13 For more on the public works prisons see Alyson Brown, *English society and the prison: Time, culture, and politics in the development of the modern prison, 1850–1920* (Suffolk: Boydell, 2003), Ch. 5.
14 Mayhew and Binny, *The criminal prisons of London*, p. 473.
15 Zedner, *Women, crime and custody*, p. 147.
16 Zedner, *Women, crime and custody*, p. 47.
17 William Douglas Morrison, *Crime and its causes* (London: Swan Sonnenschein & Co., 1891), p. 152.
18 For several good examples of these complaints and debates see Bennett, 'Bad for the health of the body'.
19 Florence Elizabeth Chandler Maybrick, *Mrs Maybrick's own story: My fifteen lost years* (London: Funk & Wagnalls Company, 1905), p. 188.
20 Sarah Amos, 'The prison treatment of women', *Contemporary Review*, 73 (1898), 803–813, p. 809.
21 LMA, WA/6/006, Minute Book, September 1850–December 1852, 9 November 1850.
22 Mayhew and Binny, *The criminal prisons of London*, p. 189.
23 Report from the Departmental Committee on Prisons (London: 1895), p. 13.
24 Victor Bailey, *The rise and fall of the rehabilitative ideal, 1895–1970* (Abingdon: Routledge, 2019), p. 18.
25 For a more thorough discussion of some of the key areas addressed by the Gladstone Committee see Christopher Harding, '"The inevitable end of a discredited system"? The origins of the Gladstone Committee report on prisons, 1895', *The Historical Journal*, 31:3 (1988), 591–608, https://doi.org/10.1017/S0018246X00023505.
26 Report from the Departmental Committee on Prisons, p. 189.
27 Jane Lewis, *The politics of motherhood: Child and maternal welfare in England, 1900–1939* (London: Croom Helm, 1980); for an examination of the developments in the education of mothers see pp. 89–113. Rima Apple also identified the mid-nineteenth century as a key period in which it was increasingly argued in the United States that mothers required the medical and scientific knowledge of experts to raise their

family. See Rima Apple, *Perfect motherhood: Science and childrearing in America* (London: Rutgers University Press, 2006); for a discussion of the early decades of the twentieth century see pp. 34–55.
28 Anna Davin, 'Imperialism and motherhood', *History Workshop*, 5:1 (1978), 9–65, https://doi.org/10.1093/hwj/5.1.9; Lewis, *The politics of motherhood*; Deborah Dwork, *War is good for babies and other young children: A history of the infant and child welfare movement in England 1898–1918* (London: Tavistock Publications, 1987). In her study of the United States, Apple identified a similar link between the growing maternal and child health movement of the early twentieth century and concerns raised about the poor physical condition of some of the armed forces during recruitment for the First World War, which was traced back to a failure on the part of the nation's mothers. See Apple, *Perfect motherhood*, p. 37.
29 Ellen Ross, *Love and toil: Motherhood in outcast London, 1870–1918* (Oxford: Oxford University Press, 1993), p. 5.
30 Tania McIntosh, *A social history of maternity and childbirth: Key themes in maternity care* (Abingdon: Routledge, 2012), pp. 24–44.
31 Zedner, *Women, crime and custody*, pp. 265–267.
32 Report of the Inter-Departmental Committee on Physical Deterioration (London: 1904).
33 *British Medical Journal*, 20 August 1904, p. 397.
34 Report of the Commissioners of Prisons and the Directors of Convict Prisons for the year ended 31 March 1904 (London: 1904), p. 31.
35 Stephen Hobhouse and A. Fenner Brockway, *English prisons today: Being the report of the prison system enquiry committee* (London: Longmans, Green and Co, 1922), p. 179.
36 'Prison babies: The case of infants in Holloway Jail', *Illustrated London News* (9 January 1909), p. 56.
37 'Baby Week', *The Times* (3 July 1917), p. 6.
38 Trudi Tate, 'King baby: Infant care into the peace', in Trudi Tate and Kate Kennedy (eds), *The silent morning: Culture and memory after the Armistice* (Manchester: Manchester University Press, 2013), pp. 104–130, p. 115.
39 Linda Bryder, 'Mobilising mothers: The 1917 National Baby Week', *Medical History*, 63:1 (2019), 2–23, https://doi.org/10.1017/mdh.2018.60, p. 4.
40 For an example of these late nineteenth- and early twentieth-century debates see Mary Scharlieb, 'Alcoholism in relation to women and children', in T.N. Kelynack (ed.), *The drink problem of today in its medico-sociological aspects* (London: Methuen & Co., first published 1907, revised edition 1916), pp. 128–156, p. 129.

41 Report of the Commissioners of Prisons and the Directors of Convict Prisons for the Year Ended 31 March 1918 (London: 1918), pp. 8–13.
42 Report of the Commissioners of Prisons and the Directors of Convict Prisons for the Year Ended 31 March 1922 (London: 1922), pp. 14–15.
43 Report of the Commissioners of Prisons, and the Directors of Convict Prisons for the Year Ended 31 March 1923 (London: 1923), pp. 11–18.
44 Mary Size, *Prisons I have known* (London: George Allen & Unwin, 1957), p. 45.
45 MRC, MSS/67/4/24/18, Holloway Discharged Prisoners' Aid Society Annual Report 1 January 1938, p. 5.
46 Size, *Prisons I have known*, p. 109.
47 Size, *Prisons I have known*, p. 125.
48 Cicely McCall, *They always come back* (London: Methuen, 1938), pp. 134–135.
49 'Lectures on mothercraft in prison', *Newcastle Evening Chronicle* (17 July 1945), p. 1.
50 D.W. Dean, 'Education for moral improvement, domesticity and social cohesion: The Labour government, 1945–1951', in Liz Dawtry, Janet Holland and Merril Hammer, with Sue Sheldon (eds), *Equality and inequality in education policy* (Avon: Multilingual Matters, 1995), pp. 18–30, p. 19.
51 Ann Dally, *Inventing motherhood: The consequences of an ideal* (London: Burnett Books, 1982), p. 92.
52 Laura King, 'Future citizens: Cultural and political conceptions of children in Britain, 1930s–1950s', *Twentieth Century British History*, 27:3 (2016), 389–411, https://doi.org/10.1093/tcbh/hww025.
53 Kathleen Lonsdale et al., with introduction by Ethel Mannin, *Some account of life in Holloway Prison for women* (London: Prison Medical Reform Council, 1943).
54 Report of the Commissioners of Prisons for the year 1952 (London: 1953), p. 15.
55 TNA, HO 45/19893, Prison and Prisoners: Overcrowding in prisons, minutes from the Prison Commission, 23 April 1945.
56 *British Medical Journal*, 31 January 1948, p. 206.
57 Becky Taylor and Ben Rogaly, '"Mrs Fairly is a dirty, lazy type": Unsatisfactory households and the problem of problem families in Norwich 1942–1963', *Twentieth Century British History*, 18:4 (2007), 429–452, https://doi.org/10.1093/tcbh/hwm019, p. 436.
58 John Welshman, *Underclass: A history of the excluded 1880–2000* (London: Hambledon, 2006), p. 69.
59 Taylor and Rogaly, '"Mrs Fairly is a dirty, lazy type"', p. 431.

60 Pat Starkey, 'The feckless mother: Women, poverty and social workers in wartime and post-war England', *Women's History Review*, 9:3 (2000), 539–557, https://doi.org/10.1080/09612020000200259, p. 540.
61 Hobhouse and Brockway, *English prisons today*, p. 337.
62 TNA, MH55/1572, Courses in mothercraft delivered to women in prison, 1952, Mary Steel, 'Babycraft Behind Bars', 1952.
63 MRC, MSS 121/CH/3/4/2, Lady Allen of Hurtwood, 'An Alternative to Prison for Neglectful Mothers', 2 April 1945.
64 MRC, MSS.67/4/24/35, Fifty Second Annual Report of Holloway Discharged Prisoners' Aid Society, 1955.
65 TNA, PCOM 9/1435, Women convicted of child neglect investigations in prisons, 1946–50.
66 TNA, PCOM 9/1435, Women convicted of child neglect.
67 National Justice Museum, Nottingham, Prison Nursing Advisory Committee Reports on Prison Visits, 1928–1954, 24 May 1951.
68 Joan Henry, *Women in prison* (London: White Lion Publishers, 1952), p. 84.
69 Report of the Commissioners of Prisons for the year 1952 (London: 1953), p. 56. It was noted by the Prison Commissioners that during the course of the year 1952, 1035 evening classes were delivered across the prison estate to 901 men and 134 women and they were run by the City Education Committee in the form of Evening Institute activities.
70 TNA, MH55/1572, Courses in mothercraft ..., Report by A.E. Girling, Public Health Nursing Officer, 19 August 1952.
71 MRC, MSS 121/CH/3/4/1, Lady Allen of Hurtwood speaking in Liverpool, 24 February 1945.
72 Report of the Commissioners of Prisons for the Year 1952, p. 40, p. 59.
73 TNA, MH55/1572, Courses in mothercraft ..., Home Nursing Syllabus for Neglectful Mothers Course.
74 TNA, MH55/1572, Courses in mothercraft ..., Mary Steel, 'Babycraft Behind Bars'.
75 TNA, MH55/1572, Courses in mothercraft ..., Women Public Health Officers' Association Superintendents Group Meeting, 13 March 1953.
76 TNA, MH55/1572, Courses in mothercraft ..., Mary Steel, 'Babycraft Behind Bars'.
77 Henry, *Women in prison*, p. 60.
78 TNA, MH55/1572, Courses in mothercraft ..., Women Public Health Officers' Association Superintendents Group Meeting, 13 March 1953.
79 TNA, MH55/1572, Courses in mothercraft ..., letter from Dr Ian McCracken to Dr G. Lilico, 22 May 1953.

80 TNA, MH55/1572, Courses in mothercraft …, letter from Dr Herbert, Welsh Board of Visitors, to the Ministry of Health, 16 March 1953.
81 Report of the Commissioners of Prisons for the Year 1952, p. 40.
82 LRO, 347 MAG 1/2/2, Minutes of Visiting Justices 1870–1878, 27 April 1870.
83 Lewis, *The politics of motherhood*, p. 61, p. 68.
84 McCall, *They always come back*, p. 12.
85 MRC, MSS.67/4/24/32, Holloway Discharged Prisoners' Aid Society Annual Report 1 January 1952, p. 7.
86 Report of the Commissioners of Prisons for the Year 1952, pp. 41, 59.
87 MRC, MSS.67/4/24/34, Holloway Discharged Prisoners' Aid Society Annual Report 1 January 1954, p. 8.
88 Report of the Departmental Committee on Persistent Offenders (London: 1932), pp. 38–40.
89 Size, *Prisons I have known*, pp. 141–145.
90 Henry, *Women in prison*, pp. 105–106.
91 Size, *Prisons I have known*, p. 149.
92 Size, *Prisons I have known*, p. 185.
93 Size, *Prisons I have known*, p. 161.
94 Report of the Commissioners of Prisons for the Year 1952, p. 38.
95 At the time Wakefield and Maidstone, closed prisons for men, each had a small open camp attached. There were also two open male prisons at Sudbury and Falfield and a medium-security establishment at Portland. They could collectively accommodate up to 1,500 male prisoners.

4

Born in prison: a heritage of woe?

In 1903 Arthur Griffiths lamented that to be born in prison carried with it an 'inalienable heritage of woe'.[1] Griffiths had been a British military officer before joining the prison service. He served as a governor in several prisons before his appointment as an Inspector of Prisons in 1878. Describing Wormwood Scrubs Prison, he focused especially on those inmates he encountered who were of an 'entirely distinct class ... detained within the walls, and for no fault of their own ... the poor, blameless infants who have drawn their first breath in the prison or are so young that they cannot be separated from their mother, and are thus cradled in crime'.[2] Despite the initial pessimistic tone adopted by Griffiths, he captured a long-standing contradiction within debates about prison births and the presence of infants in prisons when he added that, in many cases, 'the prison born are better off than the free born'. He detailed the care provided to prison babies and the influence of the institution in allowing the development of 'purer maternal instincts', facilitated by there being 'no incentives to neglect of offspring, no drink, no masterful men, no temptation to thieve or go astray'.[3] While Griffiths' comments would not have been out of place within the commentaries on domesticity and mothercraft discussed in Chapter 3, they also encapsulate a much deeper, and more contentious, question that has long faced the prison system, namely, whether prison was, or could ever be, an appropriate place for the birth and care of infants.

The nineteenth century witnessed intense debate about providing for the children of the poor and destitute in public institutions and in the community. The workhouse was often at the centre of discussion and has been richly explored in the scholarship examining contemporary questions of state responsibility, parental agency and the development of child welfare agencies and legislation.[4] Those who advocated admitting children to the workhouse argued that their care and upbringing could be properly regulated by the state, but others pointed to the negative physical and moral influence of the workhouse environment and instead supported alternatives such as emigration abroad or boarding out to families in the community.[5] However, the institutionalisation of the children of female prisoners within prisons during the same period has received very minimal examination. This chapter demonstrates that similar debates played out in prisons. There were those who argued that they were places where mothers and their babies could receive medical care, refuge and education as part of heavily regulated regimes. Others warned of the dangers of the moral contamination of children by the physical prison space, their criminal mothers and the other women they would encounter. Nowhere were these debates more intense than when addressing the question of whether babies should be born in prison.

Throughout this period, several voices expatiated on the question of prison births. Some focused on the issue from the perspective of the institution, including the maternity provisions in place and the impact of infants on the discipline of the prison. Others focused more upon the benefits for the mothers of having their children with them during their sentence instead of being forced to separate. As the period progressed, voices claiming to advocate for the infants of prison mothers also became louder. However, it is important to acknowledge here that the mother's voice was often lost within debates about the conditions in which they would give birth. There were some who argued that their prison sentence equated to a forfeit of their right to choose, a question which the chapter delves into in greater depth in relation to the mid-twentieth century. Recurring arguments supporting and opposing prison births were interleaved with questions of health, discipline, stigma and choice. Within this, the use of language was important. As in Griffiths' commentary, babies born in prison were often described as innocents who found themselves as inmates, not convicted of any crime but destined to be tainted by association with the criminal justice system.

When Brixton was opened as a female convict prison, there were provisions for more than thirty mothers with children. This included babies born in the prison and children brought into prison with their mothers. While babies continued to be born in Brixton until its closure for women in 1869, there were efforts to prevent women taking their children into the prison with them when they were transferred from local prisons. This was most likely to address the issue of limited space to accommodate them and the additional considerations required for their containment. Research has also shown that within his annual reports to the Directors of Convict Prisons, Brixton's Medical Officer, James Rendle, often spoke of how the poor health of many women who entered the prison put pressure on the institution's already stretched resources, as it meant they required accommodation in the infirmary and could not be subject to the ordinary rigours of the prison regime, something which also applied to mothers with babies.[6] In 1854 the Home Office issued instructions to local prisons that no female prisoners with children should be sent to Brixton unless 'circumstances render it necessary that the mother and child should not be separated'.[7] By the early 1860s, if women were transferred to Brixton from other prisons, older children were to be given to relatives or put into the care of the parish. However, those already in the prison often stayed with their mother until the end of her sentence. When Mayhew and Binny visited Brixton Prison, they met a four-year-old child with his mother who knew no other life beyond its walls.[8]

Following Brixton's closure as a female convict prison in 1869, women serving sentences of penal servitude were sent to either Woking, Millbank or Fulham instead. It appears that after the closure of Brixton, in most cases where women were identified as being pregnant at the time of sentencing to a term of penal servitude in a convict prison, they would be held in a local prison until they gave birth and to nurse the child, likely up to the age of nine to twelve months. Helen Johnston identified cases where women who had commenced their sentence in a convict prison were sent back to a local prison to give birth when it was discovered that they were pregnant.[9] Following the birth and nursing period, the women would then be transferred to a convict prison to serve their sentence and their children would be handed over to relatives or sent into the care of the parish in which their mother had been arrested. In local prisons, such arrangements would be made by the matron upon receiving a written certificate from the prison doctor stating that a child could be safely removed from its mother.[10] However, a reading of the available records indicates that the age, and circumstances, at which it was deemed that children could be separated from their mothers varied between different prisons and across this period. An account by a 'prison matron', which was likely written by Frederick William Robinson using accounts from those who had worked in the prison system, spoke of children remaining with their mothers beyond infancy, rather than being given over to the care of the parish. The account mused that for these 'prison flowers' it was difficult to say which course of action was the more merciful.[11]

This contentious question of whether babies should be born or accommodated in prisons was grappled with from social, ideological and medical standpoints by those administering and working in prisons, those advocating for their reform and observers beyond the confines of the prison system. While this chapter examines the arguments levied for and against prison births, it is too simplistic to suggest that there was a clear line separating the opposing sides. Instead, a reading of the myriad of medical, social and ideological justifications and rejections of prison births reveals that the issue posed something of a Gordian knot in a system that sought absolute uniformity but was faced with distinct challenges in containing and caring for this part of the prison population. The chapter examines how those responsible for the management of prisoner health and institutional discipline on a daily basis, and observers both within and beyond the prison service, attempted to untie this often contradictory and contentious knot when justifying and rejecting the practice of prison births, and how these efforts impacted upon the experiences of mothers and their babies in prison.

Prison births and the question of health

Cicely McCall, a psychiatric social worker who worked as an officer in both Holloway and Aylesbury prisons, argued in 1938 that instead of focusing upon the question of a prison address on the birth certificate, the questions of real importance with regard to births in prison were the vital ones of health and the impact of the prison environment upon a mother's personal relationship with her child both before and after birth.[12] Across the period under examination here, many of the women who entered an English prison either pregnant or with infants came from the poorest sections of society. In February 1851, John Lavies, the doctor in Westminster's Tothill Fields Prison, informed the prison's Visiting Justices of the case of a woman who had arrived in the prison dangerously ill, malnourished and close to her confinement. She gave birth only days after commencing her sentence. Lavies reported that the care she had received in the prison had very likely saved her life and that her health had gradually improved. He used her case to stress the need for greater provisions to be put in place to care for the health of people who entered into the prison.[13] Although occurring during the infancy of the modern prison system, the argument made by Lavies in this case captures a question that permeated its subsequent development. Namely, the role, if not obligation, of the prison to provide for the health of those confined within its walls and its ability to do so.

Olwen Purdue has highlighted the medical arguments made against admitting children under the age of five into workhouses, which were deemed to pose a danger to the health of very young children in terms of the development of their teeth, bones and general constitution.[14] However, Lara Marks found that by the 1890s attitudes towards unmarried and poor mothers giving birth in public institutions, including workhouses, had shifted somewhat among Poor Law guardians. They increasingly argued that detaining them for weeks after the birth was beneficial to the mother's health, and also that of her infant. Marks found evidence to suggest that although sanitary conditions remained poor, rates of maternal morbidity were lower, thus justifying the mother's place there for the birth of her child.[15] This positioning of public institutions as places to offer maternity care to the poorest sections of society had already been used in the debate about prison births.

Arguments were repeatedly raised throughout the century following the 1850s that prison was used by the poorest sections of society as a place of refuge to gain food and shelter. Ex-prisoners, both men and women, testified to Hobhouse and Brockway that they sought short-term imprisonment, especially in the winter months.[16] In 1936, twenty-three-year-old May Amos was found guilty of stealing clothes and money from her employer and was sentenced by the Marylebone police court to six months in prison for the theft. She was pregnant at the time. One of the detectives in the case stated that May had seven previous convictions and she had met with difficulties at different hospitals because she was single, and he believed she had committed the crime to get back into prison for the birth of her child. The magistrate gave May an assurance that there were 'adequate places in prison for looking after expectant mothers'. He added that he was sending her to prison for a period sufficiently long to allow the baby to be born and for her to 'regain her health and strength'.[17]

At the outset of the creation of the modern prison system, medical officers such as John Lavies in Westminster and James Rendle in Brixton had noted the frequency with which pregnant women and those with infants entered prisons, and the poor condition in which they often arrived. They had used this to argue that greater provision was not only required to care for this distinct group of inmates, but was also vital to ensure the more efficient running of the prisons on a daily basis. In the first few months following the allocation of Tothill Fields Prison in Westminster as a prison for women and male juveniles in 1850, Governor A.F. Tracey repeatedly reported to the Visiting Justices of the need to adapt the prison for the reception and containment of women. In a meeting in November 1850, he reported that, following consultation with the prison doctor, a large room had been allocated as a nursery. He added that the 'probability of a very considerable increase as the winter advances' in committals of women with infants rendered further adaptations an immediate concern.[18]

David Morris, appointed chaplain in Liverpool Prison in 1874, dedicated a substantial section of his first report to the Visiting Justices in October to the condition of mothers bringing young infants with them into the prison. He attributed the crowded nature of the female side of the prison to the living conditions of the working classes in the surrounding community. He criticised the short sentences handed down for crimes such as drunkenness and the lack of any preventive effect on the criminality of these women. He complained that their entering the prison close to the date of their confinement and with young infants converted it into something of a hospital or a refuge, which exacerbated the issue of overcrowding and removed any semblance of deterrence.[19] Reports of a similar nature were repeatedly raised from within different female prisons, but were largely not properly addressed at policy level. However, alongside complaints and concerns about the pressures that containing this group of prisoners posed to the institution there were enduring arguments that prison played a vital role in caring for these women and their infants.

Even Griffiths, who viewed a prison birth as a 'heritage of woe', acceded that prison nurseries, 'though no doubt still a cell', were bright, clean spaces where prison babies were given wholesome food, received the care of matrons and visitors alike and were able to sleep in a comfortable cot – amenities they may not have had if born outside of the prison.[20] Writing of the many women she encountered serving sentences in Liverpool, Manchester, Leeds and Holloway prisons, Mary Size stated that the women serving short sentences, often less than three months, brought 'ill-nourished little creatures, bearing the stamp of poverty and neglect' into prison with them. However, during their short confinement babies were given care and proper feeding and Size noted that their health often improved.[21] McCall wrote that in many cases it was likely that mothers and babies had better medical attention in prison than most of them would have at home. Although critical of what she believed were systemic missed opportunities to achieve effective reformatory intervention while women served their prison sentence, McCall praised the daily arrangements in place for mothers and their babies. Women did not have to do hard work during late pregnancy, as they may have done on the outside, they had time to recover from the birth and their children were looked after in the prison crèche while the women carried out their daily work. In the evening, babies slept in a cot beside their mother. There was also a sense of community within the prison, where every woman in the prison knew the names of the prison babies and when a mother walked down the prison corridors with her child, 'every head is turned and every woman makes the same admiring comments that she would make standing at her own door in a back street tenement dwelling'.[22]

In addition to those who stressed the role prisons played in providing at least some care to the pregnant women and those with young infants who entered them, others developed this point further to argue that prison sentences were opportunities for greater medical intervention in the case of mothers and their infants. William Sullivan, part of the medical staff at Liverpool's Walton Gaol and later the medical officer at Holloway, took great interest in the relationship between maternal inebriety and the health of children. In the late

1890s he undertook a study involving 120 female prisoners in Liverpool. Collectively they had given birth to 600 children, some during prison sentences and others in between shorter-term prison sentences. Of these 600 infants, only 265 had lived over two years. Sullivan lamented that the majority of women, including those who were pregnant, entered Liverpool to serve short sentences and thus there was limited time to exercise any perceptible influence on their inebriety.[23]

Drunk and disorderly behaviour had accounted for around 22 per cent of convictions where women ended up serving shorter sentences in local prisons. This had risen to 37 per cent by 1890, around the time of Sullivan's study.[24] To support his argument for longer prison sentences to achieve intervention in cases of female inebriates, especially mothers, Sullivan detailed the case of a woman who had been an alcoholic for over ten years. She had served previous short prison sentences, in between which she had given birth to four children. However, they were all either stillborn or died in very early infancy. When she entered Liverpool Prison to serve a longer sentence, she was pregnant again. This time she spent the majority of her pregnancy in prison and gave birth behind bars, and the child survived. Sullivan claimed to have documented several similar cases to justify not only the practice of women giving birth in prison, but also the detaining of mothers and their babies beyond their immediate confinement so as to ensure provisions for their longer-term health.[25]

The positioning of the prison as an institution to not only provide medical care to mothers and their infants in prison, but also regulate the relationship between them was an argument that developed further in the early twentieth century as the question of whether babies should be born and confined in prisons at all became more greatly contested. At the time of journalist Annesley Kenealy's visit to Holloway Prison in 1905, babies were generally handed out to family or friends, or into the care of the parish if no one could take them, when they reached the age of twelve months. However, if a child was deemed to be in ill health or malnourished or as having been subject to neglect before they entered the prison, the doctor could recommend that they be kept there for longer under medical supervision. Kenealy used this to further support her observation that caring for babies in prison provided them with an element of protection and, by extension, the regulation of their mother's interactions with them.[26] Well into the twentieth century, in some cases children as old as three remained with their mothers.[27]

The medical officer in Lancaster's local prison recounted a case in 1910 of an unmarried woman who was serving a nine-month sentence for neglecting her infant. She had fifty-four previous convictions for drunkenness, theft and neglect. During her latest sentence her infant accompanied her into the prison and was taken into the care of the prison staff.[28] Similarly, the medical officer at Holloway Prison recalled a case in the early 1920s of a woman serving a sentence for neglecting her seven children. She brought the youngest infant into prison with her. The medical officer took the infant into the care of the prison as it was found to be underweight and malnourished.[29] Despite intervention in the care of these infants for the benefit of their health while in prison with their mothers, the influence of the prison was limited, because at the end of their sentence mothers walked back out of the prison gates with their infants. However, cases such as these provided further support to the arguments for greater education in domesticity and mothercraft, as detailed in Chapter 3. They also reveal how questions of providing for, and regulating, motherhood in prison intersected with issues of middle-class ideals of motherhood, a point to which the chapter now turns.

A touch of something human: the impact of babies on the management of prisons

In addition to addressing the question of prison births from the perspective of health and medical care, prison staff, reformers and commentators also spoke of the broader impact of babies upon the management of the prison institution and female prisoner behaviour. Thomas Carter, a chaplain in Liverpool Prison, commented in January 1872 on the hundreds of women who were committed to the prison time and again for short sentences. He contemplated that while 'it may be just to drive them off the streets; it would be generous and humane to tell them what to do and show them how to do it' in order for them to return to their lives upon release.[30] Chapter 3 explored the attempts to reclaim women, or 'show them how to do it', through education in domesticity and mothercraft during their prison sentence. The present chapter enhances this by demonstrating the importance placed upon the presence of babies and young children in the prison environment, including their ability to promote the more humane environment advocated by Carter.

In her evidence to the Departmental Committee on the Education and Moral Instruction of Prisoners in Local and Convict Prisons in 1896, Mrs Sheldon Amos, who for some time had taken a great interest in prisons and had visited several, stated that 'it seems to me you should encourage the tender side in a woman instead of crushing it, and in this connexion I have been very much struck by the good effect of babies in prison'. Despite prison placing restrictions on womanliness, Amos talked about many women being better off there as 'they are saved from bad and brutal husbands, they have not the worry of life, and they have quiet undisturbed nights'.[31] While of course we must acknowledge that for many women a prison sentence was not the beneficial respite suggested by Amos, the argument that caring for their babies behind bars was an opportunity to save mothers from themselves, and perhaps from their lives outside, is key to our understanding of the intersections between motherhood, criminality and imprisonment.

Accommodation in the prison nursery and having the opportunity to care for their children was believed to be a benefit, or perhaps even a privilege, for prison mothers throughout this period, and one that could be taken away if women did not adhere to the prison rules. Alongside this, the prison nursery was described as a place of care, if not a home, for prison babies. But it was also sometimes posited as a place to regulate motherhood and, where necessary, safeguard prison babies from their mothers. When journalist Annesley Kenealy visited Holloway in 1905, she remarked in detail on the prison crèche. She stated that while prisons would rarely be considered to be desirable places of residence, in the case of the prison babies it was the 'only happy, comfortable home many of them are likely to experience'. The babies slept in cots in their mothers' cells at night and spent their days in the crèche, where their mothers were permitted to visit them twice per day. They were well fed, regularly weighed to ensure they were putting on weight and provided with comfortable clothes, cots and bedding. They were also believed to benefit from the company of other infants and the care given to them by the prison staff. Crucially, according to Kenealy, prison crèches served as a vital protection for the infant prison population, not only from the often harsh realities they would face outside, but also from the neglect of their mothers in the prison itself.[32] Although accounts such as this one provide valuable descriptions of the daily running of prison crèches, we cannot accept the almost idyllic scene painted by Kenealy entirely at face value. Kenealy's observations come from a piece she wrote for *The Lady's Realm*, a contemporary illustrated magazine with a middle- to upper-class readership. Her article was written at a time when Edwardian health politics repeatedly raised concerns about the ability of poorer women to care for their infants, as discussed in detail in Chapter 3.

Throughout this period, treatises on the benefits of having babies in prisons were shot through with commentaries on class, gender and crime. Henry Maudsley, a psychiatrist who wrote widely on moral degeneracy as a cause of crime, argued that when a woman sank into criminality and ended up in prison she lost all sense of shame, modesty and womanliness.[33] The Reverend William Morrison, a long-serving prison chaplain, wrote that child-rearing among the poorer classes could actually mitigate against female tendencies towards crime and foster in women the qualities of compassion and altruism.[34] He went further, to argue that inculcating the qualities of motherhood in prison could be a check on the degrading effects of industrialism and poor living conditions upon their more feminine nature that women would face upon their return to society.[35]

During their visit to Brixton, Henry Mayhew and John Binny remarked that the prison nursery was 'the most touching portion of the female convict prison' and a place in which tolerance and goodness could be learnt.[36] Upon witnessing the daily running of the nursery in Tothill Fields, they stated that even the sternest of observers would 'tingle with compassion to note the wretched mother caressing the little things' and that for many women these infants were the only thing that 'made life bearable to them'. They continued, 'the women in the nursery do not glory in their shame as some others do'. Instead, they argued, motherhood made them feel the degradation of their position and, perhaps, made them more malleable to reform.[37] Despite the importance placed upon motherhood as a reformatory tool, a reading of debates about having babies in the prison environment reveals that there was acknowledgement of additional benefits to the institution in terms of discipline and also the management of prisoner health.

Writing of her time in Holloway Prison following her involvement in the suffragette campaign for the right to vote in the early twentieth century, Constance Lytton spoke of a feeling that overcame many women in prison, namely that of being forgotten about and cut off from everyone outside.[38] This feeling of separation and being cut off was perhaps further exacerbated for mothers who gave birth in prison and for those whose children were taken away at a certain age, and for the mothers who left children on the outside. In 1895 Dr Robert Glover, Medical Inspector of Local Prisons and Superintending Medical Officer of Convict Prisons, gave evidence to the Gladstone Committee, an enquiry into issues such as accommodation, labour and discipline in prisons. Glover recounted reports of women who had given birth while in local prisons suffering from depression when their infants were taken away at around nine months of age. When asked about the power of the prison medical officer in such matters, he replied that in extreme cases they could recommend that the child remain in the prison for longer with their mother.[39] The present study has found evidence of some children remaining with their mothers beyond the age one year, but countless others suffered the pain of being separated from their children, either at the point of entering the prison or when their children were sent outside.

Basil Thomson, a former Deputy Governor in Liverpool Prison, remarked in 1925 that having babies in prisons caused disorganisation among the staff and the prisoners. He added that their presence could cause excitement, but also jealousy, among the other women prisoners, some of whom may have been mothers themselves with children on the outside.[40] However, in their extensive examination of conditions in English prisons in 1922, ex-prisoners and reformers Hobhouse and Brockway wrote of the potential remedial effects of having babies in the prison. They stated that the advantages to the mother of their presence in the prison were obvious, but added that 'into the cold existence of other women too, the children bring a touch of something human. The crowing of a baby breaks the silence, a scrap of ribbon on its sleeve marks a touch of unwonted colour, and to many women the mere sight of a child is a relief.'[41] While this study is primarily focused upon the experiences of mothers who gave birth to their babies in prison or brought in young children with them, it is important to acknowledge that many women had been separated from their children on the outside. The impact of this separation has been examined in the more recent history of female imprisonment.[42] However, it has a longer history of impacting upon the experiences of incarcerated women and factoring into debates about the running of female prisons, including in terms of the management of female prisoner behaviour and health.

Mary, a woman serving a nine-month sentence in Westminster Prison in 1881, was placed in the prison's sick cells by the doctor after he concluded that she was suffering from temporary insanity due to the effects of being separated from her three children, who were outside. While in her infirmary cell Mary, like the other women in the prison, was supposed to spend a substantial amount of time picking oakum each day. However, she instead made toys for her children. Upon her return to her normal cell she was given another monotonous labour task, of sorting waste paper, but she managed to set a stack of paper on fire in her cell and was again placed in the infirmary for much of her remaining sentence.[43] Recent research into the management of female prisoner health in the convict prison estate in the mid-nineteenth century revealed that concern for their children on the outside, and the heavy restrictions placed upon communication, prompted violent conduct in some women. The research argued that a belief that this behaviour stemmed from the mothers' pains of separation from their children, as opposed to deliberate infractions of the prison rules, meant that it was more likely to be responded to with medical treatment than disciplinary sanction.[44]

In terms of the management of behaviour in female prisons, Kenealy observed the benefits offered by having babies and young children within the walls of the prison. Female prisoners could be placed on duty in the prison crèche to help care for the babies during the day while their mothers carried out their own prison labour. These women, Kenealy had been informed by one of the prison warders, were selected 'by reason of their love for little children', and, crucially, their good conduct.[45] A Lady Visitor recounted to Hobhouse and Brockway the case of a woman named Alice. She was twenty-eight years of age and had already served several short sentences for drunkenness. She was described as 'a bright and pretty girl but unmanageable sometimes'. She was subject to ungovernable fits of rage where she screamed, sang songs loudly and banged on her cell door. She had been sent to a punishment cell and placed in a strait jacket, but to no avail. When attempting to identify a means to calm Alice, the matron found that she talked of longing to spend time with babies and young children. Following consultation between the matron and the medical officer, it was decided that Alice would be allowed to spend time with the prison babies. When an improvement in her conduct was noted, she was given the job of walking the toddlers around the exercise yard on certain days of the week. Alice told the matron that when she left prison she would have a child of her own.[46] Although Alice does not appear again in the records, and it is not clear whether she had children on the outside that she had been separated from, or perhaps had lost children prior to her commission of the crime that led her to prison, her case offers a valuable insight into the broader impact of children in the prison environment.

'It is not the baby's fault': balancing stigma and health

Alice Cook, of no fixed address, was sentenced at the North London Police Court in July 1939 to four months in prison for stealing clothing and £148 from her employer. During sentencing, the magistrate Mr Basil Watson stated, 'you are going to have a baby and you must receive proper attention. Your baby will be born in prison. It is not a reflection on the baby. It is not the baby's fault.'[47] Watson's comments offer a glimpse into the complex and contradictory question of whether babies should be born in prison. He was acknowledging that Alice would receive medical care in prison, maybe better than she might expect outside, and perhaps using this point to justify the custodial sentence despite his reticence in condemning her child to a prison birth. Again, the use of language is important here, as Watson states that 'it is not the baby's fault', and stresses that the circumstances of their birth should not be a reflection upon them. However, this chapter demonstrates that the question of stigma was a vital one in shaping debates about prison births. For some, both within and beyond the prison system, it eclipsed considerations of medical care, maternal choice and the relationship between a mother and her baby.

In her study of the social and legal impact of illegitimacy upon mothers and children in the late Victorian period, Ginger Frost argued that the 'crimes' of the mother, of engaging in sexual intercourse out of wedlock and bearing an illegitimate child, served to exclude that child from being part of the highly idealised Victorian notion of the family.[48] It was denied the name of its father, and the social and legal protections that accompanied this, and in many cases it was excluded from the broader family unit if its mother did not have, or was excluded from, her own family. For the children, both legitimate and illegitimate, of women who committed and were convicted of legally defined and punishable crimes by the courts, their mother's imprisonment impacted on them in a myriad of ways. Some children were left in the care of their fathers, the broader family or the parish; others were sent to the workhouse; while some younger children and infants accompanied their mothers into the prison. While each scenario arguably carried with it an element of exclusion from the Victorian family ideal, this chapter primarily focuses upon one group of children, namely those who were born behind bars, although some of the evidence presented also discusses those infants who were taken into the prison with their mothers.

In the 1860s and 1870s, social reformer Isabella Tod campaigned for legislation to compel the Boards of Guardians administering the Poor Law to remove children from workhouses as, she argued, containing them there was 'an outrage on nature' and a danger to their physical and moral health.[49] A case highlighted by the Birmingham Petty Sessions in April 1896 further illuminated this issue in prisons. Archie Callaghan, a child under the age of nine years, was convicted of the theft of a spade and sentenced to ten days' imprisonment and then five years in a reformatory school. The Visiting Justices of Birmingham's Winson Green Prison argued that Archie should not be in the prison, as 'there are no arrangements in the prison here for the care of children and the placing of this child in a cell by himself for the time of his detention could not possibly be adopted'. They recommended that Archie be transferred either straight to a reformatory school or to a workhouse instead, a recommendation that appears to have been upheld.[50] This case is interesting, as it demonstrates not only the importance of the use of language, referring to Archie as a child instead of a prisoner, but also the argument that the rigours and environment of the prison were not appropriate for someone of his young age. This argument was one that was even more pronounced in the case of the children of prisoners, but arguably more complex because the question of their containment was also bound up with issues of maternal health and discipline as well as logistical questions and those of choice.

Chaplain David Morris went beyond complaining of the spatial and physical challenges caused by the overcrowding of Liverpool Prison in the 1870s, to stress the moral danger to the young infants in prison with their mother. He particularly stressed the case of a woman who had frequently accompanied her own mother into prison as a child to illustrate the dangers of moral contagion. At the age of twenty-eight she had already been committed to Liverpool thirty-five times, bringing her own young children in with her on the majority of occasions.[51] Recidivism and the cyclical nature of short-term imprisonment were of great concern within commentaries on the efficacy of the prison system in the late nineteenth and early twentieth century.[52] While research has examined how habitual female criminality and inebriety were believed to pose especial danger to the family unit, debates about prison births and the impact of the prison environment upon infants, including the question of stigma, have been largely overlooked.[53]

Mary Carpenter, an educational and social reformer who had visited women's prisons, provided a detailed testimony of her visit to Mountjoy Prison in Dublin in 1862. She described feeling shocked that infants should be 'bred in a gaol'.[54] Carpenter was a supporter of theories of physiognomy that explored the relationship between an individual's physical appearance and their criminal tendencies.[55] She spoke of the dangers of moral contagion where children were surrounded by faces exhibiting 'every species of hideous vice and degradation'. Even when children experienced their mother's love, this was tainted by the wickedness of the other women, many of them mothers. She used these theories to argue that children were in danger of developing criminal habits if left under the care and influence of their mothers. Carpenter raised this concern, but recalled being assured by a prison officer that the children were not negatively impacted because they were not conscious of their position of being in prison.[56] However, even if the infants themselves were not conscious of the circumstances of their birth, those debating the matter pointed to the potential long-term impact in the eyes of others.

Following his visit to Brixton Convict Prison in 1856, Henry Mayhew wrote an article about the 'convict nursery' for the *Cheltenham Chronicle*. Upon meeting the mothers and their children living and working in the nursery, Mayhew praised the provisions for them and noted that the nursery was a place where toleration and goodness could be learnt. However, he questioned the lives the children would lead once they left the prison. He contemplated whether they would have the same opportunities as 'the honest man's child' or if they would meet with 'gibes in years to come for their felon extraction'. He put it to his readers, 'would you like to take them into your household and your family, when they grow up, to tend your own little ones?'[57]

In 1901, in an attempt to avoid the stigma of a prison birth, the Home Office issued an order to all prison governors dictating that the prison address must not appear on a child's birth certificate. Instead, the street name where the prison was located would be used. This was referred to as a 'pious fraud'.[58] This is an important moment in the history of prison births, as it marked at least some acknowledgement on the part of the prison hierarchy that to be born in prison had the potential to negatively impact upon the children of female prisoners. However, crucially, this harm was not believed to stem from the prison itself but, rather, from perceptions and attitudes beyond the prison gates. As the early twentieth century progressed, debates about the provisions in place to adequately care for mothers and babies continued, with additional measures being taken to improve this care. However, even when acknowledging, and even praising, improvements in the standard of care, and the fact that the prison address would not appear on the birth certificate, for many the stigma of a prison birth was inescapable.

Alice Hawkins, a suffragette from Leicester who served five terms in prison for acts committed as part of the Women's Social and Political Union's militant campaigns for the vote, raised the issue of prison births when chronicling the plight of women in prison. Writing of her time in Holloway in February 1907, she recalled observing women with babies in the garden. At this time babies born in prison remained with their mothers up to the age of twelve months. Hawkins acknowledged that they appeared to be well looked after but lamented that 'a young life just born into the world should have to spend its first months of life in prison'. She added that this 'was one more injustice added to our cry for the right to stop some of these horrible things being allowed'.[59] Hobhouse and Brockway included an account from an ex-prison matron in their examination of the prison system in the early 1920s. She recalled the case of a woman who brought a baby aged nine weeks into prison with her to serve a six-month sentence for fortune telling. The woman had another five older children who remained with their father on the outside. The matron felt it was 'an abominable thing' to condemn the youngest child to pass the first six months of its life behind bars.[60] She was alluding to a belief that the child would be marked out from its siblings due to its association with the prison system on account of its mother's criminality.

In 1937 Sir Samuel Hoare, the Home Secretary, gave a speech at the opening of the Elizabeth Fry Exhibition in Norwich. A great, great nephew of Fry, and a long-term advocate for penal reform, he addressed the question of prison births. Hoare pointed to the fact that the prison address had not appeared on the birth certificates of babies born in prison for decades and that mothers themselves received a good standard of care, arguing that, on balance, the present policy was the best one.[61] When highlighting the standard of medical care, he captured a long-standing debate in the history of incarcerating expectant mothers, namely, whether prisons offered medical care women would not have had access to on the outside or if a prison birth could potentially cause harm to the mother and child.

One such case where these debates came to the fore was that of Florence Osborne. In March 1892 she pleaded guilty to larceny and perjury and was sentenced to nine months 'with such hard labour as is consistent with her weak condition'.[62] She was weeks away from giving birth. Her husband, Captain Osborne, immediately began a petition for her release on medical grounds. He sent a petition to the Home Secretary stating that she was hysterical at the thought of giving birth in prison and submitted evidence of her history of being subject to attacks characteristic of a highly neurotic temperament and culminating in outbreaks of hysteron-epilepsy. Captain Osborne requested that the Home Secretary use his power to order Florence's release on medical grounds, as her 'continued imprisonment might seriously imperil her life or the life of a child about to be born'.[63] In connection with her case, the *BMJ* published several reports which were used in support of Osborne's petition and were signed by many eminent leaders of the medical profession in London, attesting to the danger to life likely to accrue from the imprisonment of Mrs Osborne over the period of her confinement. An article on 16 April 1892 stated the belief that her further detention and the stress of a prison birth would expose her nervous system to such strain as might well terminate in puerperal mania and endanger her life and that of the child. Attesting signatures included those of consulting surgeons at St Bartholomew's Hospital, University College Hospital and St Mary's Hospital.[64]

An order for Florence's immediate release on medical grounds was made in early May. Following her release, it was reported that 'it will readily be believed that both the governor of the gaol and the infirmary department ... are not sorry to be spared the responsibility' attached to her case. The article continued that if her life and that of her child had truly been endangered by her continued imprisonment there was no complaint to be made. However, it stated that 'something less than justice had been done', and warned that if such releases became common practice where female prisoners could be relieved of a large proportion of their punishment 'because they are in a certain condition, the results might be very undesirable indeed'.[65]

The early twentieth century witnessed several cases where pregnant women in prison and their families petitioned the Home Office to be temporarily removed to an outside hospital for their confinement. These cases were comparable to that of Florence Osborne in that they sought to avoid a prison birth. However, the petitions primarily centred upon the question of stigma and were more overt in their opposition to this consequence of a prison birth than questioning the health implications for the mother, as in Florence's case, or offering criticism of the care the women would receive in prison.

The case of Ivy Cusden in 1924 provides an interesting case study of how health-centred debates have complex broader resonances, and reveals an important interplay between choice, medical care and entitlement to health as well as perceptions of the social ramifications of being born in prison. Ivy was twenty years old when she met Morris Jones, a man who promised to marry her when she announced that she was pregnant. However, it later transpired that he had married another woman, named Mabel, who found out about Ivy and began to spread 'dreadful tales of her character'. Ivy threw sulphuric acid in Mabel's face and was sentenced to eighteen months in prison at the Berkshire Assizes. Ivy was around five months pregnant when she began her prison sentence.

Petitions were immediately sent to the Home Office following Ivy's sentencing in January 1924, asking for arrangements to be made to ensure that she would be removed to an outside hospital entirely disassociated from penal life for one month to allow for the birth and her recovery. The petition claimed to be signed by 53,000 people in support of Ivy's family and was sent to Home Secretary Arthur Henderson from the Reading Trades Council. It stressed that their chief concern in sending it was focused on the unborn child rather than Ivy herself. The petition stressed sympathy with Mrs Jones, the victim of Ivy's crime, but added that the child too was blameless in the crime.[66] Reporting upon the petition, one newspaper entreated the Home Secretary to show mercy to the unborn child, lamenting, 'can there be any handicap in this life more cruel than the dreadful fact of being brought into the world by a convicted parent behind prison walls?' The article continued by stating that English law forbids a child under seven being sentenced to prison under any circumstances, as children cannot judge between right and wrong and must therefore not be exposed to the stigma of life behind bars.[67]

The Criminal Justice Administration Act of 1914 enabled the Home Secretary to order that a prisoner might be taken to an outside hospital if they could not be adequately treated in the prison. However, the usual reasons for removal on the grounds of health, namely urgency and necessity, were not believed to be readily applicable to confinements, although there was some precedent for releasing women early on the medical grounds of pregnancy. The evidence gathered in this research suggests that in the majority of cases such release was granted if the woman's expected date of confinement coincided with her release date, to avoid her being detained beyond her original sentence. This appears to be particularly evident in cases of advanced pregnancy where women had been sentenced to short sentences, usually of less than three months. In 1904 Durham Prison reported to the Prison Commissioners that in the preceding year they had released ten women on account of advanced pregnancy, all but one of whom had been sentenced to less than one month in prison, and it was believed to be expedient to release them early, in some cases after only a matter of days. In the same year Holloway Prison reported eleven such cases.[68]

In the two years prior to March 1924, forty babies were born in the eighteen prisons that held female prisoners. However, an additional twenty-seven women were discharged on account of their advanced stage of pregnancy, because if their confinement took place within prison it was likely that they would be detained beyond the term of their original sentence.[69] In these cases it is clear that early release was more dependent upon the length of the original sentence and the timing of the woman's confinement, as opposed to more detailed examinations of her health or the issue of the stigma that many feared would be attached to a child born in prison. The medical report which would be completed by the prison doctor when pregnancy was identified would be sent to the Home Office only if it was deemed probable that giving birth during her sentence would mean a woman was detained longer than her original sentence.

In Ivy Cusden's case, despite it being clear that her sentence was long enough to cover the remainder of her pregnancy and her confinement, the public interest in the case prompted the Home Office to seek regular reports on her condition from Holloway's doctor. Shortly after her committal, he reported that he had every reason to expect a normal confinement. He added that Ivy had been placed in the lying-in ward of the prison hospital upon reception so that her weight, food intake and sleeping patterns could be closely monitored.[70] It was the usual practice that women would be moved to the prison hospital in the final month of pregnancy, if at all. Ivy was most likely placed there from the outset of her sentence due to the intense interest her case had generated. In March the *Daily Mail* reported that the petition was still under consideration by Home Secretary Henderson, due to the serious nature of Ivy's crime, but expressed hope that, although Ivy was reportedly being properly cared for in prison, the focus would be upon her child.[71] This is a crucial point to note because, while some of the correspondence sent to the Home Office mentioned how Ivy herself was anxious at the thought of having her baby in prison, the calls for mercy in the form of granting her temporary release for her confinement were centred on the innocent child, as opposed to the mother who had committed the crime. This marked a difference from Florence Osborne's case, where, although the health of her child was mentioned, it was Florence's own mental state that was more greatly highlighted. In April, the Home Secretary's office formally responded to the petition from Reading to state that the Home Secretary had no power to release Ivy temporarily in order that her child might be born outside of the prison and, after careful consideration of her case and the medical reports, he had concluded that it would be neither justified nor consistent with the public good to recommend the great reduction of her sentence which would be required to ensure her discharge before her confinement.[72] Ivy gave birth to a daughter on 20 May, with the mother and child reported to be doing well and released at the expiration her sentence.[73]

A case that occurred in the early 1930s reignited the debate not only about prison births but also about the treatment of expectant mothers by the criminal justice system. Olive Kathleen Wise was sentenced to death at the Old Bailey in January 1931 for the murder of her nine-month-old son Reginald. Olive had separated from her husband in 1928, and he had left her to support their three children. She later met Alfred Wheatley, with whom she had Reginald. Alfred stated his intention to marry Olive if she could prove that she was free to marry. However, in the meantime Olive had struggled to feed and care for her children. On Christmas Eve of 1930 she went to her neighbour's house and claimed that she had killed Reginald by placing him in the oven. He was found to have died from coal gas poisoning. At her trial one of the detectives in the case stated that when she was arrested, she stated that she 'must have been mad to do it'.[74] Olive was found guilty and, despite the jury's recommendation to mercy, she was sentenced to death. However, Olive was around eight months pregnant at the time and thus, on her defence counsel's application, the judge stayed her execution and a jury of matrons was empanelled to ascertain her condition. It was reported that it had been many years since a jury of matrons had been empanelled at the Old Bailey.[75]

Since the thirteenth century, women could be empanelled to sit on a jury of matrons. Their purpose was to discern whether a woman convicted of a capital offence was 'quick with child', that is, whether the child had started to move in the womb. If a woman successfully 'pled the belly' her execution would be stayed until after she had given birth. In many cases, the original death sentence would then be commuted to either transportation to America and, later, Australia in the eighteenth and early nineteenth century, or imprisonment thereafter. Kevin Crosby notes that there had long been a distaste among judges in criminal cases for formally sentencing a pregnant woman to death, knowing that the sentence would not be carried out.[76] Although rare, these cases continued into the early twentieth century.

Demands were made from several quarters for Olive's immediate reprieve. Mr Valentine La Touche McEntee, the Labour MP for Walthamstow, petitioned the Home Secretary on her behalf and stated his view that 'it is really barbarous to sentence her at all, and if the law is as it appears to be from the action of the judge, then some amendment of the law ought to be made so that no woman could be sentenced until after she has given birth'.[77] Olive's capital sentence was commuted to penal servitude for life on 19 January 1931, three days after her original conviction.[78] This case is interesting for several reasons. It not only brought into sharp focus the need to change legal practices surrounding the treatment of pregnant women convicted of capital crimes but also reignited debates about the broader treatment by the criminal justice system of pregnant women and those who gave birth while in prison.

Olive's case prompted Edith Picton-Turbervill, MP for The Wrekin in Shropshire, to introduce a Private Member's Bill to abolish the death penalty for pregnant women.[79] During the second reading of the Bill, which would eventually become the Sentence of Death (Expectant Mothers) Act of 1931, Lord Sankey, the Lord Chancellor, cited the case of Olive Wise as an example where the judge and all present had to go through the trying ordeal of formally sentencing the woman to death even though everyone in the court knew the sentence would not be carried out. He labelled this as a 'solemn farce' that brought no benefit to the administration of the law.[80] The Act ended the formal recording of the death sentence against pregnant women convicted of capital crimes. Where a woman convicted of an offence punishable by death was found in accordance with the Act to be pregnant, the sentence passed against her would instead be penal servitude for life. The Act also abandoned the empanelling of a jury of twelve matrons to ascertain whether a woman was pregnant. Instead, this would be decided by the jury in the case, based on expert medical evidence put before them.[81]

Following the commuting of Olive's death sentence to one of penal servitude for life, public interest in her case did not wane. Instead, interest in the case refocused on the question of whether she should be forced to give birth behind bars. Mr McEntee asked the Home Secretary whether he would consider arranging for the removal of Olive to a private maternity home for the period of her confinement and whether he would also consider her early release from prison so that her child would not have the stigma of association with the criminal justice system. Mr Short, the Under-Secretary to the Home Office, answered that there was no power to order this removal, as proper provision was made in the prison for her necessary care.[82]

Olive gave birth to twins, a boy and a girl, on 6 February 1931 in Holloway Prison hospital. Miss Madeline Crisp, Olive's sister, told reporters that she and their father had been informed of the birth by the prison and intended to visit the following week. She added, 'my father was naturally a little disappointed that the children were born in the prison hospital' after all the efforts that had been made to have Olive removed.[83] The twins were baptised by the prison chaplain days later.[84] Mrs Clynes, the wife of the Home Secretary, visited Olive in Holloway the week after the birth. She described how Olive was 'in a bright, cheerful room with about six other women' and attested that 'she is having every attention' to meet her needs.[85] However, this still did not end calls for Olive's release.

Petitions were continually sent to the Home Office asking for her release, in a campaign led by McEntee and Olive's family. On 12 February 1931, only days after the birth of her babies in Holloway, Mr Greenwood, the Minister of Health, was asked in Parliament about Olive's plight in the months before she committed her crime. It was noted how Olive had previously been in receipt of indoor and outdoor relief but had been unable to obtain help in the days leading up to Reginald's death, which had prompted her to take such desperate action.[86] Alongside the circumstances surrounding the commission of her crime, the prospect of a better life thereafter was also levied in support of petitions for Olive's early release from prison, namely that Alfred Wheatley had visited Olive in prison and stated his intention to marry her and help to care for the babies.

Olive was released from prison in July 1932, having served seventeen months of her life sentence.[87] In September 1932, Olive married Alfred Wheatley in the Stratford Register Office. The *Sheffield*

Daily Telegraph reported upon comments made by McEntee, who described how their romance and Alfred's determination to marry Olive had only been strengthened by the 'terrible ordeal' of her imprisonment and the birth of the twins behind bars.[88] Of course Olive was not unique in that the length of her prison sentence would inevitably mean she would give birth in prison. Similarly, hers was not the only case to attract the attention of the Home Secretary and require their office to justify a refusal to temporarily release women to give birth, on account that there was maternity provision in female prisons. However, the decision to release her after only seventeen months of a sentence of penal servitude for life was likely swayed by the wide publicity and attention that her case generated, and her place within public and parliamentary debate about the treatment of pregnant women convicted of capital crimes. Some of the coverage of the case was also shaped not by the crime Olive had committed but by the dire circumstances that had prompted it. In turn, reports on efforts to first prevent Olive's giving birth in prison and then secure her early release centred on the fact that Alfred wanted to marry her, and her twins, despite their prison birth, would have a respectable family unit.

Prison births: should the mother have the last word?

During the Second World War, the number of pregnant women released early on medical grounds increased. Although officially this was a practice intended to prevent women being detained beyond the expiration of their sentence, it may also have been the case that the shortages of staff and provisions in prisons during the war played a part in the decision-making process. In 1943 the figure was sixty-four women, as compared to the pre-war figure of twenty-eight in 1938.[89] The figure remained high in the wake of the war as conditions in women's prisons occupied a greater place on the agenda of the prison service and again prompted extensive outside commentary. Despite the efforts to improve the education and training of women in domesticity and mothercraft, detailed in Chapter 3, the contentious question of whether babies should be born in prison at all continued to rage on. Similar to earlier cases and debates, a reading of government and public discourse reveals that it was often the case that the standard of medical care in prisons was not at the centre of criticism of prison births. Rather, it was the issue of the right of the child not to be stigmatised. However, in the mid-twentieth century an additional question dominated the argument, namely the extent to which women in prison had the right to choose the conditions in which they gave birth.

In April 1948 Tom Garnett, a city councillor and Justice of the Peace in Sheffield, asked the question, 'how long will the British public tolerate the brutal system under which children, born of mothers undergoing a prison sentence, are condemned to go through life carrying the stigma of their place of birth attached to them?'[90] In June 1948 in the House of Lords, Lord Llewelin argued for an extension to the Sentence of Death (Expectant Mothers) Act of 1931 to now also allow the Home Secretary the power to release a pregnant woman from prison for the duration of her pregnancy so that the child was not born in prison; then, if necessary, the woman could be taken back to prison.[91] In answer to these debates, Section 60 of the 1948 Criminal Justice Act empowered the Home Secretary to authorise the temporary release to an outside hospital or maternity home of any pregnant woman who wished for her confinement to take place outside the prison. It would be the practice for women to be asked well before their due date whether they would prefer to be removed to an outside hospital so that suitable arrangements could be made.

Despite heaping high praise on the facilities in place to care for expectant mothers and mothers with babies in Holloway, Mary Size commented that, following 1948 Act, the majority of women were glad of the opportunity to save their children from the stigma of a prison birth.[92] This is interesting, as it was the birth itself that was the source of stigma, despite acknowledgements of the beneficial health care and provisions to be found in the prison. However, there continued to be some women who preferred to give birth within the confines of the prison. This prompted intense debate. A report from Manchester's Strangeways Prison detailed that since the Criminal Justice Act had come into operation, eleven women had stated their preference to remain within the prison for the birth of their baby, as they 'had confidence in the prison staff'. In response to this, a meeting of Manchester City Magistrates in January 1949 stressed their determination to persuade the Home Secretary to take more urgent steps to prevent prison births.[93] In a letter to Home Secretary Chuter Ede in September 1948, Jean Hardy, secretary of the Farnworth Labour Women's Section, stated their belief that no baby should be born in prison. The letter stressed that 'we are not concerned at this point with the comfort of the mothers and contend that all women should be removed from the prison precincts for the period of their confinement, irrespective of their desires'.[94]

When refuting the argument that the stigma was obviated by the prison address not appearing on the birth certificate, Manchester Councillor Arthur Donovan recounted the case of a Manchester businessman who went to visit his birthplace, listed as No. 1 and 3 Southall Street, and how this was actually the address of Strangeways Prison. Donovan stated the man had been 'mentally wrecked by the news' of his start in life.[95] He told the Manchester Justices' Annual Meeting in January 1950 that it was wrong for children to be born in prison and questioned the legality of a mother having the right to decide. An article reporting upon the meeting similarly asked the question 'should the mother have the last word?'[96]

One of the most significant problems facing mothers in prison, identified in Phyllis Baunach's research, is the question of loss. Whether women have positive relationships with their children or strained ones, a prison sentence engenders feelings of loss and failure. Baunach explores the importance of the belief that this loss and separation from their children is a consequence of their own behaviour in shaping feelings of ostracism and failure among mothers in prison.[97] Heather Cahill posits the history of maternity care as one in which women's ability to exercise real choice and make informed decisions is limited, and where questions of medical intervention and legal regulation have undermined the autonomy of mothers.[98] Despite being based upon research into more recent experiences of maternal imprisonment, their arguments are valid when considering the historic issue of maternal choice and agency in prison, especially in relation to the question of whether mothers in prison retained any right to make the choice of where they gave birth. This question was not only considered from a medical perspective but was also steeped in social and moral concerns.

In February 1949, Home Secretary Chuter Ede explained to the House of Commons that he was not prepared to take steps to force all women to give birth in an outside hospital, as the prison hospitals were fully equipped to provide all necessary care and attention in maternity cases as well as having experienced doctors, nurses and midwives on hand to attend all confinements. He added that it was 'natural that some expectant mothers had come to trust these people and did not want to go outside', and thus 'to insist upon their removal from prison would, besides inflicting hardship, have a bad effect on the mother's mental and physical health or prove detrimental to the child'.[99]

An article in *The People* in January 1949 lamented the 'sentimental campaign' against prison births. It also quoted Dame Lilian Barker, the first woman to become Assistant Commissioner of Prisons, who stated in relation to Holloway Prison that 'some women are determined to have their babies in a prison hospital. And why not? The medical attention there is the best in the world.' The women were supplied with advice, baby clothes, cots and toys and trained in babycraft. Barker added, 'can you blame the poor girl who has no hope of getting a hospital bed, who cannot afford a nursing home and who cannot provide for her new baby, for committing a crime to have her child in prison?'[100] We must exercise caution against taking comments such as these entirely at face value, as the prison authorities themselves were anxious to avoid public criticism of conditions in prisons. In addition, previous chapters have shown how the standard of care given to women in prison continued to vary considerably; there were cases throughout the period of very poor standards and a lack of any consistent practices, which resulted in pregnant women being locked up in isolation for hours at a time and giving birth in their cells. Nevertheless, they do reveal the continuation of a historic question facing the prison system, namely, whether having maternity provision in place in prisons could ever obviate the stigma of a prison birth upon the child.

It is clear that while the Act of 1948 did not end the practice of women giving birth in prison, it was a notable shift in policy and led to a distinct decline of prison births as the 1950s progressed. For example, in the year preceding the Act, of one hundred women imprisoned during their confinement, twenty-two were granted early release and three were temporarily removed on medical grounds, but seventy-five gave birth in prison.[101] However, in March 1951 Ede noted in the House of Commons that since the Act came into force in December 1948, fifteen babies had been born in prison in

England and Wales compared to ninety-two confinements taking place in outside hospitals.[102] Despite petitions against prison births from several quarters and a decline in prison births in practice, the government was reluctant to change the legislation to ensure that there were no prison births at all, as politicians such as Ede were aware not only of the potential difficulties of finding suitable hospital places for the women but also of the possibility that they could not be removed in time, especially if labour came on quickly or prematurely, which could result in greater censure on the prison system.

Joan Henry served an eight-month sentence in Holloway and Askham Grange in the early 1950s, during which she spent time in Holloway's hospital for treatment on her foot. She recounted her observations of the experiences of some of the other women she met in the hospital. Her account demonstrates that pregnant women expressed different desires for the conditions in which they would give birth. Pat, a woman whom she described as a prostitute and as having an 'aggressive and difficult personality', wanted to have her baby in the prison hospital.[103] There were other cases where women had expressed a desire to give birth in an outside hospital and arrangements had been made. However, the date of their confinement was miscalculated, either by the prison doctors or due to irregular menstruation, or they went into premature labour. In the early 1950s Betty, a young woman confined in Holloway's hospital due to advanced pregnancy, went into labour earlier than she or the prison staff had expected. One night, when locked in the ward with fellow prisoners, Betty began to cry out in pain. Joan Henry rang the bell to alert the attention of the night sister, who examined Betty and found it to be too late to transfer her to an outside hospital. She gave birth to a baby boy in Holloway's labour room.[104] Issues of logistics and consistent practices in place in maternity cases continued, and still continue today, to impact upon the ability of mothers in prison to exercise control over the conditions in which they gave birth.

The decline in prison births in the early 1950s was due to a combination of factors, including maternal choice and more consistent arrangements being made by prisons themselves to facilitate the removal of women to outside hospitals. By the end of the Second World War, the majority of births in the community took place in a hospital for the first time, reaching 63.7 per cent of all births by

1954.[105] Angela Davis has demonstrated that, within the spheres of pregnancy and childbirth, there was no one unified position among general practitioners (GPs), midwives and other practitioners about best practice for mothers.[106] In addition, with the introduction of the National Health Service in 1948, it initially seemed as though the role of GPs would be central to maternal care. Despite this, by the 1950s hospitals had become the locus for childbirth and antenatal care.[107] Although prison births declined significantly as the 1950s progressed, they did not end entirely. Despite the intention that women will give birth in outside hospitals, today there continue to be babies born inside prisons if mothers are not transferred to hospital outside on time. The standard of mothers' care, including their treatment in outside hospitals as well as when they return to prison, with and in some cases without their babies, continues to garner intense debate.

Conclusion

Should babies be born in prison? Have prisons ever been, and could they ever be, suitable places for the care of expectant mothers and their infants? These are questions that have faced the modern prison system since its creation. While they evolved with changing circumstances and policy shifts throughout the century following the 1850s, they remained without definitive answers. The commentary by Griffiths quoted at the beginning of this chapter highlighted the contradictions that permeated debates about prison births and the suitability of the prison environment for mothers and their children. Those within the prison system questioned whether babies should be born there at all, at the same time justifying the provisions in place for their care. Prison staff, administrators and external commentators stressed the role motherhood could play in offsetting the criminal tendencies of those who walked through the prison gates pregnant and with young infants, while also lamenting their potential to negatively influence them.

The chapter has demonstrated that there was not a clear dichotomy between the arguments for and against prison births. A deeper examination of the material gathered reveals that it was not the case that prison births were consistently opposed on moral grounds but justified on medical grounds or vice versa. Instead, the requirements of containing this distinct group of inmates prompted debate interleaved with questions of discipline, care, health, supervision and choice. There were those who vehemently opposed on the grounds of the stigma to the child and the danger of its moral contagion, but did not address, or in some cases dismissed, the issues of separation and choice for the mothers themselves. Others ardently defended provisions in place in prisons to care for this group of inmates but complained of the pressures this could place on their already stretched resources and the impact their presence could have on the efficacy of the disciplinary requirements of the institution. Some pointed to the role the prison could play in offering care and regulation of criminal mothers which was not likely available elsewhere, while questioning the potentially negative impact on prison babies and the disruption of a system striving for uniformity.

By the end of the period under examination here, women were predominantly transferred to outside hospitals for the birth of their babies. As the second half of the twentieth century progressed, Mother and Baby Units (MBUs) replaced prison crèches as the part of these penal institutions reserved for the containment of mothers and their children. There are currently MBUs in six English women's prisons. They are a separate part of the prison, enabling women to have their children with them in prison. Women need to apply for entry to the MBU and each application is considered by a board. MBUs usually have accommodation for up to twelve prisoners, the intention being that, following the birth of their babies in an outside hospital, women will be able to be accommodated with their babies up to the age of eighteen months. However, there are still instances of women giving birth alone in their cells due to the historic logistical and practical challenges and inconsistences of their care.

Notes

1 Major Arthur Griffiths, 'In Wormwood Scrubs Prison', in George Sims (ed.), *Living London: Its work and its play, its humour and its pathos, its sights and its scenes*, Vol. III (London: Cassell, 1903), pp. 126–131, p. 127.

2 Griffiths, 'In Wormwood Scrubs Prison', p. 126.

3. Griffiths, 'In Wormwood Scrubs Prison', p. 127.
4. For select key works see Jane Humphries, 'Care and cruelty in the workhouse: Children's experiences of residential poor relief in eighteenth- and nineteenth-century England', in Nigel Goose and Katrina Honeyman (eds), *Childhood and child labour in industrial England: Diversity and agency, 1750–1914* (London: Routledge, 2013), pp. 115–134; Alysa Levene, *The childhood of the poor: Welfare in eighteenth-century London* (Basingstoke: Palgrave Macmillan, 2012); Lydia Murdoch, *Imagined orphans: Poor families, child welfare, and contested citizenship in London* (New Brunswick: Rutgers University Press, 2006).
5. Olwen Purdue, 'Nineteenth-century NIMBYs, or what the neighbour saw? Poverty, surveillance, and the boarding out of Poor Law children in late nineteenth-century Belfast', *Family & Community History*, 23:2 (2020), 119–135, https://doi.org/10.1080/14631180.2020.1920719, p. 120.
6. Rachel Bennett, 'Bad for the health of the body, worse for the health of the mind: Female responses to imprisonment in England, 1853–1869', *Social History of Medicine*, 34:2 (2021), 532–552, https://doi.org/10.1093/shm/hkz066.
7. For an example of this letter see LMA, WA/G/007, Minute Book, December 1852–November 1855, 9 September 1854.
8. Henry Mayhew and John Binny, *The criminal prisons of London and scenes of prison life* (London: Griffin, Bohn and Company, 1862), p. 191.
9. Helen Johnston, 'Imprisoned mothers in Victorian England, 1853–1900: Motherhood, identity and the convict prison', *Criminology & Criminal Justice*, 19:2 (2019), 215–231, https://doi.org/10.1177/1748895818757833, p. 222.
10. LMA, WA/G/P/1866/001, House of Correction Westminster Regulations and Rules, 1866, p. 42.
11. *Female life in prison, by a prison Matron, Vol. II* (London: Hurst and Blackett Publishers, 1862), p. 10.
12. Cicely McCall, *They always come back* (London: Methuen & Co., 1938), p. 107.
13. LMA, WA/G/006, Minute Book, September 1850–December 1852, 1 February 1851.
14. Purdue, 'Nineteenth-century NIMBYs', p. 122.
15. Lara Marks, 'Medical care for pauper mothers and their infants: Poor Law provision and local demand in East London. 1870–1929', *Economic History Review*, 46:3 (1993), 518–542, https://doi.org/10.1111/j.1468-0289.1993.tb01347.x, p. 540.

16 Stephen Hobhouse and A. Fenner Brockway, *English prisons today: Being the report of the Prison System Enquiry Committee* (London: Longmans, Green and Co., 1922), p. 15.
17 'Mother sent to gaol', *Daily Herald* (25 February 1936).
18 LMA, WA/G/006, Minute Book, September 1850–December 1852, 9 November 1850.
19 LRO, 347 MAG 1/2/2, Minutes of Visiting Justices 1870–1878, 24 October 1874.
20 Griffiths, 'In Wormwood Scrubs Prison', p. 127.
21 Mary Size, *Prisons I have known* (London: George Allen & Unwin, 1957), p. 72.
22 McCall, *They always come back*, p. 107.
23 William Sullivan, 'A note on the influence of maternal inebriety on the offspring', *Journal of Mental Science*, 45 (1899), 489–503, p. 492.
24 Lucia Zedner, *Women, crime and custody in Victorian England* (Oxford: Oxford University Press, 1991), p. 220.
25 Sullivan, 'A note on the influence of maternal inebriety', p. 496.
26 Annesley Kenealy, 'Prison babies: Holloway's comfortable provision for its child population', *Daily Mirror* (28 November 1905), p. 11.
27 Hobhouse and Brockway, *English prisons today*, p. 347.
28 Hobhouse and Brockway, *English prisons today*, p. 17.
29 Hobhouse and Brockway, *English prisons today*, p. 17.
30 LRO, 347 MAG 1/2/2, Minutes of Visiting Justices 1870–1878, 25 January 1872.
31 Report of the Departmental Committee on the Education and Moral Instruction of Prisoners in Local and Convict Prisons (London: 1896), p. 120.
32 Kenealy, 'Prison babies', p. 11.
33 Henry Maudsley, 'Review of female life in prison', *Journal of Mental Science*, 9 (1863), 69–87.
34 W.D. Morrison, *Crime and its causes* (London: Swan Sonnenschein, 1891), p. 152.
35 Morrison, *Crime and its causes*, p. 158.
36 Henry Mayhew and John Binny, *The criminal prisons of London and scenes of prison life* (London: Griffin, Bohn and Company, 1862), p. 189, p. 191.
37 Mayhew and Binny, *The criminal prisons of London*, p. 475.
38 Constance Lytton and Jane Warton, *Prisons and prisoners: Some personal experiences* (London: William Heinemann, 1914), p. 103.
39 Report from the Departmental Committee on Prisons (London: 1895), p. 46.
40 Quoted in Zedner, *Women, crime and custody*, p. 147.

41 Hobhouse and Brockway, *English prisons today*, p. 347.
42 Phyllis Jo Baunach, *Mothers in prison* (New York: Transaction Publishers, first edition 1983, this edition 2020); Lucy Baldwin (ed.), *Mothering justice: Working with mothers in criminal and social justice settings* (Hampshire: Waterside Press, 2015).
43 Susan Willis Fletcher, *Twelve months in an English prison* (New York: Charles T. Dillingham, 1884), p. 353.
44 Bennett, 'Bad for the health of the body', pp. 546–547.
45 Kenealy, 'Prison babies', p. 11.
46 Hobhouse and Brockway, *English prisons today*, p. 17.
47 'Baby will be born in prison', *Gloucester Citizen* (25 July 1939), p. 9.
48 Ginger Frost, *Illegitimacy in English law and society, 1860–1930* (Manchester: Manchester University Press, 2016), p. 50.
49 Isabella Tod, 'Boarding-out of pauper children', *Journal of the Statistical and Social Inquiry Society of Ireland*, 7:5 (1878), 293–299, p. 297.
50 Birmingham Library, PS/B/4/5/1/2, Birmingham Petty Sessions 1896–1906, letter from Mr Stone, Chairman of the Visiting Justices Committee to the Visiting Justices, 11 April 1896.
51 LRO, 347 MAG 1/2/2, Minutes of Visiting Justices 1870–1878, 24 October 1874.
52 Neil Davie, *Tracing the criminal: The rise of scientific criminology in Britain, 1860–1918* (Oxford: The Bardwell Press, 2005); Victor Bailey, *The rise and fall of the rehabilitative ideal, 1895–1970* (Abingdon: Routledge, 2019).
53 See in particular Zedner, *Women, crime and custody*. For case studies of female offenders who entered into cycles of recidivism and the types of crimes they committed see Lucy Williams and Barry Godfrey, *Criminal women 1850–1920: Researching the lives of Britain's female offenders* (Barnsley: Pen & Sword, 2018). For an early twentieth-century commentary on the issue of female inebriety and the family see Mary Scharlieb, 'Alcoholism in relation to women and children', in T.N. Kelnack (ed.) *The drink problem of today in its medico-sociological aspects* (London: Methuen & Co., first published 1907, revised edition 1916), pp. 128–156.
54 Mary Carpenter, *Our convicts, Vol. II* (London: Longman, 1864), p. 266.
55 Russell P. Dobash, R. Emerson Dobash and Sue Gutteridge, *The imprisonment of women* (Oxford: Basil Blackwell, 1986), p. 104.
56 Carpenter, *Our convicts, Vol. II*, p. 266.
57 'The convict nursery at Brixton', *Cheltenham Chronicle* (1 July 1856), p. 4.
58 Hobhouse and Brockway, *English prisons today*, p. 346.

59 Quoted in Caitlin Davies, *Bad girls: A history of rebels and renegades* (London: John Murray, 2018), p. 269.
60 Hobhouse and Brockway, *English prisons today*, p. 11.
61 'Mothers appreciate their treatment', *Western Daily Press* (2 August 1937), p. 4.
62 Florence Ethel Osborne, Reference Number t18920307-337, oldbaileyonline.org.
63 'Case of Florence Osborne', *Lakes Chronicle and Reporter* (22 April 1892), p. 2.
64 *British Medical Journal*, 16 April 1892, p. 830.
65 'Release of Mrs Osborne', *Henley Advertiser* (7 May 1892), p. 2.
66 TNA, HO 144/3982, Prisons and prisoners: Childbirth in prison. Memorandum on existing practice and the arguments for temporary removal 1924, Ivy Cusden petition, 26 March 1924.
67 'Ivy Cusden', *John Bull* (9 February 1924), p. 3.
68 Report of the Commissioners of Prisons and the Directors of Convict Prisons for the year ended 31 March 1904 (London: 1904), p. 157.
69 TNA, HO 144/3982, Prisons and prisoners: Childbirth in prison. Memorandum on existing practice.
70 TNA, HO 144/3982, Prisons and prisoners: Childbirth in prison. Memorandum on existing practice …, statement from the Medical Officer at Holloway Prison, March 1924.
71 'Ivy Cusden petition', *Daily Mail* (25 March 1924), p. 4.
72 TNA, HO 144/3982, Prisons and Prisoners: Childbirth in prison. Memorandum on existing practice …, letter from John Anderson, Undersecretary of State, to G.W. Goodwin, 1 April 1924.
73 'Ivy Cusden', *Daily Mail* (21 May 1924), p. 2.
74 'Trial of Olive Kathleen Wise', *Leeds Mercury* (27 December 1930), p. 4.
75 'Olive Wise', *Dundee Courier* (17 January 1931), p. 4.
76 Kevin Crosby, 'Abolishing juries of matrons', *Oxford Journal of Legal Studies*, 39:2 (2019), 259–284, https://doi.org/10.1093/ojls/gqy037, p. 276.
77 'Olive Wise', *Taunton Courier and Western Advertiser* (21 January 1931), p. 6.
78 TNA, CRIM 1/534, Defendant: Wise, Olive Kathleen. Charge: Murder. Session: January 1931. For Olive's pardon see CRIM 1/584/99, Pardon: Wise, Olive Kathleen.
79 Crosby, 'Abolishing juries of matrons', p. 279.
80 Hansard HL Deb. 18 June 1931, vol. 81, col. 292–4.
81 TNA, HO 45/24517, Capital Punishment: Sentence of Death (Expectant Mothers) Act 1931.

82 Hansard HC Deb. 23 January 1931, vol. 247, col. 511–2W.
83 'Olive Wise gives birth in prison', *Portsmouth Evening News* (9 February 1931), p. 8.
84 Davies, *Bad girls*, p. 270.
85 'Visited in prison by Home Secretary's wife', *Taunton Courier and Western Advertiser* (18 February 1931), p. 4.
86 Hansard HL Deb. 12 February 1931, vol. 248, col. 611.
87 TNA, HO 144/17929, Criminal Cases: Wise, Olive Kathleen, convicted at Central Criminal Court on 13 January 1931.
88 'Romance that began when woman was in prison', *Sheffield Daily Telegraph* (5 September 1932), p. 8.
89 Report of the Commissioners of Prisons for the year 1952 (London: 1953), p. 99.
90 TNA, RG 48/1882, Registration of births occurring in prison 1948–51, Tom Garnett, 'Removing the stigma', *The Observer* (22 April 1948), p. 5.
91 TNA, RG 48/1882, Registration of births occurring in prison 1948–51, extract from a House of Lords debate on prison births, 15 June 1948.
92 Size, *Prisons I have known*, p. 125.
93 'Magistrates urge: No prison babes', *Dundee Courier* (4 January 1949), p. 2.
94 TNA, HO 45/23580, Birth of children in prison 1924–1949, letter from Jean Hardy to Secretary of State's office, 4 September 1948.
95 'Prison births', *Daily Express* (4 January 1949), p. 3.
96 'Should the mother have the last word?', *Manchester Evening News* (2 January 1950), p. 4.
97 Baunach, *Mothers in prison*, p. 1.
98 Heather A. Cahill, 'Male appropriation and medicalisation of childbirth: An historical analysis', *Journal of Advanced Nursing*, 33:3 (2001), 334–342, https://doi.org/10.1046/j.1365-2648.2001.01669.x, p. 334.
99 TNA, HO 45/23580 Birth of children in prison 1924–1949, letter from J. Chuter Ede to Arthur Donovan, 19 December 1949.
100 TNA, PCOM 9/467, Births and infants in prison 1930–1949, Peter Forbes, 'Waste no pity on these babies who are born in prison', *The People* (30 January 1949).
101 TNA, HO 45/23580, Birth of children in prison 1924–1949, memorandum on prison births, 7 July 1948.
102 TNA, RG 48/1882, Registration of births occurring in prison 1948–1951, extract from a House of Commons debate on prison births, 1 March 1951.
103 Joan Henry, *Women in prison* (London: White Lion Publishers, first published 1952, this edition 1973), p. 56.

104 Henry, *Women in prison*, p. 91.
105 Angela Davis, 'Wartime women giving birth: Narratives of pregnancy and childbirth, Britain c. 1939–1960', *Studies in History and Philosophy of Biological and Biomedical Sciences*, 47:2 (2014), 257–266, https://doi.org/10.1016/j.shpsc.2013.11.007, p. 265.
106 Angela Davis, *Modern motherhood: Women and family in England, c. 1945–2000* (Manchester: Manchester University Press, 2012), p. 209.
107 Davis, *Modern motherhood*, p. 84.

Conclusion

Should pregnant women and mothers with babies be placed in prison? Is prison a place of safe custody for this distinct group? Can it ever be? Exploring the history of women's prisons, the study has illuminated how these questions challenged the modern prison system in the century following its inception. They were propelled to the forefront of government and public debate again in September 2019, following the death of a baby whose mother had given birth alone in her cell in HMP Bronzefield. Speaking at a debate about the issue in the House of Lords, Liberal Democrat peer Meral Hussein-Ece commented 'this Victorian incident of a woman giving birth alone in a prison cell illustrates the lack of care and support for pregnant women in prison, many of whom should not even be there'.[1] Labelling this case as 'Victorian' was intended to evoke images of an unyielding and uncaring system; crucially, one that was, or as Hussein-Ece alluded, should be, confined to a distant past. However, rather than being an isolated reversion to practices long since disappeared, the case is a stark demonstration of the historic and indelible challenges mothers and babies have posed to the criminal justice system.

In September 2021 a report was published by the Prison and Probation Ombudsman, Sue McAllister, following an independent investigation into the 2019 case. It identified several concerns about the care and management of pregnant women in prison and made a number of recommendations for the improvement of maternity services in the prison. The report found that the baby's mother, identified as Ms A, had been placed on 'extended observations' by the deputy head of health care. This meant she should have been checked by a nurse every morning, afternoon and evening and a minimum of twice during the night. However, this did not happen. Ms A rang the bell in her cell twice on the evening of 26 September. Although on one of the occasions an officer spoke to her via the cell call system, no nurse was called. The officer stated that they could not remember the conversation. Ms A's cell was checked later that evening and in the early hours of the morning, but the officers did not report anything out of the ordinary. On the morning of 27 September two other women prisoners alerted the on-duty officers that there was blood in Ms A's cell. It was discovered that she had given birth and her baby was unresponsive. Attempts to resuscitate the baby failed. The report's findings placed significant importance upon the staff in charge of Ms A not having a full history of her pregnancy or of her complex needs. More broadly, it labelled the maternity services at Bronzefield as 'outdated'.[2]

Undoubtedly significant, and founded in thorough investigation, the recommendations made in 2021 are perhaps best viewed not as a new departure in thinking about the imprisonment of pregnant women but as part of a wider narrative debating their custody and care. The tragic details of the case, the responses to it and the recommendations made thereafter have a long and contested history, one that continues to shape the justice system today. The Duchess of Bedford's 1919 landmark enquiry carried out in Holloway Prison was the first of its kind and placed maternity care in prison at its centre. A *History & Policy* article marking its centenary in 2019 demonstrated the longevity of several of the issues raised, including the conditions in which pregnant women are imprisoned and their access to specially trained maternity staff before, during and after the birth of their babies. It underlined how, despite the continued efforts of organisations and individuals to improve conditions, it is difficult to produce consistent and fully effective change.[3]

Reform organisations such as the Howard League and non-governmental organisations (NGOs) have campaigned for improvements in the conditions in which pregnant women and those with infants are imprisoned; provided evidence of the impact of imprisonment upon their physical and mental health; and made recommendations regarding the arrangements in place for women to regularly receive antenatal care and to ensure the safe delivery of their babies in hospital. In 1995 and 1996 cases of female prisoners being shackled during their labour prompted campaigns from within and beyond the prison system to end this practice. The National Childbirth Trust petitioned the Home Secretary, Michael Howard, to overturn the policy of handcuffing pregnant women during birth and supported a report made by the Howard League on the issue.[4] An article published by the Association for Improvements in the Maternity Services focused upon the case of a woman named Annette who gave birth in Whittington Hospital in 1996 in shackles and was placed in chains even when walking with her baby in her arms to a scan after the birth. The article encapsulated an issue that surrounds the conditions in which women give birth while under a prison sentence when it stated she had been sentenced to prison for stealing a handbag but 'she was not sentenced to public humiliation and degradation'.[5] Home Office minister Ann Widdecombe eventually announced in the House of Commons in 1996 that handcuffing during labour would cease. Although this was a key moment of change and improvement, it was acknowledged by reform organisations and charities alike that further significant improvements to maternity services in prisons were required.

The 1919 enquiry explicitly stated the belief that pregnant women in prison, 'whatever their delinquencies', and their babies, who were innocent in the eyes of the law, were entitled to proper care while in the charge of the state.[6] Today in the UK all mothers and babies have the right to high-quality maternity care. When babies are born to women in custody the midwives who attend them have a statutory duty of care which is governed by the Nursing and Midwifery Council's rules and codes of practice. However, following the case in HMP Bronzefield, the Royal College of Midwives released a position statement reiterating the need to ensure equality of care in prison, stating that 'maternal and new-born healthcare should not be compromised by imprisonment'.[7] Ethnographical research, including that carried out by Dr Laura Abbott and Birth Companions, a women's charity dedicated to tackling inequalities and disadvantage during pregnancy and birth, has identified continuing difficulties in ensuring this right to maternity care on a consistent basis for both mothers and babies. This is variously due to women having limited agency in prison, not having the ability to maintain regular contact with a midwife during their pregnancy and not being taken out to hospital in time when they go into labour.[8]

A position statement issued by the Royal College of Obstetricians and Gynaecologists in September 2021 recorded that the number of babies born to women serving prison sentences was sixty-seven in 2018–19 and that one in ten women delivered their baby before they reached a hospital. The statement recommended that maternity services located near to women's prisons should have a designated obstetric lead for the care of pregnant women in prison.[9] The investigation following the 2019 case in HMP Bronzefield concluded that all pregnancies in prison should be treated as high risk 'by virtue of the fact that the woman is locked behind a door for a significant amount of time' and there is likely to be a higher percentage of women who have experienced trauma and others who are fearful of engaging with any authorities, including maternity services. Among some of its main recommendations were that health care staff should have clinical expertise with pregnancy cases and that the midwifery services in prisons should be tailored to the specific needs of pregnant women in a custodial setting.[10]

By tracing how prison administrators, doctors, officers, reformers and prisoners themselves have attempted to untangle the exigencies of pregnancy and birth in prison, this study has illuminated this often overlooked aspect of England's penal history. It has illustrated the conflicts that were played out in a variety of ways between containment and care, health and discipline, and how these debates manifested in a skein of experiences for mothers in prison. When they walked through the prison gates, pregnant women and those with young infants were entering into physical spaces that were not designed for their accommodation. Uniformity was a key principle underpinning the rules and regulations decided upon at policy level, which very rarely considered the specific needs of mothers and their children, in some cases to the detriment of their physical and mental health. However, this study has shown that these women and their children were a consistent feature of life in prison and that the terms of their incarceration were negotiated and adapted by prison staff and prisoners alike.

Heather Cahill explored the concept of visibility in relation to developments in maternal health care and how the importance of the appearance of safety promoted by scientific medicine was reinforced by politicians needing to be seen to be contributing to the protection of future generations.[11] Prisons offer a unique means of exploring this idea of medical care being visible, and pose something of a paradox. Physically, they had the appearance of heavily controlled environments and the regimes intended left little room for variation. However, the different realities prompted a range of experiences for women facing childbirth and mothering in prison. These experiences were shaped by physical factors such as the prison structure, the cells and the prison hospitals in which women gave birth. However, they were also shaped by factors that are far less visible in official records and instead have to be unearthed and pieced together from the testimonies of those who lived, worked and were incarcerated in prisons.

The Duchess of Bedford's 1919 enquiry was a significant step on a long path towards the acknowledgement, or indeed making more visible, of the fact that maternity cases in prison required distinct consideration. It more explicitly recognised the changes required and made strides towards enacting them. The impetus for the enquiry was born out of notable cases, such as those of May McCririck and Ellen Sullivan, who had given birth alone in prison cells and whose cases had made more visible the inadequacies of the system for pregnant women. Their cases coincided with broader debates about health in prison and the staffing of women's prisons which fuelled an official and public desire to look behind Holloway's high walls and open up the regime within to a greater level of scrutiny. A notable area focused upon, which had in many ways been part of the very bedrock upon which the modern prison system was built, was the practice of cellular confinement and women spending long periods of time isolated from the hundreds of prisoners occupying the cells around them.

Defenders of the principle of separation in prison have historically pointed to its indispensability in encouraging prisoners to repent of their crimes and achieve meaningful reform before the expiration of their sentence. Others have focused upon the logistical benefits of separation as a means of more effectively separating the first-time offender from the recidivist, the older prisoner from the younger, and its importance in managing the discipline of an institution. However, the consequences of imprisoning pregnant women in isolation for long periods of time, often with limited means of communication, were highlighted by the 1919 report and used to express in the most explicit of terms that such a practice required revision. However, a century later the need to address the conditions in which pregnant women are confined were starkly illustrated again. Perhaps 'Victorian' due to the omnipresence of the principles of isolation and separation, the safe custody of this group poses a perennial rather than an 'outdated' question, one for which the twenty-first-century justice system is yet to find a definitive answer.

Although it was significant and led to, or hastened, notable developments in the provisions for mothers in prison, the path to change in the wake of the 1919 enquiry was not a linear one. The allocation of resources and staff, and indeed the strength of the impetus for change, was dependent on a myriad of factors in the decades that followed, including funding, circumstances in individual institutions, public opinion and the proclivities of governments towards the administration of the criminal justice system. In the second half of the twentieth century it was also dependent upon the building and rebuilding of prisons for women in attempts to address the constant questions about female imprisonment.

The Report of the Departmental Committee on Persistent Offenders in 1932 found that in the case of the great majority of women, 'prison buildings of the fortress type are unnecessary for purposes of security and the effect of such buildings seems to be in many respects worse than on men'.[12] At the time, Holloway was the principal penal institution for women. In 1938, three years into her role as Britain's first female Assistant Prison Commissioner, Lilian Barker proposed rebuilding Holloway as something of a 'prison in a park', on more open land and without the heavily secured fortress-type buildings. Although the plan did not progress and the question of rebuilding prisons for women was halted due to the outbreak of war in 1939, its proposal was nevertheless significant. It was developed further still by Joanna Kelley, appointed as Holloway's Governor in 1959. She advocated rebuilding Holloway in London. In 1966, following her appointment as Assistant Director of Prisons, with responsibility for women's prisons, plans were in place to rebuild the prison. Rock labelled the process of razing and reconstructing Holloway on the same site as unprecedented.[13]

In December 1968, Lord Stonham, Minister of State for Home Affairs, spoke of the Holloway Redevelopment Project. He declared that 'crime is almost exclusively a man's disease', and continued that women who committed serious and violent crimes were exceptional, posing the question of whether prisons were the correct places for them and, if so, how they could ensure their effective treatment.[14] His comments echoed those made a century before during debates about the deficiencies and eventual closure of Brixton Convict Prison in the 1860s, discussed in Chapter 1. Like Holloway, it was considered the main penal institution for women at the time. However, also like Holloway, the efficacy of its structure and regime in containing women, and in many cases their children, came in for continued scrutiny. Reports upon the progress of the new establishment at Woking following Brixton's closure in 1869 placed great emphasis on arrangements in place to care for the health of women in prison, which had been found deficient in the old system.[15]

Despite these intentions, a recent study concluded that addressing the health needs of the hundreds of women who came to prisons from different backgrounds, with complex needs, and indeed pregnant women and those with young infants, continued to be a 'vital spoke on the problematic wheel of female incarceration'.[16] The new establishment at Woking did not, and perhaps could not, address the perennial problems that continued to face prisons attempting to balance the maintenance of health with the management of penal discipline. Similarly, the intention of the newly built Holloway in the 1960s was to develop an entirely different approach to the imprisonment of women, one shaped by 'a humane environment for the treatment and rehabilitation of women and girls'.[17] Despite these intentions, the female prison estate continued to face criticism, including for the care offered to pregnant women and women with babies.

In 2015 the 'problematic wheel' of considerations when incarcerating women, including mothers, turned again when Chancellor George Osborne announced that Holloway would be closed and the land sold for housing development. He stated that in future women would serve their sentences 'in more humane conditions, better designed to keep them away from crime'.[18] The rhetoric again was reminiscent of previous reviews of the provisions in women's prisons. Despite criticisms of conditions and enquiries into medical care in the prison, Holloway was regarded as central in the criminal justice system for women, especially in terms of location, and its closure without provisions in place beyond the removal of female prisoners to other establishments across the country was criticised. Holloway's situation in London meant that women could be held closer to their families and communities and have access to agency support when they finished their sentence. One article spoke of the importance of location in terms of Holloway's visibility, reminding those who might see it daily of the impact of inequalities in society and of the need to redress the treatment of women by the criminal justice system. The building of luxury homes on the site was labelled as 'cruelly ironic'.[19] Holloway has been primarily a site of incarceration and suffering, but also one of medical care, a home as well as a site in the fight for the rights of women. Its long history of shaping the experiences of women reinforced arguments and petitions to repurpose the site for services supporting women. Currently, plans are ongoing for the demolition of the site and the building of almost a thousand new homes, which are intended to include affordable housing.

The history of motherhood in the modern prison system is a long and storied one, contested and complex, emotive and evocative. When they walked through the prison gates May McCririck, Ellen Sullivan, Annette and Ms A, like countless others, entered into a system not designed with the health needs of pregnant women at the forefront of consideration. Although each had her own individual story and set of experiences, their pregnancies and the conditions in which they gave birth to their babies were impacted upon by circumstances beyond their control and by perennial, historic and systemic questions that have been asked time and again of the criminal justice system in the past two centuries. Is prison a place for mothers and babies? Can it ever provide them with safe custody? Historically, it has been acknowledged by policy makers and reformers alike that mothers and babies are a distinct group with distinct needs. However, meeting the challenges of containing and caring for them has been dependent upon a range of logistical, ideological and political factors which impact upon the health outcomes for mothers and babies. Despite significant changes, policy shifts, major efforts by reform organisations and individuals and even the closure, building and rebuilding of establishments for women, perennial conundrums remain. So too does the question of if, when and how we can truly and completely confine 'Victorian' incidents to the prisons of the past.

Notes

1. Hannah Devlin, 'Revealed: 47 pregnant women in prisons in England and Wales', *The Guardian* (1 November 2019).
2. Independent investigation into the death of Baby A at HMP Bronzefield on 27 September 2019, Prisons and Probation Ombudsman (London: 2021), pp. 1–2.
3. Rachel Bennett, 'Maternity care reform in English prisons: A century of unanswered concerns', *History & Policy* (2019).
4. Wellcome Library [hereafter WL], SA/NCT/J/2/2/7, 'A cause to campaign for?' *New Generation*, 15 (1996), pp. 28–29.
5. WL, SA/WHL/1/28, Beverley A. Lawrence Beech, 'Shackled women', *AIMS Journal*, 7 (1995/96), p. 3.
6. TNA, PCOM 7/40, Report of committee presided over by Adeline, Duchess of Bedford to inquire into various matters concerning Holloway Prison, May 1919, p. 44.
7. Rebecca Gilroy, 'RCM demands equal maternity care for prisoners in wake of baby death', *Nursing Times* (November 2019).
8. For extensive research exploring the experiences of mothers in the criminal justice system see the collection of chapters in Lucy Baldwin (ed.), *Mothering justice: Working with mothers in criminal and social justice settings* (Hampshire: Waterside Press, 2015). For a discussion of the experiences of pregnant women see Laura Abbott's chapter 'A pregnant pause: Expecting in the prison estate', pp. 185–210. See also the findings and recommendations set out in Birth Companions' *Birth Charter for women in prisons in England and Wales* (March 2016).
9. Royal College of Obstetricians and Gynaecologists position statement: Maternity care for women in prison in England and Wales (September 2021), pp. 2–3.
10. Independent investigation into the death of Baby A at HMP Bronzefield on 27 September 2019, Prisons and Probation Ombudsman (London: 2021), p. 3.
11. Heather A. Cahill, 'Male appropriation and medicalization of childbirth: An historical analysis', *Journal of Advanced Nursing*, 33:3 (2001), 334–342, https://doi.org/10.1046/j.1365-2648.2001.01669.x, p. 340.
12. Report of the Departmental Committee on Persistent Offenders (London: 1932), p. 39.
13. Paul Rock, *Reconstructing a women's prison: The Holloway Redevelopment Project, 1968–88* (Oxford: Oxford University Press, 1996), p. 109.
14. Quoted in Rock, *Reconstructing a women's prison*, p. 86.

15 Report of the Directors of Convict Prisons for the year 1869 (London: 1870), p. 369.
16 Rachel Bennett, 'Bad for the health of the body, worse for the health of the mind: Female responses to imprisonment in England, 1853–1869', *Social History of Medicine*, 34:2 (2021), 532–552, https://doi.org/10.1093/shm/hkz066.
17 Rock, *Reconstructing a women's prison*, p. 120.
18 James Morris, 'Holloway Prison to close George Osborne announces', *Islington Gazette* (25 November 2015).
19 Sara Hyde, 'Closing Holloway Prison to make room for luxury flats isn't a triumph, George Osborne – it's just cruelly ironic', *Independent* (26 November 2015).

Bibliography

Primary sources
Library of Birmingham (LB)
PS/B/4/5/1/1, Birmingham Petty Sessions, 1878–1892.
PS/B/4/5/1/2, Birmingham Petty Sessions 1896–1906.
QS/B/23/3, Birmingham Quarter Sessions, October 1854–June 1859.

Hull History Centre (HHC)
TCGL, Draft Reports for the Gaol Committee 1856–57.
TCGL 15, Gaol Committee Report, 1851.

Liverpool Record Office (LRO)
347 JUS 4/1/2, Minutes of the Visiting Justices 1864–1870.
347 JUS 4/2/1, Rules and regulations for the government of Liverpool Prison 1855.
347 MAG 1/2/1, Minutes of the quarterly and annual meetings of the Visiting Justices of the Borough Gaol 1852–1864.
347 MAG 1/2/2, Minutes of the Visiting Justices 1870–1878.

London Metropolitan Archives (LMA)
CLA/003/ME/01/001, Matron's Journal 27 December 1933–23 November 1937.
WA/G/006, Minute Book of the Visiting Justices for the House of Correction, Westminster, September 1850–December 1852.
WA/G/007, Minute Book of the Visiting Justices for the House of Correction, Westminster, December 1852–November 1855.

Bibliography

WA/G/008, Minute Book of the Visiting Justices for the House of Correction, Westminster, November 1855–November 1857.
WA/G/009, Minute Book of the Visiting Justices for the House of Correction, Westminster, November 1857–January 1860.
WA/G/010, Minute Book of the Visiting Justices for the House of Correction, Westminster, February 1860–October 1862.
WA/G/011, Minute Book of the Visiting Justices for the House of Correction, Westminster, November 1862–October 1865.
WA/G/012, Minute Book of the Visiting Justices for the House of Correction, Westminster, November 1865–May 1868.
WA/G/013, Minute Book of the Visiting Justices for the House of Correction, Westminster, May 1868–April 1871.
WA/G/P/1866/001, House of Correction Westminster Regulations and Rules, 1866.

Modern Records Centre, University of Warwick (MRC)

MSS/67/4/24/4, Holloway Discharged Prisoners' Aid Society Annual Report, 1924.
MSS/67/4/24/5, Holloway Discharged Prisoners' Aid Society Annual Report, 1925.
MSS/67/4/24/6, Holloway Discharged Prisoners' Aid Society Annual Report, 1926.
MSS/67/4/24/7, Holloway Discharged Prisoners' Aid Society Annual Report, 1927.
MSS/67/4/24/8, Holloway Discharged Prisoners' Aid Society Annual Report, 1928.
MSS/67/4/24/9, Holloway Discharged Prisoners' Aid Society Annual Report, 1929.
MSS/67/4/24/10, Holloway Discharged Prisoners' Aid Society Annual Report, 1930.
MSS/67/4/24/11, Holloway Discharged Prisoners' Aid Society Annual Report, 1931.
MSS/67/4/24/12, Holloway Discharged Prisoners' Aid Society Annual Report, 1932.
MSS/67/4/24/13, Holloway Discharged Prisoners' Aid Society Annual Report, 1933.
MSS/67/4/24/14, Holloway Discharged Prisoners' Aid Society Annual Report, 1934.
MSS/67/4/24/15, Holloway Discharged Prisoners' Aid Society Annual Report, 1935.

MSS/67/4/24/16, Holloway Discharged Prisoners' Aid Society Annual Report, 1936.
MSS/67/4/24/17, Holloway Discharged Prisoners' Aid Society Annual Report, 1937.
MSS/67/4/24/18, Holloway Discharged Prisoners' Aid Society Annual Report, 1938.
MSS/67/4/24/19, Holloway Discharged Prisoners' Aid Society Annual Report, 1939.
MSS/67/4/24/20, Holloway Discharged Prisoners' Aid Society Annual Report, 1940.
MSS/67/4/24/21, Holloway Discharged Prisoners' Aid Society Annual Report, 1941.
MSS/67/4/24/22, Holloway Discharged Prisoners' Aid Society Annual Report, 1942.
MSS/67/4/24/23, Holloway Discharged Prisoners' Aid Society Annual Report, 1943.
MSS/67/4/24/24, Holloway Discharged Prisoners' Aid Society Annual Report, 1944.
MSS/67/4/24/25, Holloway Discharged Prisoners' Aid Society Annual Report, 1945.
MSS/67/4/24/26, Holloway Discharged Prisoners' Aid Society Annual Report, 1946.
MSS/67/4/24/27, Holloway Discharged Prisoners' Aid Society Annual Report, 1947.
MSS/67/4/24/28, Holloway Discharged Prisoners' Aid Society Annual Report, 1948.
MSS/67/4/24/29, Holloway Discharged Prisoners' Aid Society Annual Report, 1949.
MSS/67/4/24/30, Holloway Discharged Prisoners' Aid Society Annual Report, 1950.
MSS/67/4/24/31, Holloway Discharged Prisoners' Aid Society Annual Report, 1951.
MSS.67/4/24/32, Holloway Discharged Prisoners' Aid Society Annual Report 1 January 1952.
MSS.67/4/24/33, Holloway Discharged Prisoners' Aid Society Annual Report 1 January 1953.
MSS.67/4/24/34, Holloway Discharged Prisoners' Aid Society Annual Report 1 January 1954.
MSS.67/4/24/35, Fifty Second Annual Report of Holloway Discharged Prisoners' Aid Society, 1955.
MSS 121/CH/3/4/1, Lady Allen of Hurtwood speaking in Liverpool, 24 February 1945.

Bibliography 187

MSS 121/CH/3/4/2, Lady Allen of Hurtwood, 'An Alternative to Prison for Neglectful Mothers', 2 April 1945.

National Justice Museum, Nottingham

Prison Nursing Advisory Committee reports on prison visits, 1928–1954.

The National Archives, Kew (TNA)

CRIM 1/534, Defendant: Wise, Olive Kathleen. Charge: Murder. Session: January 1931.
CRIM 1/584/99, Pardon: Wise, Olive Kathleen.
HO 8/129, Quarterly returns of prisoners in hulks and convict prisons, September 1856.
HO 8/133, Quarterly returns of prisoners in hulks and convict prisons, September 1857.
HO 8/137, Quarterly returns of prisoners in hulks and convict prisons, September 1858.
HO 8/141, Quarterly returns of prisoners in hulks and convict prisons, September 1859.
HO 8/145, Quarterly returns of prisoners in hulks and convict prisons, September 1860.
HO 8/149, Quarterly returns of prisoners in hulks and convict prisons, September 1861.
HO 8/153, Quarterly returns of prisoners in hulks and convict prisons, September 1862.
HO 8/157, Quarterly returns of prisoners in hulks and convict prisons, September 1863.
HO 8/161, Quarterly returns of prisoners in hulks and convict prisons, September 1864.
HO 8/165, Quarterly returns of prisoners in hulks and convict prisons, September 1865.
HO 8/169, Quarterly returns of prisoners in hulks and convict prisons, September 1866.
HO 8/173, Quarterly returns of prisoners in hulks and convict prisons, September 1867.
HO 8/177, Quarterly returns of prisoners in hulks and convict prisons, September 1868.
HO 8/181, Quarterly returns of prisoners in hulks and convict prisons, September 1869.
HO 45/10429/A53867, Nursing Staff in the Prison Service 1892–1919.

HO 45/19893, Prison and Prisoners: Overcrowding in prisons, minutes from the Prison Commission, 23 April 1945.
HO 45/19977, Prisons and Prisoners: Women Medical Officers at Holloway and Aylesbury Prisons (1918–20).
HO 45/23580, Birth of children in prison 1924–1949.
HO 45/23653, Prisons and Prisoners: Report on the Conditions in Holloway. Treatment of Pregnant Prisoners (1940–49).
HO 45/24517, Capital Punishment: Sentence of Death (Expectant Mothers) Act 1931.
HO 45/24643, Prisons and Prisoners: Prison Governors and Medical Officers, appointment of women (1913–1938).
HO 144/3982, Prisons and Prisoners: Childbirth in prison. Memorandum on existing practice and the arguments for temporary removal 1924.
HO 144/17929, Criminal Cases: Wise, Olive Kathleen, convicted at Central Criminal Court on 13 January 1931.
HO T1/12409, Staffing of the prison service: Improvement of arrangements for medical care of prisoners, 1919.
MH55/1572, Courses in mothercraft delivered to women in prison, 1952.
PCOM 2/164, Millbank Book of Questions and Suggestions 1855–1863.
PCOM 7/40, Holloway Prison: Duchess of Bedford's Committee of Enquiry into Various Matters 1919.
PCOM 7/40, Report of committee presided over by Adeline, Duchess of Bedford to inquire into various matters concerning Holloway Prison, May 1919.
PCOM 9/467, Births and Infants in Prison 1930–1949.
PCOM 9/1435, Women convicted of child neglect: Investigations in prisons 1946–1950.
PCOM 9/1443, Women prisoners: Introduction of maternity dresses.
RG 48/1882, Registration of births occurring in prison 1948–51.

Wellcome Library (WL)

SA/NCT/J/2/2/7, 'A cause to campaign for?', *New Generation*, Vol. 15 (1996).
SA/WHL/1/28, Beverley A. Lawrence Beech, 'Shackled women', *AIMS Journal*, Vol. 7 (1995/96).

Statutes

1774 Health of Prisoners Act (14 Geo. III c.59)
1823 Gaol Act (4 Geo. 4 c.64)
1853 Penal Servitude Act (16 & 17 Vict. c.99)
1857 Penal Servitude Act (20 & 21 Vict. c.3)

1877 Prison Act (40 & 41 Vict. c.21)
1898 Prison Act (61 & 62 Vict. c.41)
1898 Inebriates Act (61& 62 Vict. c.60)
1902 Midwives Act (2 Edw. VII c.17)
1908 Prevention of Crime Act (7 & 8 Edw. VII c.59)
1913 Mental Deficiency Act (3 & 4 Geo. V c.28)
1914 Criminal Justice Administration Act (4 & 5 Geo. V c.58)
1931 Sentence of Death (Expectant Mothers) Act (21 Geo. V c.24)
1933 Children and Young Persons Act (23 & 24 Geo. V c.12)
1948 Criminal Justice Act (11 & 12 Geo. VI c.58)
1948 National Assistance Act (11 & 12 Geo. VI c.29)

Commissions and annual reports

First Report from the Select Committee on Transportation together with the minutes of evidence and appendix (London: 1856).

Independent investigation into the death of Baby A at HMP Bronzefield on 27 September 2019, Prisons and Probation Ombudsman (London: 2021).

Nineteenth Report of the Inspectors appointed under the provisions of the act 5 & 6 Will. IV c.38 to visit the different prisons of Great Britain (London: 1854).

Report of the Commissioners appointed to inquire into the operation of the acts relating to transportation and penal servitude (London: 1863).

Report of the Commissioners of Prisons and the Directors of Convict Prisons for the year ended 31 March 1904 (London: 1904).

Report of the Commissioners of Prisons and the Directors of Convict Prisons for the Year Ended 31st March 1918 (London: 1918).

Report of the Commissioners of Prisons and the Directors of Convict Prisons for the Year Ended 31 March 1922 (London: 1922).

Report of the Commissioners of Prisons and the Directors of Convict Prisons for the Year Ended 31 March 1923 (London: 1923).

Report of the Commissioners of Prisons for the year 1952 (London: 1953).

Report of the Departmental Committee on Persistent Offenders (London: 1932).

Report of the Departmental Committee on Prisons (London: 1895).

Report of the Departmental Committee on the Education and Moral Instruction of Prisoners in Local and Convict Prisons (London: 1896).

Report of the Directors of Convict Prisons for the year 1853 (London: 1854).

Report of the Directors of Convict Prisons for the year 1854 (London: 1855).

Report of the Directors of Convict Prisons for the year 1855 (London: 1856).

Report of the Directors of Convict Prisons for the year 1856 (London: 1857).

Report of the Directors of Convict Prisons for the year 1857 (London: 1858).

Report of the Directors of Convict Prisons for the year 1858 (London: 1859).
Report of the Directors of Convict Prisons for the year 1859 (London: 1860).
Report of the Directors of Convict Prisons for the year 1860 (London: 1861).
Report of the Directors of Convict Prisons for the year 1861 (London: 1862).
Report of the Directors of Convict Prisons for the year 1862 (London: 1863).
Report of the Directors of Convict Prisons for the year 1863 (London: 1864).
Report of the Directors of Convict Prisons for the year 1864 (London: 1865).
Report of the Directors of Convict Prisons for the year 1865 (London: 1866).
Report of the Directors of Convict Prisons for the year 1866 (London: 1867).
Report of the Directors of Convict Prisons for the year 1867 (London: 1868).
Report of the Directors of Convict Prisons for the year 1868 (London: 1869).
Report of the Directors of Convict Prisons for the year 1869 (London: 1870).
Report of the Directors of Convict Prisons for the year 1870 (London: 1871).
Report of the Directors of Convict Prisons for the year 1871 (London: 1872).
Report of the Directors of Convict Prisons for the year 1872 (London: 1873).
Report of the Directors of Convict Prisons for the year 1873 (London: 1874).
Report of the Directors of Convict Prisons for the year 1874 (London: 1875).
Report of the Directors of Convict Prisons for the year 1875 (London: 1876).
Report of the Directors of Convict Prisons for the year 1876 (London: 1877).
Report of the Directors of Convict Prisons for the year 1877 (London: 1878).
Report of the Inter-Departmental Committee on Physical Deterioration (London: 1904).
Report of the Select Committee of the House of Lords on Gaol Discipline (London: 1863).

Medical journals

British Medical Journal
The Lancet

Newspapers

Cheltenham Chronicle
Daily Express
Daily Herald
Daily Mail
Daily Mirror
Dundee Courier
Gloucester Citizen
Henley Advertiser
Illustrated London News
Independent

Islington Gazette
John Bull
Lakes Chronicle and Reporter
Leeds Mercury
London Evening Standard
Manchester Evening News
Manchester Guardian
Newcastle Evening Chronicle
Portsmouth Evening News
Sheffield Daily Telegraph
Taunton Courier and Western Advertiser
The Guardian
The Observer
The People
The Times
Western Daily Press

Primary printed sources

Amos, Sarah, 'The prison treatment of women', *Contemporary Review*, 73 (1898), 803–813.

Birth Companions, *Birth Charter for women in prisons in England and Wales* (March 2016).

Carpenter, Mary, *Our convicts*, Vol. II (London: Longman, 1864).

Chesterton, George Laval, *Revelations of prison life with an enquiry into prison discipline and secondary punishments* (London: Hurst and Blackett Publishers, 1856).

Devon, James, *The criminal and the community* (London: J. Lane, 1912).

Female Life in prison, by a prison matron, Vol. II (London: Hurst and Blackett Publishers, 1862).

Fletcher, Susan Willis, *Twelve months in an English prison* (New York: Charles T. Dillingham, 1884).

Fry, Elizabeth, *Observations on the visiting, superintendence and government of female prisoners* (Norwich: S. Wilkin, 1827).

Gordon, Mary, *Penal discipline* (New York: George Routledge & Sons, 1922).

Griffiths, Arthur, *Memorials of Millbank and chapters in prison history* (London: Chapman and Hall, 1884).

Griffiths, Arthur, *Secrets of the prison house*, Vol. 1 (London: Chapman and Hall, 1894).

Griffiths, Major Arthur, 'In Wormwood Scrubs Prison', in George Sims (ed.), *Living London: Its work and its play, its humour and its pathos, its sights and its scenes*, Vol. III (London: Cassell, 1903), pp. 126–131.

Harris, Vernon, 'The female prisoner', *The Nineteenth Century and After*, 363 (1907).
Henry, Joan, *Women in prison* (London: White Lion Publishers, first published 1952, this edition 1973).
Hobhouse, Stephen and Brockway, A. Fenner, *English prisons today: Being the report of the Prison System Enquiry Committee* (London: Longmans, Green and Co., 1922).
Howard, John, *The state of the prisons in England and Wales* (Warrington: William Eyres, 1777).
Jebb, Joshua, *Modern prisons: Their construction and ventilation* (London: John Weale, 1844).
Lonsdale, Kathleen, et al., with introduction by Ethel Mannin, *Some account of life in Holloway Prison for women* (London: Prison Medical Reform Council, 1943).
Lytton, Constance and Warton, Jane, *Prisons and prisoners: Some personal experiences* (London: William Heinemann, 1914).
Maudsley, Henry, 'Review of female life in prison', *Journal of Mental Science*, 9 (1863), 69–87.
Maybrick, Florence Elizabeth Chandler, *Mrs Maybrick's own story: My fifteen lost years* (London: Funk & Wagnalls Company, 1905).
Mayhew, Henry and Binny, John, *The criminal prisons of London and scenes of prison life* (London: Griffin, Bohn and Company, 1862).
McCall, Cicely, *They always come back* (London: Methuen & Co., 1938).
Morrison, William Douglas, *Crime and its causes* (London: Swan Sonnenschein & Co., 1891).
Royal College of Obstetricians and Gynaecologists position statement: Maternity care for women in prison in England and Wales (September 2021).
Scharlieb, Mary, 'Alcoholism in relation to women and children', in Kelynack, T.N. (ed.), *The drink problem of today in its medico-sociological aspects* (London: Methuen & Co., First Published 1907, Revised Edition 1916), pp. 128–156.
Size, Mary, *Prisons I have known* (London: George Allen and Unwin, 1957).
Sullivan, William, 'A note on the influence of maternal inebriety on the offspring', *Journal of Mental Science*, 45 (1899), 489–503.
Tod, Isabella, 'Boarding-out of pauper children', *Journal of the Statistical and Social Inquiry Society of Ireland*, 7:5 (1878), 293–299.

Websites

oldbaileyonline.org
prisonhistory.org

Secondary sources
Books

Apple, Rima, *Perfect motherhood: Science and childrearing in America* (London: Rutgers University Press, 2006).

Badinter, Elisabeth, *Mother love: Myth and reality: Motherhood in modern history* (Basingstoke: Macmillan, 1981).

Badinter, Elisabeth, *The conflict: Woman and mother* (Melbourne: Text Publishing, 2010).

Bailey, Victor, *The rise and fall of the rehabilitative ideal, 1895–1970* (Abingdon: Routledge, 2019).

Baldwin, Lucy (ed.), *Mothering justice: Working with mothers in criminal and social justice settings* (Hampshire: Waterside Press, 2015).

Baunach, Phyllis Jo, *Mothers in prison* (New York: Transaction Publishers, first edition 1983, this edition 2020).

Bennett, Rachel E., *Capital punishment and the criminal corpse in Scotland, 1740–1834* (London: Palgrave Macmillan, 2018).

Brown, Alyson, *English society and the prison: Time, culture, and politics in the development of the modern prison, 1850–1920* (Suffolk: Boydell, 2003).

Butler, Anne M., *Gendered justice in the American West: Women prisoners in men's penitentiaries* (Chicago: University of Illinois Press, 1997).

Carlen, Pat, *Sledgehammer: Women's imprisonment at the millennium* (Basingstoke: Palgrave Macmillan, 1998).

Clark, Michael and Crawford, Catherine (eds), *Legal medicine in history* (Cambridge: Cambridge University Press, 1994).

Cooter, Roger, *In the name of the child: Health and welfare 1880–1940* (London: Routledge, 1992).

Cox, Catherine and Marland, Hilary, *Disorder contained: Mental breakdown and the modern prison in England and Ireland, 1840–1900* (Cambridge: Cambridge University Press, 2022).

Dally, Ann, *Inventing motherhood: The consequences of an ideal* (London: Burnett Books, 1982).

Davie, Neil, *Tracing the criminal: The rise of scientific criminology in Britain, 1860–1918* (Oxford: The Bardwell Press, 2005).

Davies, Caitlin, *Bad girls: A history of rebels and renegades* (London: John Murray, 2018).

Davis, Angela, *Modern motherhood: Women and family in England, c. 1945–2000* (Manchester: Manchester University Press, 2012).

Dobash, Russell P., Dobash, R. Emerson and Gutteridge, Sue, *The imprisonment of women* (Oxford: Basil Blackwell, 1986).

Dwork, Deborah, *War is good for babies and other young children: A history of the infant and child welfare movement in England 1898–1918* (London: Tavistock Publications, 1987).

Emsley, Clive, *Crime and society in twentieth-century England* (London: Routledge, 2011).

Farrell, Elaine, *Women, crime and punishment in Ireland: Life in the nineteenth-century convict prison* (Cambridge: Cambridge University Press, 2020).

Foucault, Michel, *Discipline and punish: The birth of the prison* (London: Allen Lane, 1977).

Frost, Ginger, *Illegitimacy in English law and society 1860–1930* (Manchester: Manchester University Press, 2016).

Gijswijt-Hofstra, Marijke and Marland, Hilary (eds), *Cultures of child health in Britain and the Netherlands in the twentieth century* (Amsterdam: Rodopi, 2003).

Hendrick, Harry, *Child welfare: England 1872–1989* (London: Routledge, 1994).

Hendrick, Harry, *Children, childhood and English society 1880–1990* (Cambridge: Cambridge University Press, 1997).

Higgins, Peter McRorie, *Punish or treat? Medical care in English prisons 1770–1850* (Victoria: Trafford Publishing, 2007).

Johnston, Helen (ed.), *Punishment and control in historical perspective* (Houndmills: Palgrave Macmillan, 2008).

Levene, Alysa, *The childhood of the poor: Welfare in eighteenth-century London* (Basingstoke: Palgrave, 2012).

Lewis, Jane, *The politics of motherhood: Child and maternal welfare in England, 1900–1939* (London: Croom Helm, 1980).

Loudon, Irvine, *Death in childbirth: An international study of maternal care and maternal mortality 1800–1950* (Oxford: Oxford University Press, 1992).

McConville, Seán, *A history of English prison administration, Vol. I 1750–1877* (London: Routledge & Kegan Paul, 1981).

McIntosh, Tania, *A social history of maternity and childbirth: Key themes in maternity care* (Abingdon: Routledge, 2012).

Morris, Norval and Rothman, David J. (eds), *The Oxford history of the prison: The practice of punishment in Western society* (Oxford: Oxford University Press, 1995).

Murdoch, Lydia, *Imagined orphans: Poor families, child welfare, and contested citizenship in London* (New Brunswick: Rutgers University Press, 2006).

Nelson, Claudia and Nelson, Daniel, *Family ties in Victorian England* (Westport, CT: Praeger Publishers, 2007).

Oakley, Ann, *Becoming a mother* (London: Penguin Books, 1979).
Oakley, Ann, *Women confined: Towards a sociology of childbirth* (New York: Schocken Books, 1980).
O'Brien, Patricia, *The promise of punishment: Prisons in nineteenth-century France* (Princeton: Princeton University Press, 1982).
Priestley, Philip, *Victorian prison lives: English prison biography, 1830–1914* (London: Pimlico, 1985).
Rock, Paul, *Reconstructing a women's prison: The Holloway Redevelopment Project, 1968–88* (Oxford: Oxford University Press, 1996).
Ross, Ellen, *Love and toil: Motherhood in outcast London, 1870–1918* (Oxford: Oxford University Press, 1993).
Schwan, Anne, *Convict voices: Women, class, and writing about prison in nineteenth-century England* (New Hampshire: University of New Hampshire Press, 2014).
Sim, Joe, *Medical power in prisons: The Prison Medical Service in England 1774–1989* (Milton Keynes: Open University Press, 1990).
Towler, Jean and Bramall, Joan, *Midwives in history and society* (London: Croom Helm, 1986).
Tucker, Judith E., *Women in nineteenth-century Egypt* (Cambridge: Cambridge University Press, 1985).
Walkowitz, Judith R., *Prostitution and Victorian society: Women, class and the state* (Cambridge: Cambridge University Press, 1980).
Welshman, John, *Underclass: A history of the excluded 1880–2000* (London: Hambledon, 2006).
Wiener, Martin J., *Reconstructing the criminal: Culture, law, and policy in England, 1830–1914* (Cambridge: Cambridge University Press, 1990).
Williams, Lucy, *Wayward women: Female offending in Victorian England* (Barnsley: Pen & Sword, 2016).
Williams, Lucy and Godfrey, Barry, *Criminal women 1850–1920: Researching the lives of Britain's female offenders* (Barnsley: Pen & Sword, 2018).
Wingfield, Nancy M. and Bucur, Maria (eds), *Gender and war in twentieth-century Europe* (Bloomington: Indiana University Press, 2006).
Zedner, Lucia, *Women, crime and custody in Victorian England* (Oxford: Oxford University Press, 1991).

Articles and chapters in books

Abbott, Laura, 'A pregnant pause: Expecting in the prison estate', in Baldwin, Lucy (ed.), *Mothering justice: Working with mothers in criminal and social justice settings* (Hampshire: Waterside Press, 2015), pp. 185–210.
Abbott, Laura and Lockwood, Kelly, 'Negotiating pregnancy, new motherhood and imprisonment', in Lockwood, Kelly (ed.), *Mothering from the*

inside: Research on motherhood and imprisonment (Bingley: Emerald Publishing, 2020), pp. 49–66.

Anderson, Sarah and Pratt, John, 'Prisoner memoirs and their role in prison history', in Johnston, Helen (ed.), *Punishment and control in historical perspective* (Houndmills: Palgrave Macmillan, 2008), pp. 179–198.

Beier, Lucinda, 'Expertise and control: Childbearing in three twentieth-century working-class Lancashire communities', *Bulletin of the History of Medicine*, 78:2 (2004), 379–409, https://doi.org/10.1353/bhm.2004.0056.

Bennett, Rachel, 'Bad for the health of the body, worse for the health of the mind: Female responses to imprisonment in England, 1853–1869', *Social History of Medicine*, 34:2 (2021), 532–552, https://doi.org/10.1093/shm/hkz066.

Bennett, Rachel, 'Maternity care reform in English prisons: A century of unanswered concerns', *History & Policy* (2019).

Bosworth, Mary, 'Confining femininity: A history of gender, power and imprisonment', *Theoretical Criminology*, 4:3 (2000), 265–284, https://doi.org/10.1177/1362480600004003002.

Brown, Alyson and Clare, Emma, 'A history of experience: Exploring prisoners' accounts of incarceration', in Clive Emsley (ed.), *The persistent prison: Problems, images and alternatives* (London: Francis Boutle, 2005), pp. 49–73.

Bryder, Linda, 'Mobilising mothers: The 1917 National Baby Week', *Medical History*, 63:1 (2019), 2–23, https://doi.org/10.1017/mdh.2018.60.

Cahill, Heather A., 'Male appropriation and medicalisation of childbirth: An historical analysis', *Journal of Advanced Nursing*, 33:3 (2001), 334–342, https://doi.org/10.1046/j.1365-2648.2001.01669.x.

Carrabine, Eamonn and Longhurst, Brian, 'Gender and prison organisation: Some comments on masculinities and prison management', *The Howard Journal of Criminal Justice*, 37:2 (1998), 161–176, https://doi.org/10.1111/1468-2311.00088.

Cheney, Deborah, 'Dr Mary Louisa Gordon (1861–1941): A feminist approach in prison', *Feminist Legal Studies*, 18:2 (2010), 115–136, https://doi.org/10.1007/s10691-010-9151-4.

Coulson, Hilary L., '"In the care of the supposed powerful state": Women and children in the Virginia Penitentiary, 1800–1883', in Erica Rhodes Hayden and Theresa R. Jach (eds), *Incarcerated women: A history of struggles, oppression, and resistance in American prisons* (London: Lexington Books, 2017), pp. 17–36.

Cox, Catherine, and Marland, Hilary, 'Broken minds and beaten bodies: Cultures of harm and the management of mental illness in mid- to late nineteenth-century English and Irish prisons', *Social History of Medicine*, 31:4 (2018), 688–710, https://doi.org/10.1093/shmhky038.

Cox, Catherine, and Marland, Hilary, '"He must die or go mad in this place": Prisoners, insanity, and the Pentonville Model Prison experiment, 1842–1852', *Bulletin of the History of Medicine*, 92:1 (2018), 78–109, https://doi.org/10.1353/bhm.2018.0004.

Davie, Neil, 'Business as usual? Britain's first women's prison, Brixton 1853–1869', *Crimes and Misdemeanours*, 4:1 (2010), 37–52.

Davin, Anna, 'Imperialism and motherhood', *History Workshop*, 5:1 (1978), 9–65, https://doi.org/10.1093/hwj/5.1.9.

Davis, Angela, 'Choice, policy and practice in maternity care since 1948, *History & Policy* (May 2013).

Davis, Angela, 'Wartime women giving birth: Narratives of pregnancy and childbirth, Britain c. 1939–1960', *Studies in History and Philosophy of Biological and Biomedical Sciences*, 47:2 (2014), 257–266, https://doi.org/10.1016/j.shpsc.2013.11.007.

Dean, D.W., 'Education for moral improvement, domesticity and social cohesion: The Labour government, 1945–1951', in Liz Dawtry, Janet Holland and Merril Hammer, with Sue Sheldon (eds), *Equality and inequality in education policy* (Avon: Multilingual Matters, 1995), pp. 18–30.

Derbes, Brett Josef, '"Secret horrors": Enslaved women and children in the Louisiana State Penitentiary, 1833–1862', in Erica Rhodes Hayden and Theresa R. Jach (eds), *Incarcerated women: A history of struggles, oppression, and resistance in American prisons* (London: Lexington Books, 2017), pp. 3–16.

Dyhouse, Carol, 'Good wives and little mothers: Social anxieties and the schoolgirl's curriculum, 1890–1920', *History and Education*, 3:1 (1977), 21–35, https://doi.org/10.1080/0305498770030102.

Farrell, Elaine, 'Poor prison flowers: Convict mothers and their children in Ireland, 1853–1900', *Social History*, 41:2 (2016), 171–191, https://doi.org/10.1080/03071022.2016.1144312.

Forsythe, Bill, 'Russell, Adeline Mary, Duchess of Bedford (1852–1920)', *Oxford Dictionary of National Biography*, 2004.

Forsythe, Bill, 'Women prisoners and women's penal officials 1840–1921', *British Journal of Criminology*, 33:4 (1993), 525–540, https://doi.org/10.1093/oxfordjournals.bjc.a048357.

Gilroy, Rebecca, 'RCM demands equal maternity care for prisoners in wake of baby death', *Nursing Times* (November 2019).

Harding, Christopher, '"The inevitable end of a discredited system"? The origins of the Gladstone Committee report on prisons, 1895', *The Historical Journal*, 31:3 (1988), 591–608, https://doi.org/10.1017/S0018246X00023505.

Hardy, Anne, 'Development of the prison medical service, 1774–1895', in Richard Creese, W.F. Bynum and J. Bearn (eds), *The Health of Prisoners* (Atlanta: Rodopi, 1995), pp. 59–82.

Holmes, Ann Sumner and Nelson, Claudia, 'Introduction', in Claudia Nelson and Ann Sumner Holmes (eds), *Maternal instincts: Visions of motherhood and sexuality in Britain, 1875–1925* (Basingstoke: Macmillan, 2007), pp. 1–12.

Humphries, Jane, 'Care and cruelty in the workhouse: Children's experiences of residential poor relief in eighteenth- and nineteenth-century England', in Nigel Goose and Katrina Honeyman (eds), *Childhood and child labour in industrial England: Diversity and agency, 1750–1914* (London: Routledge, 2013), pp. 115–134.

Johnston, Helen, 'Gendered prison work: Female prison officers in the local prison system, 1877–1939', *Howard Journal of Criminal Justice*, 53:2 (2014), 193–212, https://doi.org/10.1111/hojo.12043.

Johnston, Helen, 'Imprisoned mothers in Victorian England, 1853–1900: Motherhood, identity and the convict prison', *Criminology & Criminal Justice*, 19:2 (2019), 215–231, https://doi.org/10.1177/1748895818757833.

King, Laura, 'Future citizens: Cultural and political conceptions of children in Britain, 1930s–1950s', *Twentieth Century British History*, 27:3 (2016), 389–411, https://doi.org/10.1093/tcbh/hww025.

Lewis, Jane, 'The working-class wife and mother and state intervention, 1870–1918', in Jane Lewis (ed.), *Labour and love: Women's experience of home and family 1850–1940* (Oxford: Basil Blackwell, 1986), pp. 99–120.

Loudon, Irvine, 'Maternal mortality in the past and its relevance to developing countries today', *The American Journal of Clinical Nutrition*, 72:1 (2000), 241S–246S.

Loudon, Irvine, 'On maternal and infant mortality 1900–1960', *Social History of Medicine*, 4:1 (1991), 29–73.

Marks, Lara, 'Medical care for pauper mothers and their infants: Poor Law provision and local demand in East London. 1870–1929', *Economic History Review*, 46:3 (1993), 518–542, https://doi.org/10.1111/j.1468-0289.1993.tb01347.

Marland, Hilary, 'Childbirth and maternity', in Roger Cooter and John Pickstone (eds), *Medicine in the twentieth century* (London: Routledge, 2000), 559–574.

Marland, Hilary, '"Close confinement tells very much upon a man": Prison memoirs, insanity and the late nineteenth- and early twentieth-century prison', *Journal of the History of Medicine and Allied Sciences*, 74:3 (2019), 267–291, https://doi.org/10.1093/jhmas/jrz027.

Purdue, Olwen, 'Nineteenth-century NIMBYs, or what the neighbour saw? Poverty, surveillance, and the boarding out of Poor Law children in late nineteenth-century Belfast', *Family & Community History*, 23:2 (2020), 119–135, https://doi.org/10.1080/14631180.2020.1920719.

Reid, Alice, 'Birth attendants and midwifery practice in early twentieth-century Derbyshire', *Social History of Medicine*, 25:2 (2012), 380–399, https://doi.org/10.1093/shm/hkr138.

Sardadvar, Karin, 'Social construction of motherhood', in Andrea O'Reilly (ed.), *Encyclopaedia of motherhood* (London: SAGE, 2010).

Shepherd, Jade, 'Feigning insanity in late-Victorian Britain', *Prison Service Journal*, 232 (2017), pp. 17–23.

Smart, Carol, 'Deconstructing motherhood', in Elizabeth Bortolaia Silva (ed.), *Good enough mothering? Feminist perspectives on lone motherhood* (London: Routledge, 1996), pp. 37–57.

Starkey, Pat, 'The feckless mother: Women, poverty and social workers in wartime and post-war England', *Women's History Review*, 9:3 (2000), 539–557, https://doi.org/10.1080/09612020000200259.

Tate, Trudi, 'King baby: Infant care into the peace', in Trudi Tate and Kate Kennedy (eds), *The silent morning: Culture and memory after the Armistice* (Manchester: Manchester University Press, 2013), pp. 104–130.

Taylor, Becky and Rogaly, Ben, '"Mrs Fairly is a dirty, lazy type": Unsatisfactory households and the problem of problem families in Norwich 1942–1963', *Twentieth Century British History*, 18:4 (2007), 429–452, https://doi.org/10.1093/tcbh/hwm019.

Watson, Stephen, 'Malingerers, the "weak-minded" criminal and the "moral imbecile": How the English prison medical officer became an expert in mental deficiency, 1880–1930', in Michael Clark and Catherine Crawford (eds), *Legal medicine in history* (Cambridge: Cambridge University Press, 1994), pp. 223–241.

Wiener, Martin J., 'The health of prisoners and the two faces of Benthamism', in Richard Creese, W.F. Bynum, and J. Bearn (eds), *The health of prisoners* (Amsterdam: Rodopi, 1995), pp. 44–58.

Zedner, Lucia, 'Wayward sisters: The prison for women', in Norval Morris and David J. Rothman (eds.) *The Oxford history of the prison: The practice of punishment in Western society* (Oxford: Oxford University Press, 1995), pp. 329–361.

Index

Aylesbury Prison 12, 16, 39, 51, 55, 62, 75, 89, 113, 114, 140

Barker, Dame Lilian 62, 113, 114, 164, 179
Bentham, Jeremy 5
birth certificate 140, 153, 154, 163
British Medical Journal 17, 110
Brixton Prison 2, 12, 16, 36, 37, 40, 46, 47, 48, 50, 53, 56, 57, 64, 77, 83, 104, 106, 107, 138, 139, 142, 147, 153, 180

Carnarvon Committee (1863) 54
Carpenter, Mary 19, 34, 59, 102, 152
Central Midwives Board 14, 95
concealment of birth 20, 72, 80, 81, 90
creche 44, 45, 78, 97, 111, 143, 146, 147, 149, 167
 see also nursery 44, 49, 50, 59, 60, 77, 83, 105, 106, 107, 108, 142, 146, 147, 153
Criminal Justice Administration Act (1914) 156
Criminal Justice Act (1948) 25, 162
Cusden, Ivy 155, 157

debility 37, 47
diet 5, 12, 16, 17, 36, 45, 48, 50, 53, 54, 55, 82, 83, 84, 85, 121, 124
Directors of Convict Prisons 36, 37, 47, 139
discipline 1, 3, 16, 34, 36, 37, 39, 41, 44, 48, 49, 51, 54, 55, 56, 57, 64, 72, 77, 78, 81, 82, 84, 92, 104, 105, 114, 138, 140, 148, 152, 167, 177, 178, 180
doctors 4, 5, 6, 7, 14, 15, 16, 17, 19, 20, 21, 53, 54, 55, 61, 62, 76, 80, 81, 87, 90, 92, 93, 94, 95, 96, 106, 107, 109, 122, 125, 139, 141, 142, 144, 149, 157, 164, 165, 177
domesticity 23, 24, 96, 102, 104, 105, 108, 110, 113, 122, 123, 124, 130, 137, 145, 161

Exeter Prison 16, 116

femininity 3, 8, 9, 19, 102, 105, 130
Fletcher, Susan Willis 1, 18, 43, 55, 58
Fry, Elizabeth 11, 35, 56, 104, 154

Index

Gaol Act (1823) 35, 56
Gladstone Committee (1895) 44, 59, 91, 108, 109, 148
Gordon, Dr Mary 12, 19, 54, 61, 129
Griffiths, Arthur 19, 25, 55, 57, 105, 137

Health of Prisoners Act (1774) 4
Holloway Prison 2, 12, 16, 17, 18, 22, 38, 39, 44, 45, 50, 59, 61, 62, 63, 73, 74, 77, 78, 79, 80, 81, 84, 85, 86, 87, 88, 89, 91, 92, 93, 95, 96, 97, 111, 112, 113, 114, 115, 117, 118, 119, 125, 127, 128, 140, 143, 144, 145, 146, 148, 153, 157, 160, 162, 164, 165, 175, 178, 179, 180, 181
Howard, John 4

inebriety 109, 143, 144, 152

Jebb, Sir Joshua 15, 36, 41, 64

Kelley, Joanna 2, 179

Lancet 17, 76
Liverpool Prison 16, 37, 39, 42, 44, 46, 47, 54, 57, 59, 74, 76, 78, 108, 114, 122, 126, 142, 143, 144, 145, 148, 152
see also Walton Gaol

male convicts
  comparison to 6, 11, 37, 41, 42, 56, 77, 105, 106
Manchester Prison 16, 59, 63, 114, 116, 120, 121, 122, 125, 143, 162, 163
  see also Strangeways
Martin, Emma, Lady Superintendent 12, 48, 56, 57, 104

Maybrick, Florence 1, 18, 42, 58, 60, 107
McCall, Cicely 12, 19, 51, 58, 61, 79, 97, 114, 126, 129, 140
medical officer 5, 6, 11, 12, 35, 40, 45, 47, 48, 49, 50, 52, 53, 54, 55, 56, 58, 60, 61, 62, 63, 73, 74, 75, 76, 77, 80, 81, 82, 83, 84, 87, 90, 91, 92, 93, 94, 120, 125, 139, 142, 143, 145, 148, 150
  see also doctors
mental deficiency 108
mental health 12, 26, 52, 54, 175, 177
midwives 13, 14, 22, 23, 88, 90, 92, 94, 95, 96, 97, 119, 125, 164, 166, 176
Midwives Act (1902) 13
Millbank Prison 16, 19, 36, 37, 47, 48, 52, 53, 54, 55, 77, 105, 106, 139
mothercraft 20, 22, 23, 24, 96, 102, 103, 104, 105, 108, 110, 113, 114, 115, 119, 120, 122, 123, 124, 125, 127, 130, 137, 145, 161

Parkhurst Prison 16, 37, 47, 77
penal servitude 15, 35, 39, 41, 83, 139, 159, 160, 161
Penal Servitude Act (1853) 35
Penal Servitude Act (1857) 36, 52
premature birth 15, 86, 87, 93, 94, 97, 165
Prison Act (1877) 15, 38, 39
Prison Act (1898) 108
Prison Directorate 6, 12, 15, 40, 42, 48, 53, 61
  see also Directors of Convict Prisons
prison labour 11, 54, 106, 107, 149

recidivism 1, 6, 17, 40, 109, 126, 152

Russell, Adeline Marie, Duchess of Bedford 22, 73, 87, 88, 89, 112
  Duchess of Bedford's Enquiry (1919) 2, 22, 73, 87, 88, 89, 92, 96, 97, 175, 176, 178, 179

Sentence of Death (Expectant Mothers) Act (1931) 159, 162
separate confinement 6, 18, 20, 36, 41, 42, 43, 44, 45, 64, 72, 85, 86, 90, 97, 106
Size, Mary 2, 12, 19, 45, 51, 59, 61, 63, 95, 114, 128, 129, 143, 162

Strangeways Prison 57, 162, 163
suffragettes 18, 61, 63, 88

Tothill Fields 37, 106, 141, 142, 147
  see also Westminster Prison
transportation 3, 35, 159

Walton Gaol 74, 143
Westminster Prison 1, 37, 38, 42, 44, 50, 58, 59, 60, 73, 84, 106, 107, 149
Woking Prison 16, 37, 40, 139, 180
Wormwood Scrubs Prison 45, 78, 105, 110, 137

Milton Keynes UK
Ingram Content Group UK Ltd.
UKHW021520090124
435741UK00008B/49